The Motivated Mind

The Motivated Mind

A Complete Guide to Personal Change

J. M. Gracia

STONEFIELD PUBLISHING

Stonefield Publishing
1202 McKenna Boulevard
Suite 208
Madison, WI 53719

Copyright © 2004 Gracia Enterprises

Library of Congress Catalog Number 2003097865

ISBN 0-9714733-2-3

First Printing January 2004

Published by Stonefield Publishing

Composition by John Reinhardt Book Design

Printed in the United States of America

For Trace

Contents

Pillar V
Act

Pillar VI
Maintain

Introduction

Give a man a fish and you feed him for a day;
teach him how to fish and you feed him for a lifetime.
—Chinese Proverb

THE LIFE YOU DESIRE can be yours. Whether that means making small improvements, completely transforming your life, or inspiring others to achieve greater success, you can make it happen. Even if you're not sure exactly what you want, only that you want something better, you can and will find the answers you're looking for. It all begins with unlocking the power of your motivated mind.

The motivated mind is already a part of you—it's been that way ever since you were born, and it will remain in place for the rest of your life. The secret to success and fulfillment is not to gain something new, but to take control of the unparalleled power that is within you.

The principles of *The Motivated Mind* will change how you think, feel, and act in a way that brings you closer to the things you desire and farther from the things you wish to avoid. These principles will transform your mind into a high-powered machine, equipping you with the ability to choose a desire and inspire consistent action until you achieve success.

Action is the difference between realized success and wishful thinking. It is the bridge between dreams and reality. There are few skills in life as powerful as knowing how to get yourself to take action toward the things you want. The desire for success and fulfillment is universal. What is not so widespread, however, is the ability to do what it takes to attain achievement. What

1

it comes down to is not merely taking any action, but choosing the right one. Within these pages, you'll discover the solution to this puzzling dilemma.

Your life is the result of past decisions and actions. The choices to go left instead of right, say "yes" instead of "no," and give more instead of give up have combined to create your current life. It is at these critical points of choice that your future is determined. Do what you know is right, and you'll enhance the quality of your life. Fail to make the right choices, and you will be pulled further from the life you desire.

How do you make the right choices? How do you inspire yourself to do what it takes to succeed? The answers can be found within the pillars of *The Motivated Mind*. Before we move on to the details of this program, I want to tell you what it is not. Too often in life we are simply handed the answers to our questions without really understanding the process. We are given a fish to satisfy our hunger today, but haven't the slightest idea how to obtain food tomorrow.

If I were to inspire you throughout these pages, you may excel in the short-term. However, the feelings would soon wear thin. After a brief burst of energy, you would return to square one wondering what to do next. But, if you are taught how to inspire yourself step by step, you will excel for a lifetime. That is my intention: to teach you how to take control of your motivated mind so that you may satisfy your hunger for a successful and fulfilling life indefinitely.

Success requires six elements. No matter who you are or what you do, the only way you can get everything you want is to understand and utilize each of these factors. Mastering each element will give you the power to take complete control of your life and create massive and lasting change. The six critical factors of success form the pillars of *The Motivated Mind*.

Collectively, the pillars serve as a complete guide to personal change. Together, we will work through the entire process from start to finish, focusing on every aspect necessary to create the life you desire. While some programs do justice to their particular focus, I believe a program that covers each of the critical stages of success provides the most benefit to the reader. This creates an atmosphere that enhances the skills of a veteran while providing a complete set of tools for the beginner.

The pillars of *The Motivated Mind* create a road that leads to the things you desire most. With each pillar in place, the path is clear and easily traveled. However, failing to apply just one element is enough to bring about an untimely end to the dreams and goals you hope to achieve—the road becomes impossible to navigate. If you want to live a better life, utilizing each of the six pillars will equip you with the power to make it happen. To begin the process, an overview of the pillars and their corresponding principles follows.

Understand. Everyone wants to get motivated, but not one in a million truly understands what it is they are hoping to find. To begin, you will discover the true meaning of motivation, and will most likely be surprised at how different it is from what you may have thought. Fully understanding the subject will enable you to see the world in a completely new light, changing the way you think about your life and the lives of others forever.

You'll then learn the secrets of human behavior. In other words, you'll learn why you do what you do and how to take control of the process. It will also open your eyes to why others behave the way they do by replacing past frustrations with understanding and acceptance.

Desire. Once you have a clear understanding of motivation and how your mind operates, we will move onto the pillar of desire. Before success can take place, you have to *want* to change. If you lack the desire, there is nothing that I or anyone else can do to help you. While it cannot be given, you can discover and develop the desires that already exist within you.

The first principle within this pillar focuses on the elements of an authentic desire. You will learn how to choose a desire that will give you the feelings you hope to experience. If you have ever achieved a goal and felt empty afterward, you know the importance of choosing the right goal.

After you know how to choose the right goal, you will be given the opportunity to work through several brainstorming exercises to help you create a list of desires that you wish to achieve. Upon completion, you will have a complete package of goals that are certain to create the life for which you are hoping.

Finally, you will learn how to give each one of your desires the leverage it needs to inspire action and ultimate success. By inputting your goal into the pleasure/pain matrix, you will discover how to overcome fear and hesitation while creating the drive and excitement necessary for achievement.

Believe. If you don't believe something is possible, you'll exert very little time and attention to successfully accomplishing the goal. Because of this fact, the first principle will provide you with a new level of confidence that will remove all fear and doubt about your ability to create the changes you desire. Instead of simply saying, "You can do it," I will offer proof that you can, in fact, get everything you want.

We will then examine the power of control. You will discover just how much control you have over your life, and how accepting and employing this power will provide you with a mindset of self-assurance and certainty, placing the future firmly in your hands.

In the final section, we will focus on attitude. Although you may have believed a positive attitude is the best option, you will discover a more powerful way to perceive the world around you—one that erases frustration, fear, and anger and replaces it with hope, excitement, and confidence.

Plan. Without a strategy in place, you have nothing on which to act. In the fourth stage of *The Motivated Mind*, we will work through the entire process of understanding and creating an unstoppable strategy for success. We will begin by looking at the power of strategy, what it can and cannot do, and how best to go about putting one together.

You will then learn the most critical elements of an effective and efficient strategy. The more of these factors you can work into your plan, the better your chances are for achieving the desire. Putting together just any plan isn't good enough—it has to be the right plan.

To conclude this segment, you will create the three stages of your strategy, also known as the success triad. Each piece of the triad serves a unique purpose in your plan, and will ensure that it is not only acted upon, but also consistently pursued until completion.

Act. The most brilliant strategy is useless if it's not put into play. The only way you can get from where you are to where you want to be is through action. In this segment, we will examine three categories of myths that keep people from taking the first step toward a better life. Only by overcoming these obstacles will you gain the leverage you need to stop talking and start walking.

The first principle will offer compelling reasons to act on your strategy immediately. We will then move on to the myths of time—the causes of hesitation, procrastination, and ultimate disappointment. Putting these myths to rest will ensure your desires are no longer put off to another time.

Perhaps the most detrimental myth and most important principle of all will be covered in the final section. The majority of people in the world are being trapped by a self-destructive lie that keeps them from a life of pleasure and true happiness. Dispelling this myth may be the best thing that ever happens to you.

Maintain. The final pillar is often ignored, which is a costly mistake. The inspiration to act on your strategy today is excellent, but most of the things you will want to achieve require more than a single day of action. Only by taking steps to maintain the drive to excel will your objectives be accomplished. This is especially helpful to those wishing to lead others to success over the long-term.

This segment is built upon five principles that will ensure the energy, excitement, and urge to improve never dies. You will begin by learning how to create the right internal and external environments to propel you forward. Failing to do so is enough to bring about an untimely end to your plan.

We will then move to the principle of focus. You will come to realize the importance of your specific and general focus, along with the exact steps to take to get the most out of both. What you focus on becomes your reality. You need to learn how to control this influential force before it takes control of you.

The third section is dedicated to the process of linking. Linking involves injecting internal sights and sounds as well as your external senses with the passion and power of your authentic desire. You will learn how to use this power to inspire action within seconds. It is sure to become one of your most valuable tools.

If a single setback is enough to throw you off course, you're heading for disaster. To overcome this problem, you will learn how to deal with change and failure in an empowering way that actually increases your chances of success. You will no longer fear failure and instead look forward to the challenges that you are sure to meet on your road to happiness.

The final installment of this pillar and this book covers the principle of continuous learning and growth. Life is about growing and forever taking steps toward your potential. You will discover the process as well as the exciting benefits of constant improvement and how failing to follow the philosophy can lead to dissatisfaction with life. However, taking the lesson to heart can raise your life to an entirely new level.

To get the most out of *The Motivated Mind*, keep a pen or pencil close by. Using the note or exercise pages at the end of each chapter, record every thought and idea that jumps into your head along with the responses to the exercises within the chapter. It doesn't take long for those gems of thought to be forgotten, so write short notes as you go along and ensure that your ideas are never lost.

This is a book of action. If you are truly dedicated to improving your life, or the lives of others, you must begin taking action from the beginning. This includes working through the exercises you are given, writing down the answers to the questions you are asked, and especially creating and recording your strategy. This book and the principles in it only work if you do.

Whatever your version of the ideal life looks like, you can

have it. Nothing is too big or too small. This is your opportunity to dream and create your life by design. Don't allow the ghosts of the past or the fears of the future to hold you back from creating the life you have always wanted to live. You deserve what you desire.

I offer you my sincerest thanks and appreciation for giving me the opportunity to share these ideas with you. What you are about to learn has enhanced the quality of my life more than I could have ever imagined, and I am certain it will do the same for you. The life you desire can be yours—it's time to make it happen.

Pillar I
Understand

Chapter 1

Motivation: The Hidden Truth Revealed

Rather than love, than money, than fame, give me truth.
—Henry David Thoreau

MOTIVATION—WHAT'S IT ALL ABOUT? What is this mysterious "thing" that everyone craves? Let me begin by telling you that there is much more to motivation than you think. It's highly likely that your definition of motivation needs a little updating, and you're not alone. Millions of people from every corner of the world are looking for the key to motivation without actually understanding what it is they are seeking.

Before you can control and benefit from the power of positive motivation, you must understand what it is you are trying to control. Forget everything you have ever learned about the subject. I want you to enter this chapter with an open and eager mind, willing to question old beliefs and consider new ideas. The true definition of motivation is among the most empowering principles you'll learn in this book; understanding it is enough to change your mind and your life forever.

What Is Motivation?

Up to this point you have most likely imagined someone who was motivated working hard to achieve a goal or dream. Perhaps you picture an athlete training in the early morning or a businessman working by a desk lamp late into the night. For most, motivation means success and accomplishment, and being motivated is something that you either are or are not.

This is only half true. If you sit on the couch for five hours eating junk food and watching television, sleep until noon, or smoke your tenth cigarette in a row, you are just as motivated as the people in the examples above. Both groups are motivated, but in very different ways.

Before we get into the different types of motivation, let's look at the true definition of the word. The root of the word is *motive*, which is defined as an emotion, desire, physiological need, or similar impulse that serves as an incitement to action.

Nowhere do we find the terms positive, healthy, or successful. Motivation is simply taking an action, any action, stemming from a reason or motive. Motivation is not inherently positive; people have added that aspect on their own and it has caused many problems and frustration in return. Using the true meaning of the word, we can define motivation as:

A voluntary action in a given direction

Let's break down our new definition of motivation to ensure that we are absolutely clear about what it does and doesn't entail. The first half of the definition tells us that we are dealing with voluntary actions only. If someone pushes you and you trip, there was no choice involved in your action. You were not in control of your body at the time of the initial shove. Because of this, actions are split into two categories: voluntary and involuntary. Throughout the book, our focus will be voluntary actions.

Another important principle can be learned from the first three words of the definition. If you do something voluntarily, it is because you want to do it. Too often, people excuse their voluntary actions with phrases like "have to," or "no choice." As you will learn in detail in the upcoming chapters, every voluntary action you take is desired, otherwise you wouldn't do it. There is a motive, or reason, for every voluntary action you choose to take. This is true whether or not the action results in a positive or negative outcome.

Moving on to the second half of the definition, we have direction. Every action you take creates specific consequences. The results bring you closer to the things you desire or take you further from them. For example, if your desire is to quit smoking and you choose to smoke, the action of smoking takes you further from your long-term desire. The direction is opposite to where you wish to be heading. Every action you take has a reaction for which you are responsible.

A Constant Force

This idea will provide the biggest shock to your system. From what we have already covered, we know that every voluntary action results from a particular motive. When you do something, you do it for a reason. You don't have to know the specific set of reasons or motives for your action in order for one to exist. Both positive and negative actions result from motives. Therefore, every action, no matter how good or bad it is for you and your life, is motivated.

What does this mean? You have been, are, and will be forever motivated. The one thing you and the rest of the world have been searching for has always been there. You cannot *get* motivated because it is always present. The only time that you are not motivated is when you cease to live.

I know this is probably a very different perspective of motivation than you are used to. I wouldn't want it any other way. You have to look at things differently in order to create better results. The fact that you are already motivated should give you a sense of relief and unbelievable control over your future. The new definition of motivation is the secret to creating action and lasting change.

Think back to when you were younger. Have you ever lost one of your most prized possessions? Perhaps your favorite toy or stuffed animal? I can remember losing a baseball card that meant the world to me. I took more care of that card than anything else I had, and the day I couldn't find it was a day I will never forget. After hours of scouring my bedroom and closet, I came up empty handed. I fell onto my bed the saddest little boy you've ever seen.

Just when I was about to give up all hope and live the rest of my life in depression over my lost baseball card, I saw a small object poking out from underneath my bed. How I missed it I have no idea, but I do know that I felt relieved to find what I had lost. The struggle was over, and I could get back to enjoying the card.

You just found your lost baseball card. You have the motivation for which you have been wishing. Your search is finally over, and you can now spend your time and energy enjoying what it can bring into your life. While the rest of the world is searching hopelessly for their lost possession, you will be benefiting from the force that is within each one of us. You know the secret location; now you have to learn how to use it.

Second shock: Laziness is a myth. If you sit on the couch and waste hours each night staring into the television, you have just as much motivation as someone working toward their higher ambitions. You desire to sit on the couch, and you are acting from a motive. Everyone, no matter what they may say or do, is motivated to do what they choose to do.

When you find yourself "unmotivated" to take action toward your goals, you are actually motivated to do something else. When I used to tell myself that I wasn't motivated enough to exercise, I was actually more motivated to stay inside. These varying degrees of desire don't only have to be good versus bad.

The next time you feel like you need motivation to get going, realize that you are motivated at that very moment. The problem is, you are not motivated in the direction of your chosen desire. You are motivated to do something else at the time.

This aspect of motivation dramatically changes the picture. Millions of people, literally millions, are looking for someone or something to motivate them. You may have even asked someone to motivate you at some point, but you now know that this is impossible. Motivation is a constant in everyone's life.

If everyone is motivated, why aren't they getting what they want? Why do some people get positive outcomes and others deal with negative ones? Direction. The key to success is not in getting motivated, but in taking control of what's already there. The skill you have really been looking for is how to direct your motivation toward the things you want. You take thousands of actions every day. If you can learn how to direct those actions toward the things you desire most, you will succeed in creating the life you hope to achieve.

When you first read the title of this book, *The Motivated Mind*, you may have believed this was the purpose of the book—to take an unmotivated mind and transform it into a motivated one. It should now be clear that the purpose of this book is to take complete control of the motivated mind that is already within you.

A Matter of Direction

Impossible to create, motivation can only be directed. You can take a step forward or backward, but either way you go, the action is still motivated. For someone who desires to get in shape, a step forward would be working out while a step backward would be eating a gallon of ice cream. One action would result in bringing success closer and the other would push it further away.

FIGURE 1

Look at the actions in Figure 1. The left side represents common negative or neutral actions and the right side contains positive behavior. To the untrained eye, the actions to the left would be considered unmotivated while the right side would be just the opposite. All of the actions above are motivated. When you hear someone say, "I'm just not motivated," you know the truth. It isn't motivation they are looking for; it's the right direction.

The needle represents the direction of motivation. You can choose to smoke or you can choose to exercise, just as you can choose to eat too much or choose to study. The needle represents motivation regardless of where it is pointed.

Motivation is like a car whose wheels are constantly running. You are dropped into the driver's seat able to turn the wheel left and right, but not to stop the car's momentum. You are in control of the car's direction, deciding exactly where to go, and which turns to make. Some drive to easy street to enjoy the short-lived pleasures of instant gratification. Others choose the slightly longer route to their true desires and long-term fulfillment. While both types of drivers are equally motivated, the quality of their destinations is nowhere near the same.

This difference in outcomes creates two categories of motivation—negative and positive. While the first will lead you to the dead ends of life, the second will guide you to unparalleled success and happiness. Throughout the remainder of the book, your purpose will be to master the skill of positive motivation. Before you can do that, you need a clear understanding of exactly what it is you will master as well as what you must work to avoid.

Negative Motivation

Negative motivation is the cause of pain, struggle, fear, and ultimate failure. Negative motivation is the reason people are unsatisfied, unfulfilled, and unhappy. It is the reason people are lacking in the areas of their health, wealth, relationships, and emotions. By understanding what it is specifically and how you can work to decrease its strength, you can rid yourself of these pains. You can, once and for all, break negative habits and patterns that are keeping you from what you really want. Using the basic definition of motivation as our source, negative motivation is defined as:

*A voluntary action in the opposite direction
of your authentic desire*

The actions, as before, are those you voluntarily choose. The significant addition to this definition centers on direction. In this case, the direction is negative; it draws you further from your authentic desires. In other words, when you do something that makes it harder for you to achieve your long-term goals, you are negatively motivated. The term "authentic desire" is new and will be explained more thoroughly in upcoming chapters. For now, it is only important that you understand an authentic desire is one that, once achieved, will bring you the positive outcomes you seek.

The cause of negative motivation is short-term thinking; it is instant gratification at its worst. Negative motivation is spending your money frivolously and later regretting the decision when you can't pay your mortgage. It is eating junk food now and dealing with the extra weight, poor health, and disease later. It is knowing you should do one thing, but instead doing what comes quicker and easier. If you are negatively motivated, you may let someone attack your character because it's safer than standing up for yourself. Soon after you're left wishing you would have done things differently. In short, negative motivation is doing what feels good now only to deal with the painful consequences later.

Living for the short-term boost will never get you what you really want. The things you desire are patiently waiting for you, but you cannot attain them through negative motivation. The following examples of negative motivation will help demonstrate this point.

Sitting on the couch every night takes very little effort. It's fun to watch television and turn your brain off for five to six hours every day. In the short-term, it is easy and may feel better than working towards your desires. This habit, drawn out over a few months or years, paints a very different picture. Someone who spends hours every night in front of the television in a zone will never reach his potential physically, financially, mentally, or emotionally. If this is the authentic desire, to watch television and waste hours every night doing nothing of value, then success it is. However, I highly doubt you have desires such as these topping your list of priorities.

To realize the full impact of negative motivation, think of a time when you did something in the short-term that brought you further from the things you hoped to gain in the long-term. Now imagine living that way every day for the rest of your life.

In the end, you would be miles from where you wanted to be, wondering where it all went wrong. This isn't an exaggeration. Every day, people are stuck in a constant routine of short-term living and negative motivation. We all visit now and then, but you cannot live there.

It all comes down to living for the short-term versus the long-term. When I paint short-term living as a negative picture, I am not referring to enjoying the moment and showing appreciation for the present. I am talking about sabotaging your dreams through negative actions. Living for the long-term requires a small amount of sacrifice now to enjoy a massive amount of pleasure in the future. This is where most people drop the ball. They seek only what is easy now, ignoring the pain that will result later.

When you bite into a candy bar, it doesn't take long to be gratified. Almost instantly, you enjoy the taste. This instant gratification, however, is short-lived and results in pain down the road. Eating candy bars every day, following a constant patter of negative motivation, would lead you straight into disaster.

Negative motivation is passing up the opportunity to start a business now only to regret the decision later. It is doing drugs today, seeking their immediate effect, and dealing with the misery and depression tomorrow. Negative motivation is acting on a desire for instant gratification now and disliking the long-term outcome that results.

Saving money is another great example. Impulsive buying can bring fun and enjoyment in the moment. There is no waiting—you get what you want immediately with little short-term pain or sacrifice. On the other hand, saving your money requires time and effort. You have to put off getting what you want, without receiving instant gratification while you wait. Herein lies the differentiating factor between negative and positive motivation.

Saving your money until tomorrow allows you to purchase something bigger and better than you could today. Basing your daily decisions on receiving an instant, short-term high will make it impossible to enjoy the greater things in life. The majority of the things you want require time and effort to materialize—something that negative motivation cannot give. Eliminating the mindset and routine of instant gratification and instead living for the long-term rewards will create a quality of life that cannot compare to the short-term boosts offered by negative motivation.

Too many people are allowing instant gratification to slowly tear their lives apart. Everywhere you look, you see individuals seeking instant riches, instant health, and instant happiness. You can't get there from here. Creating an extraordinary life does not come in an instant. Although the thoughts and feelings of confidence, happiness, and meaning will make an early entrance into your life, the physical counterparts take time to come about. Seeking an instant pleasure at the expense of fulfillment is a road that leads only one place—ultimate failure.

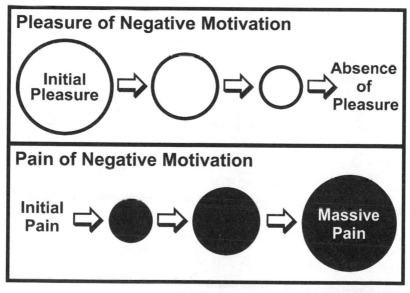

FIGURE 2

Figure 2 demonstrates how the pleasures and pains of negative motivation operate. Although the initial pleasure is instant and intense, it diminishes quickly over time. To remedy this, people increase the negative action. For example, taking drugs gives an instant result, but because of its diminishing returns, more and more is necessary to produce the initial pleasure.

The pain of negative motivation quickly grows until it is an all-consuming force. The pain of overeating starts with a poor self-image or a slightly overweight build, but progresses to self-hatred and life-threatening illness. Initially, smoking may hurt the lungs and cause trouble breathing, but the pain soon escalates into heart disease and lung cancer. In the end, negative motivation can destroy a life. It can lead to financial loss, an unfulfilling career, declining health, meaningless relationships, and ultimate failure and sadness. There is a healthy remedy to this situation. Positive motivation is the flipside of the story, and holds the solution to doing what is right for you now and enjoying the rewards in the long-term.

Positive Motivation

What do the inventor of the light bulb, an Olympian, and a successful businesswoman have in common? Each one involves positive motivation. The inventor willing to sacrifice and fail thousands of times in order to succeed, the athlete willing to work each and every day for years to reach the pinnacle of the sport, and an entrepreneur willing to risk it all on the hopes and dreams that rest within her mind have positive motivation to thank for their constant drive, dedication, and ultimate achievement. Every success, both large and small, that has ever been accomplished and that ever will be accomplished owes its achievement to positive motivation.

Positive motivation explains how someone can stay committed to one purpose over the span of a lifetime. It demonstrates why an individual would take action every day regardless of short-term failure until the desire is finally met. Everything you get in the future will come about because of positive motivation. The majority of those who have benefited from this skill seldom realize its existence. They don't know that it's there, but they do know there is an urge, an overriding desire to work toward their dreams and goals.

You have already experienced this sensation when you succeeded in the past, but understanding the process and taking control of it will enable you to take your life to the next level. You don't have to wait for the feeling to come to you. With your motivated mind, you can get positively motivated to take action whenever you wish. It literally takes only a snap of the fingers to inspire yourself to action.

The definition of positive motivation closely matches that of negative motivation with only a single change. Instead of a voluntary action resulting in greater distance from your goal, positive motivation brings you closer to what you really want:

A voluntary action in the direction of your authentic desire

It is spending wisely when you desire greater savings. It is cutting down on junk food when you want improved health. Positive motivation is creating close connections with loved ones when you desire improved relationships, and taking the risk of following your dream when you desire meaning and fulfillment. Whenever you do something that brings you one step closer to achieving what you want, you are positively motivated.

This ability sets the stage for the remainder of the program. My mission is to teach you how to positively motivate yourself to create the life you desire. Every step we take along the way will build upon the principles of positive motivation. In the end, you will be in complete control of your motivated mind as well as your future.

It is important that you understand that the hard part in getting what you want is rarely in the act itself—it is in getting yourself to do what you know you have to do. It's not hard to jog. You simply place one foot in front of the other. It is not hard to eat healthy. You buy the right foods and avoid buying the wrong ones. It isn't hard to learn how to do the things you want to learn how to do. You sign up for classes, read books, and do your research. You know what you have to do to get what you want. Even if you don't know the specifics needed to accomplish your goals, you know where to start looking for the answers.

Inspiring yourself to action is the key to achieving your desires, which is why positive motivation is so extremely vital to your

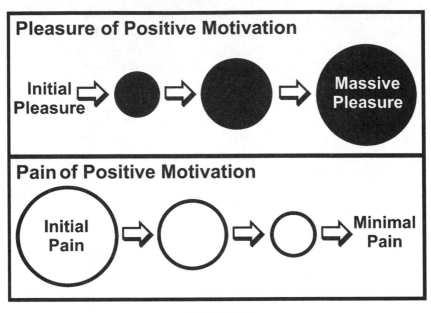

FIGURE 3

success. It doesn't matter what you know if it's never acted upon. Positive change requires action, and action is what you'll create with the skill of positive motivation. If you want it, you have only to plug your desire into the system and action ensues.

Figure 3 represents the process of pleasure and pain in regards to positive motivation. The initial pleasure of doing the right thing is rather large. You feel great about yourself and your ability to take action toward your desires. As time goes on, you realize greater and greater pleasure from coming closer to your ultimate goal. When you finally reach the point of success, the level of pleasure is incomparable to anything negative motivation can deliver.

The initial pain of taking action is somewhat large. It's a risk to put yourself out there and go for broke. I know how hard that can be. I have experienced the pain of taking that first step. You are unsure of yourself and aren't certain you can succeed. But when you take that first step, you will find that it becomes easier and easier as time goes on.

Soon the pain become
way toward your goals. T.
of positive motivation that
something that takes effort
entail great pain or sacrifice.
ent.

When I took action towar
about it. I didn't see it as pa
headed. I was so excited about
that the pain wasn't an issue. It
right path. Think of it in terms   ᴊuring a
race. He doesn't see each step as a   ₚᴄrience because he
knows each one is bringing him cₗₒₛer to the finish line.

I want to offer you a few more illustrations about the difference between positive and negative motivation to ensure that the idea really takes hold in your mind. When it comes to a change in beliefs, it takes repetition to make the new ideas stick.

Two people stand in front of an enormous pile of red bricks. Their task is simple: to move the pile of bricks from their current spot to a location five feet away. The task will be completed once every brick is moved into its new pile.

The instant gratification seeker, or one who is negatively motivated, picks up a brick and places it exactly five feet away. He doesn't want to do any more work than is necessary. The long-term thinker, or one who is positively motivated, understands his goal and places the first brick nearly ten feet from the original pile. This cycle continues for several hours. After half of the bricks have been moved, the instant gratification seeker has to stop. Because he placed the bricks only five feet away, he has no room left for the remaining bricks. He has built a wall that covers the span of five feet from his starting spot to the five-foot marker.

Our long-term thinker has more than enough space for the remaining bricks because he worked from the farthest point up. As he worked through his pile, his walk became shorter. The first set of bricks was moved ten feet away, but the next was only moved nine. This continued until he reached the five-foot

ng-term thinker had to do more work
to do less as time went on and finish the
essful while the negatively motivated worker
se.

ou may want to do the easier thing right now, move
ks as close as possible, you will only build a wall keeping
from what you truly desire. If you are willing to think long-
term and put forth intelligent effort, you will have more than
enough resources to get what you want.

Next, the two men leave their piles of bricks and walk to a ten-story building. The structure is placed in such a way that each floor up offers a progressively better view and overall experience. The view from the top, being the ultimate destination, is simply breathtaking.

The first man, seeking instant gratification, doesn't want to walk all the way up the staircase and decides to plop right down on the first floor. The view isn't that good, but at least no work or effort was involved.

The second man starts right for the stairs. Each step he takes isn't painful because he knows it is taking him one step closer to the ultimate experience. After putting forth the required effort, he reaches the top floor and opens the door to a spectacular view. It was definitely worth the walk and wait.

Both men wanted pleasure in the end. The first experienced a small amount when he decided to think short-term. After a while, he was bored and regretted not doing more. The second passed on the instant satisfaction because he knew the long-term rewards far outweighed any short-term benefits.

This is the dilemma millions of people face every day. They are so consumed with instant gratification that their view of the world is sub-par. Their daily experience and quality of life is far below what it could be. The opportunities for an exciting and rewarding life are endless. When you are positively motivated and thinking for the long-term, you will have your pick of these opportunities and the ability to make them happen.

Do I Have To?

Watching a positively motivated individual from the sidelines, you may think to yourself, "Wow. She really must be disciplined to make herself do that every day," or, "He must have tremendous willpower to make himself try again and again after failing so many times." Have you ever thought these things? I know I have, but I was missing the point of positive motivation completely.

Years ago in college, I was having a conversation with a friend about an engineering project he was working on. It wasn't for a class requirement, but rather a side project for extra credit. He worked on it every night, spending hours and hours scratching away on his notepad. Near the end of the talk, I asked him if he minded all of the time and effort he had to put in to finish the project.

With a puzzled look, he asked, "What do you mean?" You would have thought I just asked him what planet he was from. "I don't have to do it. I want to do it."

"Yeah, I'm sure you want it," I said, "but isn't it a lot of work to do every day? Don't you get tired of it?"

Again, with a confused expression, he replied, "Work? Tired of it? I love this stuff. It isn't work when you love it. I can't wait to see what this project will look like when it's finally done. If I could, I would work on it every minute of the day."

It wasn't about *having* to do anything. He *wanted* to do it. This is the power of positive motivation. It doesn't take discipline or willpower to reach your goal because you will want to take action each day. If you feel that you *have* to do something it won't last. It never lasts. Positive motivation allows you to adjust your perspective. You will feel an urge to take action and reach your goal because the final reward will be so compelling. This has nothing to do with "have to" and everything to do with "want to."

You will be able put yourself in a state in which you want to do the things that are necessary to reach your desires. Struggle and frustration don't have to accompany success. When you are doing what you enjoy doing and are working toward your authentic desires, the pain of hard work and sacrifice have no place. The satisfaction you will feel from doing what you want to be doing with your life will take center stage.

A Skill to Be Mastered

If I asked you the difference between positive motivation and painting, you might answer that one is a feeling and the other is a skill you possess. This is only half of the story. The other half is that positive motivation, just like playing the piano or acquiring any other skill or ability, is something that you can learn and master. While some are more proficient with positive motivation than others, many aren't sure where to begin. My hope is that you, by the end of this book, become as skilled at creating positive motivation as a world-renowned artist is at creating a masterpiece.

Years ago, I found myself constantly putting things off. I knew I needed to make changes in my life, but I could never get myself to do anything about them. I talked a good talk, but when it came to walking, I found a comfortable chair and sat instead. It was a frustrating situation, one that I know millions of others endure on a daily basis.

Things began to change dramatically after dedicating myself to finding the method to lasting change and success. In the early stages of piecing together the principles of *The Motivated Mind*, I found that my ability to get things done began to improve. The closer I came to completing the program, the easier it was to inspire action toward the things I wanted.

In time, my ability progressed to the point that I was able to create positive motivation within seconds. It was quite an amazing experience. I realized that I possessed something that could change my life forever—and it has. The things I had always dreamed of doing soon became a reality. Small improvements were made in some areas of my life while I enjoyed a complete transformation in others.

One experience in particular stands out in my mind that serves as a concrete demonstration of the power of positive motivation. Before I began working in this field, exercise was one of those things that I knew I had to do but never did. I knew the importance of keeping fit, and on several occasions came close to actually doing something about it. As was always the case, something came up.

After gaining the skill of positive motivation, I was able to inspire action on a consistent basis and enjoy every minute of it. When I don't feel like exercising, but know it's the right thing to do, I run the desire through the program and within a few seconds, I am in a new state of mind. Instantly I go from putting it off to enjoying the activity. What had been put off for so many years now happens on a regular basis without a hint of struggle. With improved health comes increased longevity, so I can safely say that the skill of positive motivation has not only changed my life but also extended it many years. It's truly a lifesaver.

Imagine taking your desire in mind, running it through the principles of the program, and in an instant, you are doing what it takes to succeed. This can happen in every area of your life. There is a direct correlation between your ability to create positive motivation and the quality of your life. It's definitely a skill worth learning.

So, is motivation what you thought it was? My hope is that your answer is a resounding "No!" It takes new information and new ideas to create new and exciting changes in your life. Without letting go of limiting beliefs and patterns, you have little chance of moving on to greater things. Change must happen inside before it can happen outside.

The foundational principle of positive motivation is now in place. It's time to discover how to master the skill. Uncovering the mysteries behind your behavior, why you do what you do, is the next step to replacing the patterns of negative motivation with those of positive action.

NOTES & IDEAS

Chapter 2

Solving the Mystery of Your Behavior

A man always has two reasons for what he does—
a good one, and the real one.
—John Pierpont Morgan

WHY DO YOU DO WHAT YOU DO? What process occurs behind the scenes that leads you to choose one thing over another? Discover the answer to this riddle and you'll have the secret to success. By taking conscious control of your behavior, the decisions you make and the actions you take, there is little that you cannot accomplish.

If I dropped my car off in your driveway and asked you to make it run better, would you know where to begin? An oil change and basic tune-up would help, but what about a complete overhaul of the engine? Would you be able to enhance the performance of each system within the automobile? Unless you're a mechanic, you most likely wouldn't have a clue as to what steps were required. You can't improve a system or process that you don't understand.

Although it may seem that decision-making doesn't always happen in an orderly fashion, it actually follows a very specific sequence. Not only that, but you can bring unconscious decision-making to the surface. Habits that you've been unable to break can become conscious choices under your total control. When you understand how your mind works, you can give it a major overhaul and enhance its ability to help you get what you want.

In essence, the first chapter was about the "what" behind motivation—what it is and what roles negative and positive motivation play in your life. This chapter will cover the "why" of motivation—why you choose one action over another. With these elements in place, the remaining chapters provide the "how" of motivation—how to replace negative motivation with positive action and ultimately achieve the things you desire most.

In the following sections, we will work through the process of human behavior and choice. There are many aspects of decision making that happen so quickly and automatically within your mind that you are barely cognizant of them. Nevertheless, they are in place and follow a specific sequence. The entire process always begins with desire. As you will soon discover, there is only one "have to" in life—the rest are voluntary actions under your control.

A Matter of Desire

As we touched on briefly in the opening chapter, every voluntary action is a choice or matter of desire. The only thing that you must do is cease to live. Every other action you take results from your desire to do so. It is vital that you understand this concept. It is the foundation of the entire process of human behavior.

It is important to remember what we are talking about with voluntary, desired actions. If you are hit by another car while driving to work, you did not voluntarily decide to be hit. These types of actions are the only ones that are not based in desire. Unfortunately, most people fool themselves into believing they "have to" do everything they do. They feel they have no choice in the matter and give up responsibility for their actions.

You do what you do because you want to do it. When you smoke, it is because you want to smoke. When you snap at your friends and push them away, it is because you want to do so. When you pay taxes, it is because you want to pay taxes. When you gain weight, it is because you desired to take in more calories than you burned.

I know what you're thinking: "I don't want to pay taxes. I

have to." Not true. You don't have to pay them if you don't want to. Yes, you would find yourself in a great deal of trouble should you refuse to pay, but it is still a choice. Everything you do is a choice.

You may not desire the ultimate outcome, but that doesn't change the fact that you desired the action that got you there in the first place. You cannot separate the cause and effect relationship. As we saw with instant gratification and negative motivation, the short-term payoff is what you desire, but you have to accept the long-term outcome that accompanies it. If you choose to act, you are responsible for what happens even if you aren't fully aware of the consequences.

The perfect illustration of this situation is a student with poor grades: "I want to do well in school, and I really want to do well on the next test." This statement is followed by the actions of talking on the phone, sitting around watching television, and anything else that keeps the books as far away as possible.

When the grades come back and are more than a little disappointing, you will hear, "I tried, but I'm just not smart enough." That is a cop out. The truth is that the student desired to spend time away from the books. It has very little to do with ability and everything to do with desire. Had the desire been overwhelming, sitting around the house would have been replaced with constant study.

Here's the point: If you're not taking action toward the things you desire, you don't want them enough. Instead of saying, "I want to do it," you would more accurately describe the situation by saying, "I want it to a point, but not enough to take action." The moment you have a strong enough desire will be the moment you get up and do something about what you want.

Being Honest with Yourself

You have to be honest with yourself. I know this isn't always easy to do. It sounds much better to rattle off a hundred excuses about why you don't have time to do what is good for you, but the fact is that you don't have enough desire to make it happen. It has become so common for people to lie to themselves and others about their desires that no one even thinks to look at the truth. It's time to take the blinders off. People do what they want to do, not what they have to do.

If you say you want to learn how to speak Italian and then use your free hours of the night to take a nap, it is obvious you don't want to learn Italian as much as you want to nap. "But I do want to learn Italian. I just need to rest a little each night." I believe you have a desire to learn the language, but you have to be honest enough with yourself to admit that your desire to sleep is greater than your desire to learn. If this wasn't the case, you would learn the language, not sleep.

This element of human behavior is essential because it brings the truth to light and allows you to deal with the facts. Everyone wants to live a better life. Everyone wants to improve and grow physically, financially, mentally, and emotionally, but not everyone has an equal desire. If you don't act on your desire, you don't want it enough—period.

1. I want to lose weight, but I don't eat right or exercise = you don't want to lose weight enough.
2. I want to find a satisfying job, but I'm not looking for one = you don't want a satisfying job enough.
3. I want to be the best football player in the state, but I don't practice every day = you don't want to be the best player enough.
4. I want better grades, but I don't study every night = you don't want better grades enough.

A number of years ago, a small group of co-workers put together a book club and asked me if I wanted to join. "I would, but I have other things to do," I told them. Looking back, I wasn't completely honest with them. The truth was, I wanted to join them to a point, but not enough to actually do it. I didn't *have* to do something else; I *wanted* to do something else. I desired to do other things more than be a part of the book club, otherwise I would have joined. But telling them, "I want to join you guys, but I would rather do something else," isn't as easy to say. If you are serious about making changes in your life, being honest with yourself is critical, no matter how difficult it is to do.

Bottom line: At this stage in the game, if you aren't taking action toward your goals, you don't have a strong enough desire.

Is this a depressing characteristic of motivation? Not at all. This realization is empowering. It helps to explain why you aren't getting what you want. People will rack their brains for an eternity looking for the reasons why they can't overcome procrastination, but never consider the possibility that they don't want it enough. "I'm just not worth it. I can't get myself to do anything. I'm a failure." Nonsense. You just don't have a strong enough desire to get what you want.

The strongest desire always wins out. If you aren't positively motivated, it is because your negative motives are stronger.

Let's add a little more depth to desire. You desire the actions you take based on the information you have available to you. For instance, if you desire to be in New York and have mistakenly picked up directions to Florida, you would not make it to New York. You desired to be in New York and took actions you thought would get you there, but your information was flawed. You are exactly where you are because that is where you want to be based on the information you have learned and currently have at your disposal.

One could say that if you desired to be in New York enough, you would ensure that your directions were accurate or you would get back in the car and correct your mistake. This is what it takes to get what you want. You have to learn all there is to know about your desire and overcome the setbacks you encounter.

What follows is an example of what I have experienced with people who have difficulty accepting this fact of motivation. You have to want it to the point of taking action, or nothing else matters. Follow this same example with your own desires and see if you can discover why you aren't taking action.

SALLY: I want to go back to school.
 JMG: Have you checked into classes?
SALLY: No, I don't have the time.
 JMG: Do you have five minutes to spare?

SALLY: Yes.
JMG: Then you have enough time to check into it.
SALLY: I guess I'm a little afraid to go back to school. What
    would people say?
JMG: So you want to go to school, but not as much as you
    want to protect yourself from being rejected or ridi-
    culed?
SALLY: Yes, I guess that's it.

Finally, we get to the truth. Sally desires safety and to remain
in her comfort zone more than she desires a return to higher
education. Wanting something to a degree isn't good enough if
it isn't to the degree of action.

If you're convinced that you are dealing with an uncontrollable habit, consider the following scenario: If failing to act on
your desires meant that you would be banished forever to a
deserted island, would you change your behavior? "Well, if you
put it that way," I'm often told when posing this question, "I
would do it." This proves that desire is the root of the problem.
Before the threat was made, your desire was at one point, but in
the face of the ultimatum, it leaped to a higher level.

You now have proof that a lack of time, understanding, or any
other reason people give for not doing something is simply an
excuse used to cover up a lack of desire. You can always learn
how to do something and you can always make time for things
you want to do. I know people who say they don't know how
to find a better job nor do they have the time to look, but those
same people know the intricate details of the latest Hollywood
relationships and have time to watch television every night. Ig-
norance and time restraints are excuses clouding the truth.

However, I will admit that sometimes you can't do something.
For example, you cannot become the president of the United
States if you are not a natural-born citizen. However, aside from
being president and a handful of other impossibilities, it's safe to
say that you could be taking action toward all of your desires if
you wanted them enough.

It's Not a Light Switch

Desire is not "on" or "off." There are varying levels to all of your desires, and you act on the strongest one at any given time. Think of it as a ladder. The weaker desires are on the bottom rungs, and the stronger desires are found closer to the top. The single most powerful desire, at the top of the ladder, is the one you act on.

We all want to help homeless children, but only a select few who desire it enough do something about it. Someone who fails to contribute still has a desire to help yet the desire isn't as strong as the contributor's. We all want to be happy and successful, but that doesn't mean our desire is strong enough to create lasting change.

I remember a time in high school when two of my close friends, Jenny and Julie, wanted to make the basketball team. Jenny got up at six o'clock every morning to practice, read every basketball book she could get her hands on, and played after school with anyone who was interested. When tryouts came, Jenny was chosen for the team.

Ladder of Desires

Go for a run
(Chosen Action)

Watch TV

Eat a snack

Mow the lawn

Read a book

FIGURE 4

Julie practiced every once in a while, but not nearly as much as her counterpart. She played around a bit when she could find the time, but there was so much on her plate already. Her lack of preparation and ability kept her from being chosen.

They both had a desire to make the team, but their desires were anything but equal. While Jenny's desire inspired her to take consistent action toward the goal, Julie's failed to create the same drive. This is the nature of desire—different levels create different results.

You may desire change in your life, but if it's not strong enough nothing will happen. You can't tell me that you would do it if you only knew how. If you don't know how to do something, but have a massive desire to succeed, you would read every book, talk to every person, and do everything you could to learn the necessary skills. You can't tell me that you would do it if only you had the time. With a strong enough desire, you would make the time. It isn't understanding or time you're missing—it's always a matter of desire.

When I was young I lived next door to a man named Mr. Wicker. Every time he would visit, the stories of how much he despised his job would come pouring out. This occurred on a weekly basis, and I was always around when he decided to share his thoughts with my parents.

Even as a kid, I was a little confused about Mr. Wicker's behavior. On and on he went about how much he hated his job, and yet back to work he would go every morning. I wanted to ask him why he kept going to a job that he disliked so much, but I wisely chose to keep my mouth shut.

Looking back, I now understand that Mr. Wicker didn't want to leave his job as much as he wanted to stay. Otherwise, he would have quit and found better work. If told he was choosing to go to the job he hated, he would have likely responded, "But I have to go to work. I have to pay the bills."

In reality, he didn't "have" to go to work or pay his bills. True, he would be fired and his power would be turned off, but it was still a choice. The fact was he didn't want to deal with the pain of leaving his job and finding new work.

If Mr. Wicker really wanted a new job, he would be looking

for new opportunities every day. Everyone has enough time and resources to read through the newspaper or make a few phone calls. If his desire was as strong as he wanted to make it seem, he would have been taking steps to find a more fulfilling career. Instead, Mr. Wicker showed up for work every day because he wanted to, not because he had to.

I do believe that he had a desire to leave his job. The only problem was, he didn't want it enough. Mr. Wicker was merely complaining about his plight in life because he was too afraid to do anything about it. If this closely matches your situation, you have nothing to worry about. There is a solution to this problem.

Shifting the Balance

We now reach the critical point of the topic. By now, I hope you realize that stating that you want something doesn't matter if you don't want it to the point of taking steps to achieve it. Your authentic desire must be strong enough to elicit action. If you aren't doing anything about your goals presently, it is proof that the desire hasn't reached this point. This is only the first half of the story.

Desires change. What you desire most at this point in time will not necessarily be what you desire the most tomorrow. There is a way to develop your authentic desires and diminish negative motives. You can take steps to ensure that the things you want to achieve are at the top of your list. This will inspire action and lead to success.

You are going to learn exactly how to do just that. You will have the ability to shift your desires until you get the results you seek. You will be able to take control of your behavior on a daily basis. Think back to the Ladder of Desires. Right now, your desire to change may be on a lower rung, below the desires you are acting on. In the coming sections, you will learn how to develop your desire, sending it right to the top.

We have only scratched the surface of your behavior. Questions such as what your desires consist of or why you desire one thing over another are key aspects to the process. Therefore, before we move on to shifting the balance of desire, we will answer these questions to equip you with the knowledge necessary to create changes that last.

Pleasure & Pain

Desires are all made up of the same two elements: pleasure and pain. All humans are driven to gain the former and avoid the latter. It doesn't matter what type of desire it may be, or how large or insignificant you think it is; pleasure and pain are part of its make-up.

These two factors are as strong and as real as you make them. It is for this reason that they are only perceptions, and not fixed amounts. To one person, the pain of an action may be overwhelming while another finds it of little consequence. It is your perceptions of pleasure and pain that dictate what choices you make.

Do not think of pleasure and pain in only physical terms. They also include emotional, mental, financial, and spiritual forms. Any negative force that affects your life can be seen as a pain, just as any positive force can be called a pleasure.

When someone pinches you, it results in pain. When someone says something insulting to you, it also results in pain. Losing money is painful, and so it creates stress or mental tension. Examples of pleasures include increased energy, increased salary, deepening of a relationship, and helping someone in need. It is important to look at pleasure and pain in these broader terms as we work through the material. It will help to greatly advance your ability to create positive motivation.

Consciously or unconsciously, your mind associates a certain amount of pleasure and pain to actions in question. Whatever your mind deems most desirable results in action. This could be the desire to avoid major pain or experience great pleasure.

What would you do if I told you to send me $10,000? Would you send it? I wouldn't either. The reason is because you associate a great deal of pain with the action, and little, if any, pleasure. Giving away that amount of money, or trying to raise the funds if you don't have it, would be extremely painful.

A very different outcome would result if I told you to send me a short e-mail including your name and address to receive $10,000. You wouldn't hesitate because the pleasure of receiving the money is strong while the pain of having to write the e-mail is weak. In this case, you would take action because the resulting pleasure would easily outweigh the pain.

This pattern of associating pain or pleasure to action is how your desires are constructed. The second you consider taking action toward your desires something happens in your mind. Sometimes quickly and unconsciously, sometimes slower and consciously, your brain considers how much and which type of pleasure and pain to attach to the action.

When it completes its operation you either act or you do something else. A successful person perceives a certain combination of pleasure and pain when he thinks about taking positive action. After his motivated mind takes in the information, he finds that taking action is the way to go, and he works toward his goals.

Another individual who lacks success and fulfillment follows the same procedure, only this time the combination of pleasure and pain result in negative motivation. Instead of progressing toward his goal, he chooses to head in the opposite direction and dig himself deeper into his hole.

The key is to know what you want and then work with the associations of pleasure and pain until you are happy with the result. In other words, you alter your perceptions to alter your behavior. I told you before that your desires change order. What once drove you to turn left may diminish in strength. The desire that was lower on your ladder now takes the top spot and you turn right.

Think back to the $10,000 example. Let's assume that you would take action and write to me. Would you still write the e-mail if you had to quit your job and move to Alaska after receiving the money? No. You would change your mind because you would associate more pain than pleasure. Your associations would be altered, and this in turn would alter your behavior.

Imagine walking into a kitchen containing a stove and a covered pot on one of the burners. Next to the pot you see a note that instructs you not to touch the pot because it contains boiling water. In that instant you associate pain with touching the pot and very little pleasure—you don't touch the pot.

Now you walk into the same kitchen and see the same pot. This time, the note next to the stove tells you that your favorite food is warm and waiting for you in the pot. In an instant, you associate great pleasure with taking off the lid—you touch the pot.

What caused the difference in action? What was it that made you do one thing in one situation and the opposite in another? The answer to these questions will show you the path to changing your associations and thereby changing your behavior.

The element that caused the different actions was information. In scene one, you worked with specific information that helped you form your pleasure and pain associations just as you did in the second scenario. Different information created different results. This was the case with the $10,000 example. When I added the new information about leaving your job and moving to Alaska, your associations changed and you decided against taking action.

What if the pots were actually both dangerously hot? My guess is you would have acted as if the second pot was warm, taken action, and burned your hand. What this teaches us is that our perceptions of pleasure and pain can be wrong. You can be misinformed and do something you shouldn't. Even worse, you may choose not to do something that is good for you because of false perceptions.

The latter is what typically happens to those wishing for change but not acting to make it so. They are afraid that something will happen, but aren't absolutely certain it actually will. Sally was afraid to go to night school because of what other people "may" think or say. She wasn't even certain that the pain would come or that it would outweigh the resulting pleasure. Maybe she's wrong, maybe she's right, and maybe it doesn't matter either way. The point is, your associations and perceptions of pleasure and pain can be misinformed.

Now that you have a good understanding of the nature of desire, we can expand the scope of our discussion. Up to this point, we have only dealt with the two aspects of pleasure and pain. To be more accurate, there are actually four elements that combine to form your associations about particular desires and actions.

Not all pain perceptions are bad, and not all pleasure perceptions are good. The pain you associate with not reaching for your desires is a positive pain; it drives you to action. The pleasure you associate with settling and remaining safe from taking a risk is a negative pleasure; it keeps you from the things you truly want.

This creates two worlds of pleasure and pain: positive and negative. Positives are the aspects that drive you toward your authentic desire. They are the forces that lead to positive motivation and success. Negatives keep you from heading in the right direction. They create obstacles between you and the things you want to have, experience, and become.

Below is a brief overview of each factor. Everything you do in life, from the simplest tasks to the most complex processes, is built upon a combination of these four elements. In an upcoming chapter, we will take an in-depth look at each type of pleasure and pain to complete your understanding of desire.

Pleasure of Action. These are the pleasures that you associate with acting on and achieving your goals. Examples include an improved relationship with your children after spending more time with them, the fit and healthy body you create through working out, and the extra income you earn after securing a promotion.

While these pleasures don't necessarily have to be in place to inspire action (enough pain can do this alone), they are absolutely necessary to maintaining positive motivation over the long-term.

Pain of Inaction. It may be a little odd to think about pain as a positive, but this type of pain will definitely serve as one of the most powerful motivators in your life. These are the pains you associate with not acting on and achieving your desire. If you constantly put your goals off, certain painful outcomes will result. The source of this pain is inaction (inaction simply means failing to act on your authentic desires).

Examples include being inflicted with disease if you fail to quit smoking, losing your friends if you fail to treat them with more respect, and regretting your decision to play it safe and pass up the chance to follow your dreams. This type of pain is most often utilized to initiate action, but requires the presence of pleasure to sustain positive motivation.

Pleasure of Inaction. These pleasures, also known as underlying payoffs, are enormously powerful. They represent the pleasurable things you are receiving by not working toward and achieving your desires. The pleasure of inaction holds you back from creating positive change. Wishing to lose weight but continuing to eat three ice cream cones a day is a perfect example. The authentic desire is to improve your health, and the pleasure of inaction (not working toward improved health) is the ice cream. Eating ice cream every day is a pleasurable experience that you don't want to give up.

People do what works. On some level, you are gaining pleasure by not acting on your goals. Whether it is the calming effect of a cigarette, the sense of power you get from bossing others around, or the pleasure of watching television instead of improving your life in some way, you are receiving rewards for inaction. The pleasure of inaction is not always easy to pinpoint, but however hidden it may be, it is there. Discovering and neutralizing its impact is vital to your ultimate success.

Pain of Action. This element is also a very influential force in your life. These are the pains you associate with taking action, and represent the fears you have about doing what it takes to reach your goals. Touching the hot pot was an example of a pain of action. Other examples include the physical pain of exercise, the emotional pain of making yourself vulnerable and being rejected, and the financial pain of losing your money in an investment.

Looking back to Mr. Wicker's story, let's more accurately categorize his pleasures and pains using our four-aspect model. To begin, he perceived a certain amount of pain from staying at his job. This represents the pain of inaction. Remember, by this I mean pain that would drive him to leave and find a more fulfilling career. He didn't like what he did each day, didn't respect his boss, and didn't really connect with his co-workers. These pains created the complaining nature of his conversations with my parents each visit.

The counterpart to this aspect is the pain of action. Mr. Wicker associated great pain with quitting his job. What if he couldn't find other work? What if he wasn't good enough to do anything else? What if he had to face the fact that he couldn't hack it in any other profession? These were the pains that kept him coming back day after day to a job that left him feeling empty and miserable.

What about the pleasure of action? In the mix of his complaining, he would list off a few things he looked forward to, should he find meaningful work. He desired a new direction that challenged him, new friends, and a boss that he could look up to and admire. These were pleasures that helped create a desire to leave. Unfortunately, the desire wasn't strong enough to create action.

The hardest aspect to pinpoint is the pleasure of inaction. Underlying payoffs are named for this very reason; they're under the surface and not easily recognizable. It takes practice and honesty to put your finger on these pleasures. When you do, you'll have the leverage necessary to change your behavior.

Despite what Mr. Wicker may have said, he did perceive pleasure from staying put. He had safety and security in a weekly paycheck and had no worries about paying the bills or being out on the street. He liked his routine because it was certain, and valued the protection it gave his confidence.

Taken together, the ultimate result was to remain in the job he hated. The desire to leave was there, but it wasn't strong enough to inspire the positive motivation necessary to improve the situation. The only action it created was complaining to the neighbors.

It is vital that you are able to work with these four aspects of desire, but it can be difficult to do so without an organized model from which to work. There is a solution, and it comes in the form of the scales of action. This model of human behavior ties everything together and clearly demonstrates why you choose

one action over another. The scales give you an extremely powerful and useful approach to creating a change that sticks.

The Scales of Action

As you know, all desires are not created equal. Some have more
weight than others. If you are given the choice between having
your teeth cleaned or having them removed, it's obvious that
one pain is greater than the other. The same is true of pleasure.
Doubling your raise would not give you as much pleasure as
tripling it.

The pleasures and pains that create your desires have differ-
ing strengths, also referred to as weights. Because of this, any
model used to describe this process needs to compare the rela-
tive weights of each type of pleasure and pain. Enter the scales
of action.

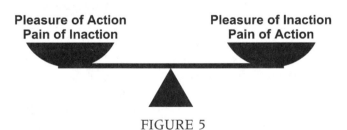

FIGURE 5

As you can see from the scales in Figure 5, the two sides
represent positive and negative motivation. The positive side
weighs the elements that inspire action (pleasure of action, pain
of inaction) while the negative side weighs the elements that
hinder action toward your authentic desire (pleasure of inaction, pain of action).

When you reach a decision point, which happens thousands
of times a day, you consciously or subconsciously weigh each of
the four factors on your mental scales. The side that carries the
most weight results in action. This is how the decision-making,
action-taking process operates, and explains why you choose to
do one thing over another.

The "tipping point" is a term we will refer to from time to time as we move along. The term refers to the factors of positive motivation (pleasure of action, pain of inaction) outweighing the factors of negative motivation (pleasure of inaction, pain of action). In other words, when your desire has reached the tipping point, positive action is the result. This is your purpose—to develop each of your desires to the tipping point. See Figure 6.

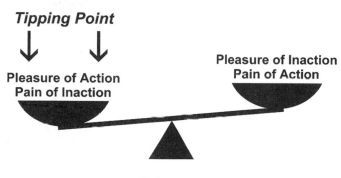

Tipping Point

Pleasure of Action
Pain of Inaction

Pleasure of Inaction
Pain of Action

FIGURE 6

As you recall, this process happens both consciously and subconsciously. When you are living by habit and running on autopilot, you will not recognize the scales working. You simply get an urge to do the things you have been patterned to do. No real thought or conscious choice takes place.

Facing new situations that you are not accustomed to would initiate conscious weighing. If you have ever had to think about the pros and cons of a decision, you have experienced the conscious operating of the scales of action.

Because habits have already found their way into your daily life, it will take focused effort on your part to bring them to the surface. You will have to stop yourself when you enter into patterned behavior and work your way through the scales. Doing this, along with other skills you will learn later, will enable you to break free of habit and negative patterns for good.

For the last time, recall Mr. Wicker's example. If you could look into his mind and see what he was thinking and feeling, even if he didn't realize it was occurring, you would see a set of scales matching Figure 7.

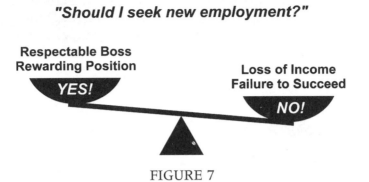

FIGURE 7

When Mr. Wicker thought about leaving his job, he immediately weighed the associations of pleasure and pain with the
action. In his case, the side of negative motivation was stronger;
the combined weight of the pleasure of inaction and the pain
of action was too much to overcome. Had the positive aspects
been increased in strength, the picture would have been very
different. As it was, Mr. Wicker's desire was far from reaching
the tipping point.

The next logical progression directs us to the source of association and perception. Why did Mr. Wicker fear failure so intensely? Why did he value fulfillment less than safety and security?
The answers can be found in the past and present.

Nature & Nurture

Do you fear rejection more than regret? Do you value independence more than close connections with others? Do you like
the color blue, or the color red? The answers to these questions
and others like them stem from only two areas in life. These two
essentials hold the key to your perceptions and associations of
pleasure and pain.

You have probably heard these terms expressed in many different ways, including genetics/environment, nature/nurture,
instinct/learned, and what you are born with/what you experience. However you put it, it comes down to a comparison between the things you possessed from birth and the things you
have learned throughout your life.

While genes have been shown to direct a portion of behavior, a great deal of control remains in your hands. As we touched on earlier in the chapter, your perceptions and associations of pleasure and pain can be changed through learning and experiencing new things in your environment. You can strengthen certain links while weakening others. In effect, the power to develop your desires to the tipping point is completely in your control. Change is possible, and your life will be a shining example of this fact.

Information is the key to altering associations. We may refer to the procedures of learning and experiencing new things, but in the end they both present us with new information. Experiencing the pain of losing your job informs you of how it feels to be without a paycheck. Enjoying the experience of finding a more fulfilling career informs you of how great it feels to achieve a goal. It all comes down to obtaining and digesting new information.

Dan Jacobs was a man in need of new information. For some reason, he simply could not inspire action toward his goals. He would talk and talk about what he wanted to do, but he never actually did anything. The situation was driving him crazy because he couldn't pinpoint the cause of his negative motivation. Dealing with a problem is one thing, but feeling powerless to improve the situation doubles the pain. The day he walked into my office, Dan was almost ready to settle and put his goals behind him.

As we worked through the program, it soon became clear that Dan associated great pain with change (pain of action). When Dan was 23, his older brother approached him with a risky business opportunity. It was more of a pyramid scheme than a business proposition, and he was uncomfortable with the idea from the beginning. After a few days of struggling with his decision, he finally accepted the invitation to join. Although he was extremely hesitant to go along with the investment, Dan didn't want to let his brother down.

To make a long story short, Dan lost money, friends, and his relationship with his brother after the dust of the scheme had settled. It was a risk he regretted taking for years after the experience. This information created the strong perception that change was a risk that equaled great pain.

Dan's story is a great example of how a personal experience can alter perception and, in turn, behavior. When confronted with future risks, including positive and healthy changes, he couldn't follow through. All he could do was recall the pain of lost friendships and faith. Information is the mother of perception, but the next example demonstrates that it can also serve as the vehicle of change.

When I first met her, Christine Stevenson was through with healthy living. To her, exercise equaled massive and intolerable pain. Every belief she had about a healthy lifestyle created absolutely no desire to exercise or eat well and an enormous desire to keep clear of the subject. This created a problem because Christine desired the benefits of keeping fit. She was dragging through the day lacking energy and vitality. She wanted to change, but it wasn't strong enough to create action.

Christine then met a woman at work who just happened to be bursting with vitality—the very thing she was after. Talking with her, she realized that exercise was a major source of her enthusiasm. Christine's new friend went on and on about how much she enjoyed being and staying in shape, and how great she felt after working out.

Over time, Christine's associations began to change. She started to think that exercise wasn't as horrible as she had imagined. If it gave her friend so much joy, maybe she could experience the same thrills. The new information altered her pleasure and pain perceptions, and finally, she decided to take action. Christine is now more fit than ever before and not only loves to exercise, but also to spread the word to others. She exemplifies the possibility of change and improvement.

I know you've experienced changes in perception. Any time you learn something new or experience a new situation, you log the new information in your mind and use it to make future decisions. This includes both positive and negative examples. Reading a book and hearing the news of a friend's car accident both impact your perceptions of the world around you. If asked, you could probably name a hundred different situations in which your perceptions changed along with your behavior.

This creates an empowering picture of success. Instead of giving credit to luck, you now know that successful people simply have the right information working for them. When the elements of their desires are weighed, positive motivation results because the information in their minds is such that the tipping point is achieved. You simply need to find the right information, and you will soon learn a method for doing just that. I must remind you, however, that I am only serving as a teacher of a skill. You will be the one to make the changes. You will be responsible for the success you achieve.

Before you can appreciate the solution, you must first fully understand the problem. All of the information we have covered in this chapter leads to a single cause of your problems along with a single solution. There is only one reason for a lack of positive motivation. Realizing the reason changed the way I looked at my life and the world around me, and explained with clarity, for the first time, why I wasn't acting on the things I desired most.

Problem: The Source of Negative Motivation

As you recall, negative motivation is choosing to take an action that brings you further from what you really want. It is acting on short-term, instantly gratifying motives that you later regret. There is a single cause to this dilemma, one that creates unnecessary pain, grief, regret, and sadness in the lives of millions of people throughout the world. Not only is it a tragic situation, it is completely unnecessary.

The essence of the problem is this: You know you should do one thing, but instead you do another. You desire change, but simply can't get yourself to follow through and actually make it happen. Improving physically, financially, emotionally, and mentally sounds fantastic before you go to bed, but it's quite a different story when the morning arrives. And the sole cause of this negative motivation? Fear.

At this point, you're probably thinking to yourself, "Afraid? I'm not afraid. I just can't get myself to do it!" Although it's never easy to admit, fear is the beast that is holding you back from a better life. You already have a good idea as to what I'm referring, but for the sake of repetition and clarity, we'll do a quick review. You fear having to give up the pleasure of inaction and endure the pain of action. Negative motivation has and always will result from these two fears.

You're not lazy, procrastinating, or putting off until tomorrow what you can easily do today—you are afraid. This fear comes in many forms, ranging from complete terror to a slight unwillingness to let go of the things you enjoy.

An employee who has mishandled a major project isn't merely putting off the call he has to make to his boss, he is afraid to make the call. The pain of action is so intense that it easily outweighs the aspects of positive motivation (pleasure of action, pain of inaction). What will the boss say? Will I be fired? Will I lose the respect of my peers? These fears keep the employee from taking action and create the negative motivation that cripples the hopes and ambitions of the most eager of spirits.

When you fail to act on your desires, it is because you are afraid. The faster you admit the fact, the faster you can move on to the solution. Below are several examples to increase your ability to recognize both types of fears in everyday situations.

Action	Afraid to Give Up	Afraid to Endure
Taking a class	Money for tuition	Humiliation
	Time spent with friends	Mental effort
Quitting smoking	Calming effect	Withdrawal
	Socialization	Weight gain
Getting in shape	Unhealthy foods	Physical effort
	Comfort of eating	Failure to succeed

Fear is never easy to admit. From birth we have been taught to be strong, confident, and fearless. This isn't about being weak. It takes more strength to admit fear than it does to merely cover it up. I have worked with many individuals who chose denial and unhappiness over truth and fulfillment. You deserve the life you desire, and owe it to yourself and your dreams to be open and honest with yourself. I'm not asking you to spill your guts to the world, just admit the truth to yourself. Recognizing the fear is the only way to overcome it.

It's important to note that fear is also not an inherently negative thing. Fear can serve many useful purposes in your life. It can be a warning that prepares you for upcoming danger, and keep you from possible hazards and obstacles. Without the presence of fear, you would end up in more physical, emotional, financial, and mental pain than ever before. The key is to avoid letting it grow into an irrational fear that has a paralyzing effect on you and your desires. You must use the fear to your advantage, better preparing yourself for success and refusing to let it take control of your life.

As we end our discussion about the problem, we enter the exciting process of the solution. If fear is keeping your desires from reaching the tipping point, your only task is to shift the balance of power. This will create the positive motivation you wish to gain and inspire you to consistent and ultimately successful action.

Solution: The Path to Positive Motivation

Imagine standing at the base of an enormous mountain. The mountain represents the things you fear, and on the other side of Mt. Fear sits everything you have ever wanted to have, experience, or become. In order to seize your desires, you must find a way to overcome your fears and scale the mountain. While the fear stems from two factors of desire, the solution is based in the remaining two elements—the pleasure of action and the pain of inaction.

Every increase in these two aspects brings you one step higher up the mountain. Develop the strength of your desire enough, and you will successfully overcome the fears that keep you from what you want. Your desire will reach the tipping point and positive action will result. The solution to replacing negative motivation with positive motivation is to increase the strength of the pleasure of action and the pain of inaction until they outweigh the pleasure of inaction and the pain of action. Do this, and you will get whatever you want.

I used to talk about wanting to learn how to play the guitar, but that's where the desire stopped. My desire was not yet at the tipping point. I feared having to give up time and money to take lessons, as well as feeling like a failure if I couldn't play well. I was negatively motivated by my fears, and was unable to get what I really wanted.

Then I heard one of my friends play—it was amazing. The sounds that came from the instrument took hold of me instantly. I was hooked and decided in that moment that I had to learn how to play. The time for talk was over. That very next day I scheduled my first lesson.

What happened in my mind that created the change? My friend's playing served as new information for my mind and increased the pleasure of taking lessons. I loved the music and wanted to create it on my own. Listening to my friend play tipped the scales in favor of positive motivation. I was able to overcome my fears and act on my desire.

Your mission is to rise above your fears and grasp the life that is waiting for you on the other side of the mountain. The beauty of positive motivation is that you don't have to wait for a friend to stop by and get you excited enough to take action. You never have to wait around for someone else to direct your motivation. Your power is within you.

Positive motivation is not about someone else doing it for you. It's not about waiting—it's about acting. If you have ever been to a live seminar, you will be able to relate well to my next story. It demonstrates the reason why having someone else inspire you for a few hours is nothing compared to being able to inspire yourself forever.

One early Saturday afternoon, I entered a large hotel room containing about a hundred other guests. I had come to take part in a four-hour seminar dealing with motivation in the workplace. I was skeptical from the start because my views clashed with the idea of "getting" motivated, but I kept an open mind and readied myself for an enjoyable experience.

What followed was four hours of an excited and animated speaker sharing stories of success and triumph with the audience. He was an excellent entertainer. Several times during his performance, I found myself sitting on the edge of my seat waiting for the next line as he recollected memories from his childhood. Taking a look around the room, it was clear that each and every participant was locked in and spellbound by his words. He had stories to share and we were more than eager to listen.

The talk was concluded with an emotional tale of achieving success after overcoming the most unbelievable odds. It was a powerful moment. With the last of the stories, we exited the room on a high note, and went our separate ways. It was an afternoon well spent.

Soon after, the excitement died down and the stories I had heard only hours before quickly lost their impact. Joining me at the seminar were several colleagues who were looking for ways to get and stay motivated at work. I met with a few of them just days after the function and our discussion soon turned to the seminar.

It was quite a telling experience. Each and every one of them told basically the same story. They were flying high on their way out the doors, but when Monday rolled around, the feelings were gone. It was back to work again as usual. The speaker was able to excite and inspire the audience, but the moment was brief. He didn't offer any tools by which someone could rekindle the excitement. He didn't teach us how to do it; he simply did it himself.

This is what any good speaker does. He increases the pleasure of action and the pain of inaction, while at the same time minimizing the pleasure of inaction and the pain of action. You feel inspired and ready to create a better life, but without knowing why you feel so good, you can't keep it going.

I'm not saying that live speakers are of no use. First, there is nothing wrong with going to hear a speaker that makes you feel good about yourself and excited about your future. Second, many speakers do teach practical skills that enable their audience members to succeed long after the talk is through. In this particular instance, that was not the case.

The moral of the story is that inspiring you is not as helpful as teaching you how to inspire yourself. You may get excited after reading this book, but if you haven't learned how to get yourself positively motivated, I will have failed. My hope is that you leave this book with the skill of positive motivation and the ability to create your own excitement and compelling future.

The Next Step

You have covered quite a span of material, and have made it out alive! Congratulations. Knowing the reasons behind your behavior, and how to replace negative motivation with positive motivation, places the power in your hands. Instead of feeling confused, frustrated, and angry about the things you do and don't do, you understand the process and are empowered to alter it at will.

The first pillar of the program, understanding *what* motivation is and *why* it is either positive or negative, is complete. It's time to discover *how* to consistently create positive motivation, which begins with the second pillar—desire. Before you can fully utilize the information you have learned up to this point, two things must happen. First, you need to fully grasp the idea of an authentic desire—what it consists of and how to choose the right one. Once you know the make-up of a truly authentic goal, we will work through several eye-opening exercises to help you discover exactly what desires will bring you the success and happiness you seek.

With a clear understanding of the "authentic desire" and a complete list of goals, the principles that you have just learned will come into play. It is at this third stage that you will develop your desires to the tipping point and inspire the action necessary to create the life you deserve.

NOTES & IDEAS

Pillar II
Desire

Chapter 3

The Authentic Desire: Your Pathway to Fulfillment

The foolish man seeks happiness in the distance; the wise man grows it under his feet.
—James Oppenhcim

YOU HAVE TO WANT IT—PERIOD. If you don't have a deep desire to change, your goals will never have a chance of reaching the tipping point. You can't enter into the process with a barely recognizable desire and expect any level of success. A deeply rooted desire to change is essential to creating positive motivation.

People may say they desire change and improvement, but that doesn't necessarily mean it's a true desire. Why would anyone falsely claim to want to change? It sounds good to others to say you have goals, and it also sounds good to yourself. It could be that you know you should change, and realize it would be a healthy and positive thing for you to do. Nevertheless, these shallow desires cannot substitute for the real thing.

Two people say they want to overcome their shyness and meet more people. One has a strong desire to fulfill the goal and realizes that he must first overcome the fears that cause negative motivation. The second thinks the idea sounds good and says he wants it to make himself feel better, but the truth of the matter is he doesn't care that much about pursuing it. The first will eventually become positively motivated to act while the second doesn't have a chance. Before any positive changes can take place, you have to really want it. But not just that—you have to want the right things.

Everyone wants to enjoy the feelings of happiness, but very few know how to gain them. It's like having an extreme appetite but not knowing what to eat. You feel hungry, but you don't know quite how to satisfy your desire. Choosing the wrong food can leave a bad taste in your mouth, causing you to regret ever eating something in the first place. That is why you must know how to successfully satisfy your need for happiness before running off in the wrong direction.

From birth, you have most likely absorbed the typical blueprint for success. Money and material things have always played an integral role in living the good life. While these things may add to your experiences, they can't be your sole reason for being. If obtaining these things guaranteed fulfillment, the stories of seemingly successful superstars meeting with self-inflicted tragedies wouldn't be so prevalent. Many of those with the goods are desperately seeking a way out of their depression and misery. Obviously, there is more to living the good life.

Before you can begin piecing together your goals and desires, you have to know what to look for. You have to choose the right path, one that will lead you to the life you deserve and far from the troubles faced by many so-called successes surrounded by money and materials, but starving for meaning and significance.

This all comes down to one thing—the authentic desire. Aside from requiring a strong initial desire to change, an authentic desire calls for three additional aspects. It must satisfy one or more of your six essential needs, be internally driven, and rest in your control. Throughout the remainder of this chapter, we will take a closer look at each to ensure that your desires have what it takes to enhance the quality of your life.

The Six Cs

As a human being, you have a very specific set of needs that must be satisfied in order to experience fulfillment. Should any of these needs go unattended, you will feel an emptiness in your life. In total, there are six needs that everyone has regardless of race, color, or creed. Happiness isn't a mystery; you simply have to satisfy these necessities.

Your job is to ensure that your desires satisfy at least one category in a healthy way. If it turns out that your goal doesn't fulfill a need, or fulfills it in a negative way, you know that your desire is inauthentic and needs to be reexamined. The needs serve as a review for potential goals to let you know if they will make you happy in the end and include control, change, center, connection, contribution, and constant growth.

Control. People need to feel that they are in control of their lives. Without a certain level of control, people live in fear. "What will happen tomorrow?" "What if I get fired?" "What if I get sick?" Thoughts like these can cause a mental, emotional, and physical breakdown, which is why introducing a healthy amount of control is necessary to a satisfying life. This can be accomplished in two ways.

First, people may try to satisfy the need by intimidating and manipulating others, or use food and drugs to control their feelings. While these actions may give you a sense of control in your life, they are neither good for you or for other people. There is a second method to gaining a sense of control in your life, and one that does so in a healthy way.

Exercise is a way to control your health and add certainty to your life. Researching a new job is another way to gain power over the situation—the more you know, the better your chances are of controlling the outcome and getting what you want. As you can plainly see, both type of actions add a level of control to your life, but the latter does it in a healthy and positive way.

Change. People need variety. Being in complete control of everything in your life would satisfy your first need, but it would also take away the excitement and anticipation of change. While you need to feel in control, you also need a sense of variety to avoid a boring, predictable life.

These two needs call for balance. Too much of one need will outweigh the other, keeping you from the feelings you desire. Just as too much control would make you bored, too much change would make you fearful and unsettled. It may take a little time and thought, but you can satisfy both of these needs simultaneously.

Again, people satisfy this need in two ways. You can add the element of change to your life with drugs, alcohol, or reckless behavior. While these things will definitely provide you with new experiences, their end result will be an increase in pain and unhappiness.

Desires that satisfy this need in a healthy way include traveling to new places or meeting new people. Both activities will add variety to your life, and leave you better off for having done them. Other examples include starting a business, going back to school, or learning a new skill.

Center. People need to feel a sense of importance and significance, that they play a central role in their world. From birth, we crave attention in our own unique ways, and need to feel that we matter, that we are here for a reason. Some people satisfy the need to feel important by putting others down. This is a quick and easy way to feel significant, but in reality, this only serves to lower your own position in life and hurt those around you.

People also fulfill this need by buying as many things as possible. With new cars and fancy homes, you can prove to everyone around you that you are important and deserve respect. Again, these actions only increase feelings of emptiness. They manufacture an inauthentic outer shell to protect inner doubt and fear. Fortunately, these are not your only options of satisfying your need for significance.

You can gain a sense of importance by finding your passion in life and sharing the joy it brings with those around you. You can become an expert in your field, the best parent you can be, or keep your mind and body in perfect shape. These desires represent healthy ways to satisfy your need to feel important without negatively impacting those around you. However, if you push your own significance too far, you will violate another human need and feel isolated and alone. That is why the need for importance is followed by a need for connection.

Connection. People need to feel connected to other individuals. Achieving everything you have ever wanted will mean very little if you are forced to enjoy the experience by yourself. People, and our connections with them, are the foundation of a happy life. Striking a delicate balance between significance and connection with others will provide you with the importance you seek, along with the sense of love and association we all hope to experience.

You have to be careful when working to satisfy this need. Gangs and other groups focused on violence and harm can make you feel strongly connected, which is why gangs in all forms enjoy an unfortunate stream of new members. People may also stay in an abusive relationship or cave in to peer pressure to be accepted. These desires are inauthentic. In the end, they will do more damage than good, create more pain than pleasure.

You can also fulfill this need by seeking out meaningful relationships with friends and family. You can join groups and organizations that empower you, and bring you closer to what you are working toward. Work teams, family gatherings, and even athletic leagues are a great way to satisfy the need to connect with others.

Contribution. People need to serve the greater good and think beyond themselves. You cannot reach the pinnacle of success and satisfaction in life without giving to others. This can take many shapes and forms, but the underlying principle of contribution must be present if you are to enjoy true happiness. Giving your time, energy, heart, and mind to others is among the most gratifying feelings you can experience. It is the perfect win-win situation; you give to others and receive just as much, if not more, in return.

There is a fine line between contributing in a healthy way and becoming a martyr. If you give everything to everyone else without ever contributing to your own happiness, you will end up resenting the ones you are trying to help. In the end, you will find that your desire to give of yourself actually drained your energy and passion in life, and robbed you of the opportunity to experience joy.

It isn't selfish to take care of yourself. You can give to others while at the same time taking care of your own needs. It doesn't have to be one way or the other. Just the opposite is true. If you constantly put the needs and wants of others ahead of your own, you won't be able to share the real you with other people—only a shell will remain. Your friends and family deserve the authentic you.

Fulfilling this need can be as simple as helping to keep your neighborhood clean or as complex as working to improve the environment on a global scale. Find a way to give to others, to improve their lives without worrying about getting something in return, and you will successfully satisfy the need to contribute.

Constant Growth. People need to grow. Meaning is impossible without it. If you're not growing and improving in some way, you will begin to feel that your life is lacking purpose. Many retirees experience a rapid decline in life satisfaction when no further opportunities for growth are present. In essence, a life without growth says to yourself and others, "I'm done. I have nothing more to do here." This type of attitude will obviously stand in your way of happiness.

Have you ever started a new project at work or home and felt a surge of energy and excitement? A sort of renewal or rebirth? This is the natural state of growth. When you learn and experience new things, you feel alive and empowered. One of the most effective ways to create a life of passion and meaning is to take positive steps toward reaching your potential. This includes learning more about your desires, your world, and yourself. Fortunately, this process of striving for self-actualization will never end, allowing you to enjoy the feelings of fulfillment for the rest of your life.

Your desires are authentic if they satisfy, in a healthy way, at least one of your human needs. For too long, happiness has been viewed as a mystery, forcing people to take stabs in the dark hoping to make the right moves. You don't have to guess about the path to happiness. When you begin to fulfill each of your needs on a consistent basis, you will experience a quality of life known to very few individuals.

Internal Drive

Have you ever felt pressured into doing something you didn't actually want to do? Peer pressure in childhood as well as adulthood is a common part of life. There are millions of people out there pushing themselves toward something they don't really want. This dilemma represents the second factor of an authentic desire—it must come from within.

The outside world creates pressure. This includes the obvious influences of television and film, but also your family, friends, co-workers, magazines, newspapers, and a handful of other areas in your life. These outside influences pressure you to look, act, feel, talk, dress, and think a certain way. It is because of these pressures that you may tell yourself you want one thing, but deep down you know you desire something else.

It happens when a housewife tries to convince herself that she is happy at home when she actually wants to be a part of the working world. People who are in perfect health and happy with their bodies are pressured into thinking thinner is always better. You would be surprised at how many people are following desires that belong to the outside world and not to themselves.

It's not hard to understand why this happens. Most people want to fit in and keep from rocking the boat. They tell themselves it's okay to ignore their true desires as long as it makes someone else happy. Your purpose in life is not to fit into someone else's plan. Your purpose is to find and follow your own.

How positively motivated would you be if I asked you to read the phone book from beginning to end? Unless you have more free time on your hands than most, we can safely assume that you would have absolutely no motivation to read the book because you don't want to. This isn't exactly how the pressure of society works. To better match it, imagine that everyone around you reads the phone book and by choosing not to follow their lead, you are alienated and humiliated. You may begin to read the book, without really wanting to, merely to fit in. Here's the main point of a pressured desire: By forcing yourself to do something merely to fit into someone else's ideal, you will have an impossible time getting yourself to take action. You may occasionally follow through, but you will struggle with it each and every time you have to do it.

Positive motivation and a pressured, inauthentic desire don't mix. If it isn't internally driven, you won't be able to inspire yourself to do what you have to do to succeed. Millions of people can't seem to get themselves to act on their goals, and feel guilty and ashamed because of it. They think they are the problem, but never stop to consider why they have the goal in the first place. Doing so would help them realize the objective they are beating themselves up over didn't start as an internal desire—it was to gratify the outside world.

Scott Dawson experienced this dilemma firsthand. He loved to help other people and found nothing quite as gratifying as giving his time and attention to others and receiving a smile and sincere appreciation in return. In particular, Scott felt that his purpose in life was to help children grow into happy and healthy adults, well prepared with the skills and lessons that are the foundation of a quality life. This authentic desire eventually led to a teaching position at Heegle Elementary School.

Everything was moving along smoothly during his first year of teaching. Scott enjoyed working with the children, and the children loved having him as their teacher. It was the perfect position, and he was ready to settle into a long and fulfilling career—then his friends stepped into the picture.

"You're wasting your time," was the typical phrase Scott heard from those around him. "You get paid next to nothing, and soon they'll replace you with some college kid who will work for even less. I can't believe you're settling for so little."

At first, Scott simply ignored their concerns. They didn't understand how much he enjoyed the kids. But then, slowly but surely, their words started to sink in. "Maybe I do deserve more," he thought to himself. "Maybe I should look for a higher paying job."

To the relief of his friends, he finally made the decision to find a position that offered more money and perks. That's where it stopped. Scott didn't do anything to find a new job, and he began to cut himself down for his lack of initiative.

"What is wrong with me?" he would think to himself. "Why can't I find a better job? I can't get motivated to do anything right. I'm a failure."

The problem wasn't that he couldn't find a better job—he didn't want one. His desire to find a higher paying position was inauthentic. His friends put money above passion, and convinced Scott that he was selling himself short. By taking on a desire that didn't come from within, he was unable to make any progress. He wasn't a failure. He was only failing to recognize his authentic desire. After a brief lapse in judgment, Scott happily refocused on teaching and regained control of his life.

Spending your time working to fulfill the demands of other people will always backfire. Life is about living by your rules. It's about doing what is right for you so you can help others do the same. This isn't about being self-centered. It's about being there for yourself so you can be there for others.

Although the majority of externally driven desires will not result in consistent action, it can happen. When the pressure is strong enough, you may be able to get yourself to take action. Instead of feeling frustrated with your lack of ability to make things happen, you'll feel unfulfilled and empty when you succeed. Achieving an inauthentic desire is a hollow victory.

The story of Claire Matthews serves as a perfect example for this type of situation. By business standards, she was well on her way to becoming a superstar. Claire not only broke through the glass ceiling, she blasted it to bits. She knew what she wanted and wasn't afraid to do whatever it took to get it. To any bystander, it looked as though Claire was living the life of her dreams. The truth of the matter was, she was miserable.

Claire was the picture of success, achieving every goal she set and making more money than she had ever thought possible, but she failed to create the happiness she thought her success would bring her. The aggressive, overly confident workaholic she saw in the mirror was not the woman she had hoped to become. Claire was quickly scaling the ladder of success, but emotionally, she had hit rock bottom.

You would have to look thirty-six years into the past to find the beginning of the problem. As far back as she could remember, Claire's mother pressured her into becoming a success. Good advice on the whole, but not when the definition of success focuses solely on money and power. "You may not always be happy, but that's not the point," was the lesson learned.

Claire didn't care about making more money than her co-workers, or about being in control of every situation. Those were her mother's desires. The pressure to please her mother drove her to start early and go home late. It forced her to push harder and harder to achieve what she thought would make her happy. In the end, when the money was in the bank account, and her name was clearly posted on her office door, Claire was one of the unhappiest successes in the world.

After following a path she linked to fulfillment, she only felt more alone and unsatisfied. Claire began to think something was wrong with her, that she wasn't good enough to feel happy. The problem wasn't Claire—it was her desire. Working toward and achieving an inauthentic desire provided none of the feelings she was looking to gain and all of the feelings she was hoping to avoid.

The desire must come from within. Working to please others will only cause pain. You have a purpose in life that is unique and independent. You should never give up your purpose to play a minor role in someone else's.

Shifting the Control

The third and final requirement of an authentic desire is choosing one that is within your control. To ensure your desires have a chance of success, they cannot be 100% externally dependent. In other words, if you rely on someone or something else to make you happy, you may be setting yourself up for a major disappointment. When it comes to your desires, you need to be in the power position, calling the shots and creating your own outcomes. The less control you have over the situation, the weaker your chances are of experiencing a meaningful success.

What is the key difference between a desire to lose weight and a desire to look good enough to please your husband or wife? Losing weight is in your control. You can take the necessary steps to improve your health and reach the goal without the consent of anyone else. You can work toward and achieve the goal on your schedule, using your chosen methods.

The second desire gives up control. What if your husband or wife demands an impossible body? What if they will never be happy with what you do? You are powerless to control the outcome. Your happiness depends on what someone else thinks, even if their judgment is unrealistic, unfair, or just plain wrong. People are constantly pinning their hopes of happiness on things they cannot control. It creates a game of chance between success and failure, with the final choice being made by someone or something else.

There are many authentic desires that have a mixture of control. Making the football team relies partially on your skill, but also the attitude of the coach. You may be the best player trying out, but that doesn't guarantee a spot on the roster. Some of the control is out of your hands. This doesn't mean the desire is inauthentic because a great deal of control remains with you. The problem is creating a desire in which the majority of control lies outside of yourself.

A close friend of mine had the deepest desire to stop her husband from drinking, but it wasn't up to her to stop it. She was not in control of the situation, and could do little to change it. After two years of failed attempts to change someone else, she decided to shift the control back into her hands. Leaving the negative lifestyle was in her control, and that's exactly what she did.

Your heart may be in the right place, and your desire may be strong, but if the control is out of your hands, you will find it nearly impossible to get what you want. There are enough things in your life that you can control to keep you happily occupied for the remainder of your days. Focus your energy in these directions, and give your desires authenticity by maintaining the control and power.

The Process of Change

Have you ever achieved a goal only to find that it left you feeling empty inside? After working toward and finally achieving what you believed to be a worthy ambition, you find yourself asking, "Is this it? Is this all there is?" It can be quite a frightening experience, leaving you feeling helpless to improve the quality of your life. Fortunately, an authentic desire does much more than put you in line with a positive outcome—it saves you from this painful situation.

Pursuing an authentic desire will ensure that the process of achievement, and not merely the end result, provides you with meaning and satisfaction. "I'll be happy when," is the tip-off to a life of disappointment. Setting your sights on a yearlong goal doesn't mean you have to put off enjoyment until the desire is finally attained. Most of your time will be spent working toward, not actually achieving, the things you want. Enjoying the process will enable you to find meaning and happiness in each moment along the path to your chosen destination.

In the next chapter, we will be working through several exercises to help you discover what you want. As we move along, be sure to choose only those goals that satisfy at least one of your human needs, are internally driven, within your control, and most importantly, deeply desired.

NOTES & IDEAS

Chapter 4

Discovering What You Really Want

Nothing happens unless first a dream.
—Carl Sandburg

WHAT IF I DON'T KNOW WHAT I WANT?" If you are among the many who have asked this question, you are about to discover the answer. Nothing else matters if you don't know what will make you happy. Everyone I speak with has the same concerns about which path will lead to happiness, but very few actually ask and answer the questions that will show the way. This is your opportunity to discover how best to satisfy your six human needs and discover your personal roadmap to happiness.

Some people wait a lifetime for their desires to come to them. "I'm not sure what I want yet, but someday it will come to me." Bad news—they're not coming. Opportunities may appear seemingly out of thin air, but you are the one who has to take advantage of the situation. You don't have to deal with a life that is far below your potential, patiently waiting for something better to come along. You have the power to choose a set of desires that will satisfy your needs. It's no longer a matter of "if"; it's a matter of "when."

The time for learning about authentic desires has come to an end. It's now time to begin the process of discovering and defining new desires along with redefining old ones. I want to remind you of an important point before we begin. The more you give, the more you'll get. If you rush through the exercises throughout the remainder of this chapter, you will come away with very few answers and many more confusing and frustrating questions. Take your time with each one, writing down your thoughts and ideas as you go. This is a book based on action, and action is what you must give in order to receive the rewards on the other end.

First Things First

Not everyone can dream to the same capacity, which has a great deal to do with how happy you are in the end. The difference between a powerfully defined desire and one that comes close is the difference between getting what you really want and meeting with disappointment. Before we jump in with both feet, I want to cover several important guidelines to keep in mind throughout the upcoming exercises.

1. Negative Restrictions. Failing in the past does not guarantee failing in the future. If you only choose desires that are certain successes, you will miss out on more than you gain. Let me save you the worry and stress—you will fail again. I will fail in the future, and so will everyone else who takes a chance at anything. Failing is a remarkably beneficial experience about which you will learn a great deal in an upcoming chapter. For now, do yourself the service of discovering desires without a fear of the past coming back to haunt you. What once proved impossible before does not have to remain impossible forever.

Once you make it through the past, you must then deal with the present. Take a look around you. What do you see? It doesn't always have to be that way. The things you want to change in your life can be changed, and the things you enjoy can be maintained. If you are afraid to choose desires that you feel are too lofty compared to your current situations, you will never be able to experience the amazing opportunities that life has to offer. You have to break free of the mold.

2. Positive Restrictions. There is one reservation I would like you to consider. When thinking of desires that you would like to achieve, it's important to do so within reason. I wouldn't put a cap on the possibilities, but some things are simply out of reach. Setting your sights on impossible dreams will only lead to a letdown.

What we're really talking about here are physical limitations. If your desire is to run a one-minute mile, you will not succeed. A desire to make it to the Olympics after only three months of training will meet with the same results. It's important to set inspiring goals, but they have to be in the realm of possibility.

3. Small, Medium, Large. Your desires must come in all shapes and sizes. Each type has its place and purpose among your list. Leave one kind of desire out and you will have a difficult time getting yourself positively motivated.

This brings us to an important characteristic of desire. What you choose now has a major impact on what you do later. If your list of desires includes only small goals, you will make small improvements, but you'll be missing the large desires that can shift your life in an entirely new and exciting direction.

It is because of this need that I suggest you choose small/short-term desires all the way up to large/long-term goals. Small desires get you started and constantly build your confidence along the way. They allow you to easily overcome the fear of action because the fear you associated with them is minimal. You may be too afraid to quit your job and start a business all in the same day, but the fear of buying a few books on the subject isn't as intense.

Examples of small desires include meeting one new person every day, walking to work a few times a week, putting a few dollars into your savings account, or watching one less hour of television at night. Small desires such as these are great at getting the process of change in motion.

But they represent only half of the picture. You also have to set large, inspiring goals. These are the desires that create excitement and exhilaration. They are long-term and far-reaching ambitions that set your sights on a compelling future filled with extraordinary joy and success. If small goals get you started, large desires keep you going.

Large aspirations, it has been said, excite the soul. If your list of desires lacks larger, long-term goals, you won't be inspired to make major changes in your life. You have to be excited about the future. You have to look forward with anticipation to what you are heading toward. You have to get pumped up when you close your eyes and picture yourself accomplishing your goals.

At this point, it isn't vital that you know exactly how you will achieve them. The important thing is to get an inspiring picture of what you want. If the desire is strong enough, you will find a way to make it happen.

The ultimate long-range desire is finding your passion in life. Finding the path you were meant to follow creates a new way of living. You think differently. You act differently. You see the world differently. You will live at another level far above what you knew before. Everyone needs to find a passion in life, and you are no exception.

The Complete Package

When I throw the term "desire" out there, the typical response always has something to do with things. People love stuff. They love to browse it, buy it, use it, store it, lose it, find it, and then sell it. There is nothing wrong with desiring material goods. They make life more enjoyable. However, material desires are only healthy and positive as long as they do not become your reason for living.

To satisfy each of your six needs, you will be working with three categories of desires: things you want to posses, things you want to experience, and things you want to become. You could also think of them as material goals, experience goals, and identity goals. Each type of desire needs to be represented in your list to create a well-rounded life. You will reach the pinnacle of success when you attain the things you want to have, do the things you want to do, and become the person you want to be, thereby satisfying each of your six needs.

Material goals are things that you buy or attain by other means. Examples include a new car or larger home. Experience goals are things you want to live through. Examples include traveling to a foreign country, scuba diving, or jumping out of an airplane. Identity goals focus on who you are and what you wish to become. Examples include becoming more outgoing, becoming a teacher, or becoming a better spouse.

Keep each type of desire in mind when you are piecing together your list of goals. Just as a body requires exercise, nutrients, and rest to function properly, your future requires desires you want to have, to do, and to be to function at the highest possible level.

Before we get into the various methods used to discover desires, let's take a look at the categories that make up the major aspects of your life. Much like the need to include each type of desire in your list, it is important to consider each area of your life when you work through your goals.

If your career is running along smoothly, but your family is slowly slipping away from you, a change is necessary. You may have close ties with your loved ones, but at the same time your health is decreasing and you can't find the time to do anything you want to do. Balance, as is usually the case in life, is the key. It's possible to have each area of your life exactly as you wish it to be as long as you are committed to bringing balance to the equation.

There are many ways to categorize the various areas of your life, and in Figure 8 you will find one such method. Don't worry if the groups don't work for you. The important thing isn't that you fit each of your desires in the sections given, but that you get all of the things you want out of your head and down on paper. If you have categories that work better for you, then by all means, use them.

Examples of the categories include:

PerG: Learning how to play an instrument, learning how to paint, learning how to write

HF: Weight-loss, exercise, dietary changes

TSM: Getting organized at home, getting organized at the office, taking control of time

ProG: Increasing salary, promotion in position and responsibilities

ET: Earning a college degree, learning new languages, learning a new skill

FIGURE 8

PF: Investing, increasing savings and college funds
RL: Learning a new sport, traveling, learning how to dance
FR: Strengthening relationships, spending time with loved
   ones, improving people skills

Self-Analysis

Because the question of what you want is so foreign to most people, the simple act of thinking about what you desire is sometimes enough to open the door to a whole world of possibilities. People never take the time to really think. Whether it's about methods to do something better, do something differently, or do something entirely new, people don't stop long enough to ask questions, let alone wait around for the answers.

This is your chance to stop and ask the questions that need asking. You are not going to accidentally bump into goals and desires that fit your needs exactly. It just doesn't happen that way. Every man or woman whom you admire succeeded because of focused, intentional thought. The same will be true of you.

It's really a crazy situation when you think about it. People put so much time and energy into choosing what clothes they wear, cars they buy, restaurants they eat at, and even which candy bar they want most. They will spend hours, days, and even months giving thought to what color they want to paint their bedroom walls or whom to invite to their wedding, but when it comes to planning out a happy and successful future, the thinking stops. People are too busy being unhappy to think about what they want.

Not all people follow this path. You are different. You are going to think about what will make you happy because you know how important it is. By reading these words, you have proven your uniqueness and individuality. You are doing something about what you want, and my hope is that you continue the habit for the rest of your life.

Now is the time to think. Without distractions or time limits, think about the life you would like to create. Think about the person you want to be. What will you have? What will you do? What kind of person will you become? Asking the right questions will turn on the light bulb of desire in your mind.

Hierarchy of Values

What do you value? Taking a look at your values and where you would rank each is a very helpful tool to discovering what changes would bring you the most satisfaction. Someone valuing close relationships would choose very different goals from someone whose top value is career. One would follow a path toward strong friendships and family ties whereas the other would find more happiness through creating an independent lifestyle.

When it comes to values, the best definition to use is your own. There isn't a right or wrong answer here. If you value it and feel it is an important aspect of your life, then it's fair game. Common examples include love, friendship, honesty, respect, fun, adventure, curiosity, freedom, creativity, and independence.

Rank your values in order of their importance to you. This list will help you in two very important ways. First, it may bring to light a new direction in which you'd like to head. Knowing what you value most will get your mind thinking about new areas of desire. Second, it can serve as a tool to help you prioritize existing goals. If you have a list of desires ranging from traveling and writing a book to starting a family and getting organized, you can bring order to it by using your hierarchy of values. For instance, if you value family above all else, you would put your relationship goals at the top of the list.

The Ideal versus The Actual

Within each of us is a picture of what is possible. We all have some idea of what our ideal life would be like if we could only get ourselves to do what we are capable of doing. It's the life we wish we could wake up to every morning: possessing the things we've always wanted to have, doing the things we've always wanted to experience, and becoming the person we've always wanted to be. These things represent your ideal life.

This ideal includes every aspect of life that you would like to improve. Whether that's doing what you love for a living or spending more time with the people you care most about, the perfect life includes whatever elements are most important to you. Without any doubts, worries, or fears, create a clear mental picture of what your ideal life would look like.

When the ideal is in place, it's time to take inventory of the actual picture. Imagine having to describe yourself to a complete stranger in fifty words or less. What would you say? Of what areas would you speak highly? Which would you be disappointed in? Create a clear representation of the current state of affairs of your life.

This is a test in honesty. While you shouldn't paint an unrealistically deplorable picture, you shouldn't ignore areas needing improvement. Doing so would miss the point of the exercise. Everyone has positive and negative attributes in their lives, things they'd like to change and things they are rather happy about.

The goal is to match reality as closely as possible without adding to or taking away from the facts. If you have a hard time getting along with others, then say so. Don't try to cover it up and make excuses. If you are overweight, then you're overweight. Be honest with yourself. The only way to improve a situation is to call it as it is. You can't fix a problem you don't identify.

On one side we have the ideal life and on the other we find the actual. The space in between presents you with an opportunity to pinpoint new desires. The difference between what you want and what you have creates the goal. This exercise will give you a clearly defined set of desires that will help you to bring your ideal picture to life.

The Past, Present & Future

Next, we will look back at the past, take inventory of the present, and plan for the future. Each stage of time will bring to light many goals and desires that will successfully satisfy your needs. Many of the answers to your happiness questions are sitting inside your mind. The following exercise will help to bring them to the surface where they can be recognized and achieved.

Past

While visiting an old friend, I bent down to say hello to his youngest son. "Your face looks funny," was his reply.

Children are amazing. They are and always will be the absolute best resource to help you understand motivation and human behavior, and they offer excellent clues as to how happiness can be attained. Their thoughts, needs, and desires aren't hidden or masked by the pressures to fit in and keep from saying the wrong things at the wrong times. They speak their heart and mind openly—a trait we would all do well to remember.

You don't lose all of your childhood qualities as you enter into adulthood; you've simply learned how to suppress them with defense mechanisms. Inside every adult is that kid that thinks the world looks a little funny. We could all benefit from reconnecting to the free spirit that directed our lives when we were younger.

By looking back at the earlier version of you, we can get a glimpse of your uninterrupted desires. You will be able to remember what it was like to want things without the worry or stress of fitting in or failing in front of others. When you hear a little kid say he wants to be a teacher, does he follow it up with a list of worries and doubts about being good enough? He simply wants to be a teacher, and leaves it at that. Children's desires are free from unnecessary worry and apprehension.

1. Future Dreams. What did you want to be when you were young? Chances are good that you were asked the question just as many times as I was, with a little pinch on the cheek to top it off. More importantly than how many times you were asked is the answer.

What did you tell them? Try to dig deeper than the occupation itself and get to the core of your desire. What was it about your dream that excited you? What parts of the career did you look forward to taking part in? Wishing to be a doctor could point to a deeper desire to help others in need. The dream of becoming a rock star when you were young may not be your ambition today, but the desire to entertain others and experience the thrill of a crowd could lead to other satisfying endeavors.

2. Memories. What are your happiest memories from your childhood? Reflecting on this question can help you to recognize things you enjoyed in the past that could have the same effect today. What were you doing? With whom were you doing it? What did you like most about the experience? A vivid memory about a positive moment in your life can hold the key to discovering authentic desires that have been pushed to the side as you grew older.

3. Hobbies. What activities did you enjoy doing when you were young? What hobbies did you have and what did you like most about them? Hobbies are a very special area of interest. There are no rewards, no short-term payoffs aside from the joy of doing the activity for the sake of doing it. Recalling the joys of the past can direct you toward authentic desires in the future.

4. Admiration. Whom did you admire when you were young? Maybe it was a family friend, an athlete, an actor, a local fireman or police officer, or a personal acquaintance? What specific things did you admire about the individual? Was it something they accomplished? Their character and integrity? Traits you deem admirable in others can often be used as desires for your own personal improvement.

Present

The past is not the only place that holds insights into your desires. Taking a closer look at your current situation can offer many ideas as to what you really want and why you want it. This will give you the leverage you need to get yourself to take consistent action over the long-term.

1. What's Working? Desiring change doesn't mean that everything in your life is in shambles. While one area could need a little tweaking, another could be making you quite happy. There is something to be learned from the things you currently enjoy. They can lead you to a discovery of your deeper desires that are rarely exposed to the outside.

What do you like about your life? What aspects do you enjoy and why? Answering these questions will help you in many ways. First, you will get a better sense of what you like and what types of things bring you happiness. Next, you can use one positive element as a launching pad for others. For example, if you enjoy working with children you may also enjoy working with adults. This could lead to a new direction in your life that gives you meaning and satisfaction. Finally, by taking note of the things that are working well, you will see that your life isn't in complete ruin. Things can always be improved, but it is also important to recognize those things that are working out well.

2. Ideal Workday. If you could choose any career you wanted, what would it be? Without fear in your mind about failing or looking foolish to others, what would you love to do with your time each and every day? What could get you out of bed in the morning bursting with energy and enthusiasm? Not only that, but it also keeps you going through the afternoon and night. Don't worry about how practical or possible it is. This is about dreaming the big dreams as well as the small. Besides, there is no reason you can't achieve the biggest dream of your life.

3. Ideal Weekend. We have just covered your career, but what about your free time? What would your ideal weekend consist of? Where would you go? What would you do and with whom would you do it? Again, don't worry about whether or not it seems possible. You may not actually achieve the ideal weekend, but getting a good understanding of what you enjoy doing is a great way to pinpoint authentic desires.

4. Present Admiration. Is there someone you currently admire? The same benefit can come from a current role model as well as one from your past, although a present admiration allows you to actually spend time with the individual. It's also important to think about people throughout history whom you admire for their accomplishments and character. It doesn't have to be someone living today. History offers a limitless amount of great men and women to look up to and exemplify.

Just as before, be specific about what you admire. Was it something the individual did in particular, or simply the manner in which she lived her life? Having a concrete example of the characteristics you admire will bring clarity to the picture of your ideal life and lead to an endless stream of potential desires.

Future

The past can offer information about what has happened, and the present slowly slides into the past, but the future is a clean slate. This is the time to look ahead to the kind of life you want to create and the memory you wish to leave behind.

1. Musts. Everyone has their list of "musts." "I must see Europe before I'm gone," or "I must write a book in my lifetime," are good examples. What things must you do during your lifetime? What regrets will you simply not accept? These will definitely serve as powerful desires to enhance the quality of your life.

Everyone may have a list of "must do" desires, but the sad truth is many of those dreams pass away with the dreamer. I wish I could say the opposite was true, but you know just as well as I do that regret is more common than realized dreams. Time will never stop ticking away. If nothing is done about the things you must do, they will join the millions of unfulfilled dreams that have come before them.

2. Impact. I believe that each human being should try to make a positive impact on the world. It is an aspiration that provides a great deal of fulfillment and should definitely be given thought. The greatest feelings in life come not only from improving your life, but also the lives of others.

What impact do you want to have on the world? What contribution do you wish to leave humanity? To come and go without a trace would be a tragedy. You have what it takes to leave your mark. It all begins with discovering what that mark should be.

3. What Will They Say? What do you want to be remembered for? What kind of person do you want others to remember long after you have gone? You have a choice in the matter. You can work to become the kind of person you would like to have in your life or put off improvement until a later time when it's "convenient."

You are not only the things you possess. You affect thousands of lives through your daily interactions with them whether you realize it or not. Are the people you deal with better off for having met you? If you're not sure, you can work to become that kind of individual. Think about what you would like people to say about you, and then take steps to fill those shoes.

4. What Will You Say? Imagine yourself as an old man or woman. You are sitting on your porch in the early morning, watching the world pass by your front door. As you wave to the newlyweds speed-walking by, you begin to reflect on your past. What memories do you want to look back on? What can you do now to ensure a happy recollection later in life?

There will come a time in most of our lives when we must take inventory of what we have accomplished and what we have failed to achieve. That time has yet to come. You can create the future you wish to remember starting today. As you sit quietly rocking in your chair, what memories will bring a smile of satisfaction to your face?

Yearly Segments

Where do you want to be exactly one year from today? Five years? Twenty years? Another method used to discover desires is to create a picture of your ideal future. From here, you work backward to the present, creating goals along the way to enable your picture to become a reality.

So much can happen in a single year. There is no telling where you'll be in that time, unless you do something about it. You can sit around and hope for the best, or you can plan out the picture you'd like to see and take steps to make it happen. You have the opportunity to decide what your future looks like.

The length of time segments is up to you. Use what works best for your situation. The point is not so much in choosing the right timeline as it is choosing a future outcome. For each segment you choose, ask yourself what you'd like your life to look like when you reach that particular stage of the game.

When looking ahead, try to include as many details as possible. The clearer you make your picture, the more opportunities you'll have to derive new desires. Consider what you'll be doing, where you'll be living, with whom you'll be spending time. Let there be no mistaking what you want and how you want it.

How do you know what you should be doing today if you don't know what you want tomorrow? People wake up each morning to see what shows up at their door. It's usually just more of the same. Life was not meant to be lived like this. You have to know where you want to be in order to know where to begin.

The Moment

Think back to a time, any time, when you felt on top of the world—nothing could stop you and everything seemed to go your way. Think of a time when you said to yourself, "This is what it's all about! This is what I want to do for the rest of my life!" Even better, try to recall one or two other situations in which you felt an amazing rush of energy and excitement run through your body.

What was it about these experiences that made you feel so

great? What specifically were you doing? How were you doing it? Just as important as the physical activity is the emotional side of the moment. How were you feeling? What emotions would you link to these times in your life? Try to pinpoint the reasons these memories stand out above all others.

If you can locate the characteristics that combined to provide you with an extraordinary experience, you can implement these same traits into future desires. It's a matter of taking what has worked in your past and making it work for you again in the future.

Dissatisfactions

All this talk about what you want may lead you to believe this is the only route to discovering desires. Fortunately, you have yet another avenue with which to work. Not only is it an important process to ask what you want but also to recognize factors with which you are unhappy. Dissatisfaction is a wonderful thing. If you are unhappy, it means that you are ready to grow. It means that you aren't willing to settle.

A man who is completely content with his life and his surroundings will in very short order become a miserable man. Unsatisfied men and women are those whom we admire and remember. They are the leaders of industry and family. Get unsettled. Get dissatisfied. Get moving.

I once met a man who claimed to be clueless about what he wanted. He then rattled off exactly what he didn't want for nearly forty-five minutes. If only he understood the potential power of being unsatisfied, he would have realized countless desires to pursue. Be careful—it's not about fruitless complaining; it's about using your complaints to improve your life. After pinpointing aspects of your life that are lacking you must work to uncover desires that will fulfill your needs in that area.

What aspects of your life are unsatisfying? What situations will you simply not deal with any longer? What will you refuse to accept? Knowing what you don't want is just as important as knowing what you hope to gain. Both paths will lead to improvement.

Creating Your Lists

After working through each of these exercises, you will have what it takes to create the three lists of desires: things you want to possess, things you want to experience, and things you want to become. Keep in mind the various categories of desires (personal growth, health and fitness, etc). It's a good idea to split each list into two categories: short-term and long-term. For each of your lists, think of as many ideas as possible—you can always edit them down later. Your short-term lists should include desires that are easily introduced into your daily life, such as giving up fast food. A long-term counterpart to this health and fitness goal could be losing twenty pounds.

It's vital that you record your lists! You can use the pages at the end of this chapter or a different method that better suits your needs. Regardless of which method you choose, make sure the lists are legible and easily retrievable. It's unrealistic to believe that you'll remember everything you think of, making it essential that you either write your lists down on paper or type them into a word-processing program. Once complete, you should have three recorded lists of short-term desires and three lists of long-term desires in the areas of having, doing, and being.

Remember to run each of your desires past the requirements of an authentic desire. If one fails to pass the test, it needs to be reexamined. You only have so much time with which to work, and you can't afford to waste it on inauthentic desires. As you recall, each goal must satisfy at least one of your six needs, be internally driven, in your control, and deeply desired.

This is, and always will be, a work in progress. The things you wish to achieve today may not resemble the things you work toward tomorrow. This is the nature of growth. You are a constantly evolving individual whose desires will shift with time. If you find that old desires don't match your current needs, ditch the desires. You always have that option. There are no rules for this process aside from the ones you create.

One of the most effective methods of discovering whether or not a particular desire will successfully satisfy your needs is testing. You have to get out there and test the waters to gain firsthand exposure and experience. Waiting around for a sure thing will leave you waiting forever. Some desires may not pan out, but the ones that hit will more than make up for the misses.

With six lists of authentic desires, it's time to develop each one to the tipping point. In the next chapter, you will learn how to give your desires the power and leverage they need to inspire action and achievement. You have learned how the human mind operates—it's time to take full advantage of that knowledge.

SELF-ANALYSIS

What kind of life would you like to create?

HIERARCHY OF VALUES
How would you rank your values?

THE IDEAL VERSUS THE ACTUAL

How would you describe your ideal life?

How would you describe your actual life?

THE PAST, PRESENT & FUTURE

Past

What did you dream of becoming when you
were a child and why?

What are your fondest childhood memories and why?

What activities did you enjoy doing as a child and why?

Whom did you admire when you were young and why?

THE PAST, PRESENT & FUTURE

Present
What do you like about your life?

How would you describe your ideal workday?

How would you describe your ideal weekend?

Whom do you currently admire and why?

THE PAST, PRESENT & FUTURE

Future

What *must* you do within your lifetime?

What will your contribution to the world be?

How do you want people to remember you?

What memories do you wish to look back on
when you are older?

YEARLY SEGMENTS

Where do you want to be in...
One Year?

Five Years?

Ten Years?

Twenty Years?

THE MOMENT
What were your best moments in life and why?

DISSATISFACTIONS

What areas of your life do you find dissatisfying?

CREATING YOUR LISTS OF DESIRES
Things you want to have:
Short-Term

Long-Term

CREATING YOUR LISTS OF DESIRES
Things you want to do:
Short-Term

Long-Term

CREATING YOUR LISTS OF DESIRES
Things you want to be:
Short-Term

Long-Term

Chapter 5

The Key to Creating Permanent Change

Change. It has the power to uplift, to heal, to stimulate,
surprise, open new doors, bring fresh experience
and create excitement in life. Certainly it is worth the risk.
—Leo Buscaglia

THE TIPPING POINT—the moment a desire becomes more than just a thought. Action is the link that connects where you are with where you want to be. It doesn't matter how good your ambitions sound if you don't back them up with action. Failing to introduce this element into the process makes improvement nearly impossible. Most people drop the ball at this stage of the game not because it is difficult, but because it is either unrecognized or misunderstood.

There is a science to inspiring successful action. It isn't a guessing game that relies on chance and circumstance. Many people fight human nature and try to force themselves to change—this never provides any lasting results. By working with human nature, and not against it, you can systematically create and maintain positive motivation whenever the need arises. This puts the power directly in your hands.

Utilizing the methods in this chapter will enable you to create a state in which you want to take action. You will be driven to do what is necessary to create better results in every area of your life. It's a radically different approach to change—one that not only leads to success, but also makes the process enjoyable and free of struggle.

Because action is such an essential element to the process of positive motivation, the remainder of this chapter will teach you how to develop any desire to the tipping point. Understanding the action equation and pleasure/pain matrix will equip you with the rare ability to take your desires and place massive action behind each one.

The Action Equation

Changing your behavior is simple, but not easy. You have only one thing to do: Associate more pleasure with your chosen desire than pain. If this is successfully done, it will reach the tipping point and positive action will result. This is a skill. It takes a thorough understanding of the key concepts as well as practice. As time goes on you will become more and more adept at creating the motivation necessary to act on and achieve your desires in record time.

As you recall, your desires consist of two elements viewed from four different angles. Positive motivation is created when the pleasure of action and the pain of inaction outweigh the pleasure of inaction and the pain of action. In other words, you will act on a desire that has more reasons to do so than not. This comparison gave us the scales of action, but it can also be viewed as a simple equation:

If

pleasure of action + pain of inaction >
pleasure of inaction + pain of action
positive motivation results

You don't have to settle with the strengths of these four elements. They are yours to increase or decrease at will. Success depends on how well you are able to alter each factor of your desire. Tip the balances and you've got action; fail to do so, and you've got disappointment. We will now cover the process of controlling these factors in detail by means of the pleasure/pain matrix.

The Pleasure/Pain Matrix

Everything you do, absolutely everything, is driven by a combination of the four factors of desire in some way. Alter the elements, and you alter your life. Taking everything you have learned about these factors, you can conclude that there are only four ways to increase positive motivation.

Do any one of these and your desire will begin to approach the tipping point. Do any combination of these and your desire will reach that point in no time at all. Implement all four techniques and you'll have an unstoppable desire on your hands that inspires constant energy, enthusiasm, and action until success is achieved.

Just as important as giving you the tools you need to succeed is making the process as user-friendly as possible. None of the information we have covered will be of any use if you feel too overwhelmed to implement it. Feeling overloaded has a tendency to create stress and frustration—obstacles to positive motivation. The solution, the pleasure/pain matrix shown in Figure 9, is a workable model that is both easy to understand and simple to use.

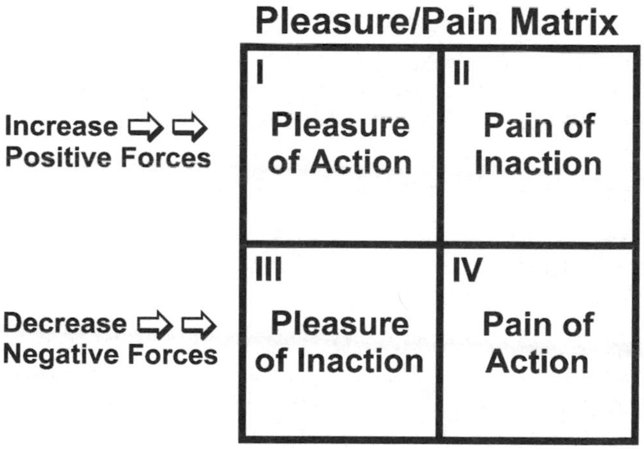

Pleasure/Pain Matrix

	I	II
Increase ⇨ ⇨ **Positive Forces**	**Pleasure of Action**	**Pain of Inaction**
	III	**IV**
Decrease ⇨ ⇨ **Negative Forces**	**Pleasure of Inaction**	**Pain of Action**

FIGURE 9

As you can see, each method to create positive motivation represents one quadrant of the pleasure/pain matrix. What you see here is only the first stage of the matrix, the simplified version. Upon completing this chapter, you will be given the full matrix to use as a reference guide for future desires.

We will now explore each quadrant of the matrix to give you a complete understanding of what it is and how best to use it. These four skills will be looked to for help when trying to inspire yourself or others to action. Once aware of the matrix and how it influences everything you think, feel, and do, the way you look at life will never be the same.

Increasing the Pleasure of Action

What will you get from accomplishing your goal? That is really the question behind the pleasure of action. It includes every positive thing that will result from reaching for and achieving your desire. These are the motives, the driving force, behind your ambitions.

When I began writing this book, my list of pleasures included helping others enjoy their lives more fully, making a positive impact in the world, the sense of accomplishment I would receive once it was complete, and the means to continue running a successful company. These reasons were always at the front of my mind, driving me to action every day. You also have reasons for wanting to change and improve. They are not empty thoughts, although they may be dormant. When activated, these pleasures have immense power.

Every pleasure of action represents a weight that can be added to your scales. The key is to collect as many pleasures as possible to reach the tipping point. If you can give your desire enough power through pleasure, you will consistently act on it. Long-term action is necessary for any lasting change to take place.

As you recall, pain is effective in initiating action, but in order to maintain it, a level of pleasure has to be present. If you do something purely to avoid pain, the positive motivation will not last. The pleasure of action ensures that you not only begin the process, but also see it through to the end.

The varying pleasures you associate with your desire are not fixed. You can change and increase them. You can add as many positive payoffs as you wish. There is no limit to how many reasons you can have for desiring your goal. You may find that a certain amount just isn't enough to get over the hump of fear. Without the ability to change the equation, you would be trapped—forced to give up what you want. Fortunately, the power to shift the balance is in your control.

Every change in your scales comes about because of new or recalled information. Everything you see, hear, touch, taste, smell, and think creates a new weight giving your desire the leverage it needs to inspire. How do you discover these weights? Many are already in your mind—you simply have to dig them out. The others are all around you, and can easily be obtained with a little effort and creativity. Before we begin this process, I want to offer two bits of advice that will greatly enhance the power and persuasion of any information you utilize. The elements of depth and detail can transform a weak thought into a powerhouse of action.

Surface desires are a great place to start, but they lack the impact necessary to move you. Wishing to get organized to free up more time isn't the ultimate desire and won't inspire action. You have to dig deeper and discover the core desire underneath the surface. To do this, you simply have to keep asking questions.

Why do you want to have more free time? What will you do with it? With whom will you spend it? What will that free time mean to you and your loved ones? What positive changes will more time allow you to make? The surface desire to free up time may actually represent a deeply rooted desire to spend more time with your children before they grow up. It should be obvious that the latter desire will have a greater effect on your behavior. For every piece of information you use for each of the four elements, dig beneath the surface to find the core pleasure or pain.

After providing depth to your desires, you'll want to give them as much powerfully denominated detail as possible. In order for the pleasures and pains of your life to affect and improve your behavior, they have to connect with you mentally and emotionally. They must be fueled by passion. Which of the following do you think would make the bigger impact?

Pleasure of Action #1: More time with children.

Pleasure of Action #2: More time spent with the children I love to ensure they enjoy health, happiness, and a life that satisfies all of their dreams. To witness every magical moment, and be a father they can admire, respect, and love.

As you can see, the same pleasure can be defined in very different ways. It may take patience and practice, but in time you will find it easy to inject emotion, passion, and power into the pleasures and pains of your desires. As you improve, you will find that creating positive motivation becomes less of a focused effort and more of an unconscious ability.

The elements of depth and detail should be used in the first two quadrants of the pleasure/pain matrix. Both the pleasure of action and the pain of inaction require power to persuade. Below is your first chance to test your skill. We will cover three methods by which compelling information can be discovered and utilized to develop any desire to the tipping point.

1. Stored. You would be amazed at how much stored up information you have in your mind. If forced, you could probably think of a handful of reasons why you want to achieve each of your desires. Why did you choose the goal in the first place? What do you want to get out of it? How will it make you feel? These are questions you have to ask yourself. If the desire is authentic, the information you already have stored in your mind will serve to create an endless stream of pleasures.

Don't stop yet. The initial reasons for your desire are easy to recognize, but I want you to dig deeper. Think about what this goal will do for you and those close to you. What short-term effects will it have? Long-term? Why should you be excited to reach the goal? Take time to really think about the pleasure of action.

The achievement of a goal is always the ultimate desire, but there are also many pleasures you can associate with the process of accomplishment. How will you feel as you work toward your desire? What benefits will you receive? What benefits will others receive?

For instance, why would someone want to get in shape? What perceived pleasures would drive them to do what it takes day in and day out? The pleasures are unique to each individual, but I'm sure the motives would look something like this:

- More energy
- Longer life
- Less physical pain
- Less emotional pain
- Save money on junk food
- Fewer visits to the doctor
- Increased confidence
- Increased pride
- Inspire others to improve

These are just a few of the common pleasures you might get from being in shape. Each one serves as a reminder as to why you would get up and exercise in the morning, eat well throughout the day, and take steps to reduce mental and physical stress and tension at night. You need to associate as many powerful pleasures to your desire as possible. It is the only way to guarantee lasting change.

2. Observed. After searching your mind for answers, it's time to move on to the minds of others. People love to do and learn things, and then share the information through the written and spoken word. This gives you the opportunity to uncover countless pleasures that can be added to your list of positive motivators.

Every single fact, figure, story, example, or snippet of information that has to do with the pleasures of your desire should be absorbed and taken advantage of. Keep your eyes open to what's out there. Reading a single book can sometimes be the difference that tips the scales to positive action. It doesn't have to be earth-shattering information to be of use to you and your desire.

I wanted to do a little traveling in the U.S. a few months ago, but wasn't doing anything about it. One night while I was working, I decided to spend a few minutes learning about the top sites to see in the country. I found a Web site about Mount Rushmore that painted an amazing story of its creation. I was really interested in seeing the monument firsthand. In a few weeks, I followed through and set out on a road trip to achieve the goal.

The moment I learned about Mount Rushmore, I changed my behavior. I associated great pleasure with traveling there and took action because of it. It took less than five minutes to look at a few Web sites, but that was enough time to create action. A few moments in the right direction can easily bring your desire to the tipping point.

The success stories of others can be among the most powerful motivators around. Biographies can serve to inspire confidence and action toward your dreams. Knowing that another individual, with the same human faults and frailties that we all possess, achieved his dreams paints an exhilarating picture of what is possible in your life. You may find a few stories that revolve around the exact desires you hope to achieve.

I suggest you start snooping around for facts and stories about your desire. Pick the brains of your friends and family, check a few books out of the library, or look online for new information. Scale-tipping resources are everywhere, and more are being created every day. Take the little time required to find them and you'll never regret it. Your desire could be on the brink of shifting the balance of power, and a single fact could lead to action and change your life forever.

3. Experienced. While in high school, I worked with a friend who was terrified of phoning customers. Every time Jenny was asked to make a call, she would find a way to pass the responsibility on to someone else. She was quite talented at maneuvering her way out of these sticky situations. The only problem was that her habit of passing the buck was beginning to catch up to her. A few more irresponsible moves and Jenny would be out of a job. She wanted to overcome her fear, but didn't know where to start.

Then one afternoon, when she was alone in the office, the phone rang. After letting the answering machine pick up the call, Jenny listened to the message with a thumping heart. It turned out that the customer needed a very important piece of information, and time was of the essence. With no way out, she was forced to make the call or risk losing a key client.

Fingers trembling, Jenny dialed the number. The customer answered the phone, and she gave him the required information. After what seemed like an eternity to Jenny, the call was over. A rush of relief came over her as she hung up the phone, but not for the reason you probably think. Jenny was relieved to realize that her fear of the phone was irrational. By experiencing the situation firsthand, she transformed pain into pleasure.

What a change of heart! Jenny went from freezing in the midst of calling customers to freeing herself of the perceived pain and actually enjoying the action. Personally experiencing the situation gave her a new list of pleasures. She learned that taking action gave her a sense of pride and confidence. When the phone rang, or a call needed to be made, Jenny was the first to get involved because she had learned something new: Action didn't equal pain, it equaled pleasure.

Experiential information is just what it sounds like—information you obtain through personal experiences. It is among the most influential methods because the information makes such a powerful impact. A friend can tell you what it feels like to see the pyramids of Egypt, but a story cannot compare to the real thing.

Jenny's story involved overcoming a single fear, but experiential information is just as useful when it comes to providing a constant flow of inspiration necessary to overcome countless obstacles and setbacks. I recently watched a program about a well-known rock band—who they were and how they made it big. All of the members agreed that going to live shows was the key to their success. Experiencing the full effect of the music and crowd instilled a drive in each member that couldn't be stopped. "Without those experiences," the lead singer said, "we never would have made it."

Get out there and experience your desire on as many levels as possible. If you want to be a professional athlete, play sports. Want to be a writer? Go to hear authors speak about their craft and write your own words. If you want to become a rock star, get out there to take in the live experience. This method isn't only for the larger of your goals; it is just as effective for your smaller, short-term desires.

If you want to be more outgoing, spend time with an outgoing friend. Taking a stroll along a college campus is a great way to gain experiential information for a desire to earn a degree. Experience is an amazingly powerful force in your life, and will stand above all others when it comes to changing your mind and behavior.

Increasing the Pain of Inaction

The second quadrant of the matrix represents the pain of inaction. These are the negatives that will result if you fail to act on and achieve your goal. If you desire a closer relationship with your spouse, the loss of the relationship would be a pain of inaction. Failing to work toward a healthier and stronger bond would make for a painful outcome.

Developing the pain of inaction is an excellent way to take advantage of the process of human behavior. People will go to great lengths to avoid pain. Instead of fighting this fact and your natural tendencies, you can use it to give you influence over your own actions. Positive motivation isn't about swimming upstream; it's about using the currents to help you get what you want as quickly as possible.

In the short-term, pain is a stronger motivator than pleasure. People will do far more to avoid pain than they will to gain pleasure. It's the difference between losing a ten-dollar bill and finding one. While the latter will give you pleasure, the former creates a more powerful emotion. Loss entails giving someone or something up to which you have grown accustomed. Pleasures are future rewards in life that have yet to be experienced. Where pleasures of action are additions, pains of inaction are subtractions.

I use the words "short-term" because you cannot maintain positive motivation over the long-term if your only motive is to avoid something painful. There has to be an element of pleasure in the desire. You don't want your desire to become more of a chore than a positive experience.

Imagine starting a small business for the sole purpose of avoiding financial pain; the bills keep rolling in and you need a supplemental income to take care of your responsibilities. This may create a drive to start the business, but it won't last. If your only reason to start a business is to avoid pain, you'll grow to hate the work. Waking up every day in a state of fear is no way to live. Positive motivation relies on an authentic desire—something you genuinely want to have, do, or be. The process can't exist if your only motive is to avoid pain without something to gain.

This doesn't mean that the pain of inaction isn't extremely beneficial. It is an absolutely critical factor that will enable you to overcome the fears that stand in your way. Without the pain of inaction, many of the greatest successes never would have occurred. I simply want you to recognize the need for both aspects. Doing so will ensure that you not only start the process, but finish it successfully.

As with the pleasure of action, we will look at the three methods to gaining compelling information with regard to the pain of inaction. Remember to add as much depth and detail to each pain, locating the core desire and injecting passion, emotion, and power into your list.

1. Stored. What painful outcomes will occur if you don't take action? What will happen to you if you don't get what you want? What will happen to your health? Your emotions? Your finances? How about the people around you? By asking these types of questions, you will find that you have more reasons to act than you may have realized. There is a constant stream of useful knowledge flowing into your mind, but it is useless if it goes untapped. Bring the stored information to the surface and use it to your advantage.

Just as important as recognizing the pains you wish to avoid is knowing which pains make a greater impact on you and your behavior than others. Think back to past experiences that involved pain of inaction. What did the situations involve? What types of pains affected you? What proved to be the strongest one? The same pain to different people will not have the same effect. Because of nature and nurture differences, people's perceptions to the same motives are unique in strength and influence. You have to learn what works best for you.

I want you to think of every pain, both small and large, which will be avoided if you act on and achieve your desire. Because newly discovered pain has the potential to shift the balance and inspire action, you have to look at it like a roomful of dollar bills. Would you stop after picking up just a few? You would keep going until you were forced to stop. This is the mindset to have as you proceed. An eagerness to find new pains of inaction will guarantee that you end up with enough compelling reasons to do what you have always wanted to do.

Seeking out the consequences of inaction may be a new experience for you. While many are familiar with the idea of rewards of action, not as many are able to discover and shape the pain of inaction with the same power and impact. Some time ago, while working with a single mother who was having difficulty staying driven to find better work, this lack of experience with pain of inaction was obvious. Pamela understood the basics of what we were talking about, but her list of pains of inaction didn't contain the necessary ingredients for positive motivation to occur.

Her list of pains provided a great starting point, including items such as a lack of money and living in a rundown apartment, but they required more depth and detail to be of any use. Working with only the information that was stored in her mind, we were able to compile a list of compelling pains that would drive her to look for better work until she achieved success. Her improved list of pains of inaction consisted of:

- LACK OF MONEY = electricity being turned off, being thrown out onto the street, not being able to feed her family, losing custody of her children
- DILAPIDATED LIVING SPACE = having to live in an unsafe neighborhood, putting her and her children in harm's way on a daily basis
- UNSATISFYING JOB = looking back on life with the painful regret of never having found passion, meaning, or fulfillment

We went into more detail with each pain, but I'm sure you get the idea. Your list of pains has to get you stirred up. It has to move you mentally and emotionally or it will merely be a list of words on a sheet of paper. Create a persuasive story and you will be captivated and inspired to take action.

This young mother had the information she needed stored in her mind. What she lacked was the experience and know-how to bring them out into the open. Give this process the time and focused thought it deserves to create a list that will inspire you to succeed.

2. Observed. I can still remember the feeling I had when the police officer showed my sixth grade class a picture of a smoker's lung. I knew at that moment I would never touch a cigarette. The sight was almost too much to take, and the image stuck in my mind forever. I learned a new piece of information that day, and it guaranteed I would never make the wrong choice when offered a cigarette. This is the power of information.

The resources are out there. If you desire a positive change in your life, you will have thousands of reasons to follow through if you take the time to look. Want to lose weight? In ten minutes on the Internet, you could find a list of illnesses, diseases, mortality rates, and a handful of other pains that result from obesity that would get you living a healthier life in no time at all. Want to control your stress levels? It only takes a single trip to your local bookstore to find scores of resources all sharing the dangers and destructive effects of a stress-ridden life. The point is, motivating information is surrounding you and it doesn't take that much effort to make it part of your desire.

I was watching a very insightful special on television a few months ago that featured a set of identical twins living opposite lifestyles. One brother was in ideal shape and enjoying boundless energy and vitality. His brother, however, was eighty pounds overweight and was obviously struggling with the consequences of his failing health.

As the show came to a conclusion, a reporter sat down with the twins to ask them a few questions about the choices they had made and their resulting consequences. At one point in the interview, the reporter turned to the unhealthy twin and asked if he was aware of the dangers of being eighty pounds overweight. As she listed several diseases that could result from his situation, the twin's expression changed from one of indifference to that of a very worried individual.

It was surprising that he didn't know the risks, but the truth was he simply didn't understand the consequences that his lifestyle created. He didn't realize his choices were so dangerous, and he let everyone in the room and watching at home know he was going to make changes. I don't never know if he followed through with his promise or not, but I do know that the information he was given changed his associations. In an instant, his scales shifted toward positive motivation.

Every new pain you recognize will drive you that much faster and further toward the things you want in life. Pain is power. Use it today to help you get to where you want to be tomorrow.

3. Experienced. This type of information gathering may be unsuited to your particular needs, but if you can work it out, it will definitely make an impression. Putting yourself through the painful experience you wish to avoid (on a less destructive scale) will serve as a constant reminder of what you will not accept in your life. It's among the heaviest weights around, and one that you should include in your list if possible.

Douglas Bentley has a lot on his plate. As a surgeon who spends the majority of his time in the emergency room, he deals with a level of stress and pressure rarely experienced by the average person. Not only does his job keep him going at a furious pace, but he also has three children and a wife at home who require and deserve his love and attention.

Some people would crack under the pressure, and take out their frustration and tension on others. If there is one thing I know for certain about Douglas, it's that he will never take his stress or frustration out on anyone else. He will never stop working to improve the relationships he has with his family. How can I be so sure? Because he's been there and knows firsthand the pain and suffering that results from an abusive home.

"My childhood was anything but pretty. After living through

what I've lived through, I know that I will never allow myself to repeat it," he told me with absolute conviction in his voice. "My desire to maintain a happy and healthy household is unshakable. I will not accept anything less."

Douglas has experienced the pain and knows full well the painful consequences of misplaced anger. This information serves to keep him heading in a positive direction. It gives him the strength he needs to deal with setbacks and work through the pressures of life. What past experiences with pain could you use to reach the tipping point?

Looking back at the past is one way to harness the power of experience, but you can also take steps to gain new information in the present. I don't suggest that you immerse yourself in the painful situation you wish to avoid. That would end up doing more harm than good. What I do suggest, if possible, is that you get a quick and relatively harmless feel for what life would be like should your pain be realized.

For someone wishing to remain an ex-smoker, spending time in a crowded bar could provide the burst of pain necessary to ensure the smoke-free habit sticks. Being surrounded by clouds of smoke, choking down every gasp for air, and taking the aroma home in their clothes may create just enough experiential information to maintain positive motivation.

Have you ever seen a child touch a flame? The instant he experiences the pain, an association is created. Touching the flame equals massive pain. The action will not happen again by choice. It may be difficult for your particular desire to fit into this method, but I'm sure you can think back to painful experiences from your past that can be taken advantage of today.

4. Burning Bridges. The last method we'll look at is a little different from the previous three. Instead of thinking about painful situations that may occur if you don't act, this time I want you to create situations that will promise pain in the face of inaction.

Burning bridges in a positive way is an excellent method for creating action. I don't want you to think of this in terms of breaking off relationships or leaving a job on bad terms. What I am advising is breaking off any chance of backing out.

Examples of this sort happen constantly. When you tell a friend that you'll be at her house in an hour to pick her up, you just created a bridge-burning situation. Because of your promise, not picking your friend up will create pain. She will be upset and you will feel guilty about saying one thing and doing another. Other examples include booking a speaking engagement to motivate the action of preparing a talk and registering for a marathon to motivate the action of training.

I know of one author who published a book that listed his weight as thirty-seven pounds lighter than the truth. He knew the public would not only read his words, but also compare them to the actual man. If he didn't lose the pounds, he would have let down his readers, his principles, and himself. By listing his ideal weight in the book for the entire world to see, he burned the bridge of weight gain. He had no choice but to move forward with his desire and see it through.

In essence, bridge burning is about setting yourself up for pain if you fail to do what you know you should do. What can you do to ensure that you follow through on your goals? What bridges can you burn in a positive way that will motivate you to stand by your word?

Developing the reasons for taking action isn't enough to guarantee success. There are obstacles in the road that must be dealt with before you can achieve your desire. By putting to rest the challenges that are produced by negative motivation (pleasure of inaction, pain of action), you will create the leverage necessary to inspire action in spite of your fears. Before you can minimize these obstacles, you must overcome the most powerful challenge of all—your story.

The Story

Human beings are excellent storytellers. Ask a man why he doesn't exercise and he'll bring you through an emotion-filled saga of the hardships and endless struggles that keep him from the gym. We all tell ourselves compelling stories that stop us from getting what we really want, but these justifications are only covering up the real source of the problem.

Stories, excuses, and rationalizations create a barrier between you and the truth. There is always a reason behind not doing something, and the only way you will ever be able to improve upon the situation is to deal with reality. In Chapter Two, you learned that negative motivation stems from the fear of giving up the pleasure of inaction and incurring the pain of action. These fears are pushed under the carpet of stories and excuses. No one wants to admit they're afraid, but everyone wants to give you a good story.

If you spend your time thinking up better excuses for inaction, you will never make any actual progress. You'll make yourself feel better for a short while, and you'll be able to satisfy your friends and family with a good rationalization, but it doesn't last. The truth is there, even if you don't want to admit it.

Think of it like a building standing in a swamp. Each day the height of the building decreases as more bricks are added to the top to correct the problem. The next day, the building sinks even deeper, and the same solution is implemented. The cycle continues forever. Without fixing the source of the problem, you could spend the rest of your life working on the wrong things. Don't waste your time thinking of a good story while your building continues to sink. Instead, fix the foundation.

There are two levels of inaction: lies and truth. Level 1 factors are the stories, excuses, and rationalizations that you tell yourself enough to eventually create a self-destructive belief. Level 2 factors represent the actual reasons you fail to act toward your desires.

Your time needs to be spent identifying and analyzing your fears along with implementing a strategy to minimize their impact. You will never be able to overcome negative motivation if you can't break through the first level. A story that covers up your fears may make you feel good in the short-term, but like most instant gratifiers, it will end up creating more pain in the long-term.

If you aren't taking action toward the things you desire, it's because you are afraid. It doesn't matter what stories you may have ingrained in your mind—they won't do you any good. Being completely honest with yourself is the only way to reach the second level and begin working on the source of the problem that is keeping you from creating a better life.

FIGURE 10

Once you break through to the Level 2 factors, your first objective will be to decrease the pleasure you get from not taking action toward your authentic desire (if you are dealing with a new desire, your objective will be to anticipate possible pleasures of inaction). Underlying payoffs are sometimes difficult to pinpoint, but with a little guidance and some focused thought, you will be able to locate the pleasure of inaction and work to neutralize its damaging effect.

Decreasing the Pleasure of Inaction

Anything you choose to do, even if it seems to be unhealthy and negative, brings you some type of payoff. You wouldn't do it if it didn't work for you on some level. When the pleasures stand in your way of success, they represent the pleasures of inaction. I'm sure you can see how receiving a reward for not acting on your desire is an obstacle that must be overcome.

An individual who constantly overeats and is depressed about his weight may seem to be receiving no payoffs for his actions. He is unhappy with his body and his lack of control.

Although his actions may seem illogical, he is getting a payoff. Perhaps food represents comfort or safety that he cannot find elsewhere. A woman who remains in an abusive relationship may cause confusion and leave people asking, "Why doesn't she just leave?" The answer contains more than the fear of pain. Many times, men and women receive a payoff for staying in an unhealthy relationship. They may believe it is the only way they can feel loved and needed.

This idea takes a little more time and thought to get a handle on. When you think of self-destructive actions, you probably don't think about payoffs or rewards. Always remember, people act on their strongest desire. This means that a negative action, even if it doesn't seem to contain a positive benefit, is a desire that has one or more payoffs.

Honesty will be your most valuable asset when dealing with the pleasure of inaction. Until you can admit that on some level you are benefiting from your negative behavior, you won't be able to move forward with your goals. The pleasure of inaction is like a pair of cement shoes: You may have a brighter destination in mind, but you won't get there any time soon.

This presents such an obstacle because people do not want to give up pleasure. It scares them to think that they will have to stop getting a payoff, even if it comes from a negative situation. There is good news. You do not necessarily have to give up your pleasure. There are many instances in which it can be replaced with a positive activity.

Smoking is a prime example. For many, smoking has a calming effect that helps to reduce stress. You can do away with the negative habit and maintain the pleasures by looking to other activities that can help you relax and let off some steam (exercise, spend time with friends, take a vacation). Before you can work to positively replace or neutralize their effect, underlying payoffs must be identified and analyzed.

1. Identify. Before we get into identifying pleasures of inaction, I want to mention an important reminder. If you are dealing with a new desire, you have yet to experience inaction. Because your goal is new, you have never had the chance to put it off. If this is the case with your desire, anticipate potential pleasures of inaction. You may not be able to look at your history for the answers, but you can still pull together a list of probable pleasures that will need to be dealt with. Keep this in mind while working through the pain of action as well.

If you are having difficulty getting yourself to take action, you have to think about what pleasures you may be gaining by not working toward your goal. How is the negative motivation working for you? What are the benefits? Think about the things you would have to give up if positive action was taken.

Katherine Dean had everything laid out and ready to go. She knew what she wanted to do, when she waned to do it, and how great she would feel when it all came together. Katie was in a dead-end job and had a strategy in place to start her own business. She wanted to be her own boss, and was ready to take control of her life.

Everything may have been in place, but Katie didn't make her move. She hesitated time and again, frustrated and confused about her inability to get things moving. It wasn't fear of pain. She had enough money to keep her safe for quite a long time, and the business she desired was low risk. "If I'm not afraid of failing," she thought to herself, "what could it be?"

After carefully examining the situation, Katie realized it was the pleasure she gained from working for someone else. She kept telling herself that she wanted independence, but on some level she desired the role of a follower. Katie didn't have to think on her own or make important decisions that affected other people. She just had to show up and do what she was told.

In this case, Katie couldn't replace the pleasure with a positive activity. If she ran her own show, she would have to take on the responsibility of the boss. She had to accept the fact that she couldn't have the best of both worlds. A choice had to be made; the same may be true of your desires. Katie decided that the pleasure of taking orders wasn't worth losing her dream. She took action and gave up the smaller pleasure for the long-term reward.

Katie never would have realized what was driving her behavior if she hadn't taken the time to carefully and honestly look at her situation. She could have mentally and emotionally beaten herself up for the rest of her life feeling like a failure. Instead, she identified the problem and took steps to solve it.

Carefully examine your situation. What would you have to give up if you took action toward your goals? What pleasures do you associate with inaction? Once you have identified your pleasures of inaction, you will need to analyze each to discover how best to handle the obstacle.

2. Analyze. The next step in the process is to discover which type of pleasure you are dealing with. There are three categories of pleasure of inaction, and each one needs to be managed in a different way. Depending on the type and strength of the pleasure, you can replace the action and seek to satisfy the desire through alternate means, create a situation of compromise between your pleasures of inaction and your authentic desire, or eliminate it altogether. Each method will remove the obstacle and make it possible for you to move forward with your goal.

The first method is useful when you have multiple options to satisfy the desire your pleasure of inaction fulfills. Payoffs such as feeling important or relaxed can be experienced in many different ways. You don't have to belittle others or drink alcohol to satisfy these desires. You can replace the negative action with a positive alternative that offers the payoffs you seek.

Some time ago, I learned of a teenager who successfully utilized this method to change her behavior. She had a desire to use her time more wisely, which meant less television. She realized that she gained great pleasure from watching movies because they made her laugh. They always left her in a great mood, and she didn't want to give up that feeling.

After analyzing her situation, she was able to replace the pleasure of inaction with several activities that helped her reach her ultimate desire. She began to read books, spend more time with friends, and work with younger kids at a day camp during the summer. These healthy activities satisfied her desire to feel happy, while at the same time helping her to achieve her goal. Is it possible to replace your pleasure of inaction with a positive alternative?

The second method is necessary when you refuse to give up the pleasure of inaction. In some cases, it's possible to satisfy two opposing pleasures at once. Instead of letting go of your authentic desire, you can compromise and work to fit both into your schedule.

My own life is an excellent illustration of this method in practice. While working on *The Motivated Mind*, I had to make a compromise between time spent writing and time spent with my friends and family. Not all pleasures of inaction are negative, such as spending time with loved ones, but they can still stand in the way of a desire. Knowing that I wouldn't give in on either one, I simply had to share my time between both activities.

You don't have to toss away your authentic desire if you find that you do not want to give up your pleasure of inaction. It may take a little reworking of your schedule, but you'll be able to succeed on both ends.

The final method is best suited for pleasures of inaction that cannot exist in the presence of your authentic desire. When you are dealing with polar opposites, one of them has to go. You will either have to forget about your desire or eliminate the underlying payoff.

Remember Katherine? She dealt with this exact predicament. She couldn't have the pleasure of being led and the authentic desire of leading the way. She had to make a choice. The same is true for someone who wishes to stop eating junk food but loves the taste of candy bars. These two competing desires cannot co-exist. One has to win and the other has to lose.

It usually comes down to a choice between short-term payoffs and long-term rewards. If you want to experience an amazing quality of life, you have to let go of your negative pleasures. It may be painful initially, but when you begin to accomplish your goals you will realize that it was more than worth it.

3. Implement. When you have identified and analyzed the pleasures of inaction, it's time to implement your solutions. Like any new skill, it will take time to quickly recognize and neutralize the impact of the underlying payoffs. It's all part of the process of self-analysis. As you learn more about yourself and your behavior, you will find that creating changes in your life happens in less time and with less effort.

Remember, this is a work in progress. You may try to replace a few activities and find that they don't do the trick; you had your hopes set on a quick solution and realize it doesn't always work out that way. You have nothing to worry about. If one idea doesn't pan out, use a different one in its place.

Always keep the ultimate desire in mind. Some people go back and forth between giving up instant gratifiers or their authentic desires. There really is no comparison. You have a single span of time to create an extraordinary life. It will not come to pass through instant gratification or short-term payoffs.

Decreasing the Pain of Action

The last vehicle to tipping your scales in favor of positive motivation is overcoming the pain of action. This includes the things you are afraid to experience should you act on your desires. Fear is a strange thing. People will do almost anything to avoid it, but when they take an honest and in-depth look at the situation, they often find the fear was greatly exaggerated or completely unnecessary.

Fear is strongest when it is left unexamined. It's like a shadow on the wall. As you peak from under your covers, you see an enormous figure creeping closer and closer to your bed. The fear sends shivers down your spine and your heart feels like it is going to explode. Flipping on the lights would show you that the creature casting this fear-inducing shadow was only a kitten. By confronting your fears you will be able to flip on the lights and expose them for what they really are.

The fear of pain arises from a lack of control. You experience fear when you don't know what's going to happen. What if I fail? What if they laugh at me? What if I get hurt? Statements like these all result from a lack of control over the situation. If you knew for certain that you would succeed, be accepted, and remain safe, you would have nothing to fear. You may not be able to guarantee positive outcomes, but there are steps you can take to give you enough control over the situation to diminish or even eliminate your fear of pain.

Honesty, as with the pleasure of inaction, is the only way to make progress in this quadrant. You can give me excuse after excuse until you are blue in the face, but until you admit your fears, you will get the same negative results you have been getting. If you *want* different, you have to *do* different.

Denying fear is not strength. It does not make you more powerful or important. It takes a strong man or woman to admit fear and work to overcome it. If you take two people who are both dealing with the same situation, and one admits he is afraid while the other refuses to accept the truth, you'll have a man quickly overcoming his obstacles and succeeding while the other makes lifelong excuses about his failures. Admitting fear gives you something with which to work. It gives you a problem to focus on and solve.

The sales profession can be a scary field. Calling customers often results in a rejection most salespeople would rather avoid. I remember hearing a story about two salespeople who worked for the same communications company. Both of the salespeople were in a slump. Their conversion rates had dropped dramatically over a span of six months, and management was getting a little worried. Both were called in for one-on-one meetings to determine the source of the decreasing performance.

The first employee, we'll call him Bob, spouted off a list of excuses. The economy wasn't strong, the company wasn't offering enough support, the products were of low quality, and he was working under unrealistic expectations. In short, Bob was not the problem. Where can you go from there? Without an actual problem to solve, Bob's boss was forced to let him go.

The second employee, we'll call him Steve, took a very different approach. It came out slowly at first, but eventually he admitted that he wasn't making as many calls as he used to. Steve was having a hard time dealing with the daily rejection from customers. This pain of taking action kept him from making enough calls to be successful.

Steve's honesty gave his supervisor something with which to work. There was a definite cause to the decrease in sales, and with that came a definite solution. After working through the fear and learning how to overcome it, Steve not only regained his previous level of success, he surpassed it by nearly double.

There is always a reason for inaction toward your desires. Placing the blame on someone else won't improve the situation. Making excuses will only dig you a deeper hole. It's time to shine the light on your fears and see them for what they actually are: obstacles that can and will be overcome. This process begins with identifying and analyzing the pain of action, and concludes with the implementation of a strategy to reduce or eliminate its impact.

1. Identify. What are you afraid of? When you think about taking that first step toward your desire, what pains appear in your mind? You don't have to admit your fears to anyone else. It's just you and your thoughts. You may want to tell someone else for support or advice, but at this point, you are the only person who has to know.

When identifying your pains of action, specificity is a must. Scribbling a few words about failing or being embarrassed isn't what we're after. You have to get to the essence of the fear. Also, make sure you are working to identify personal fears and not the typical ones associated with your particular desire. It may be easier to avoid dealing with the real fears by writing down what everyone else says, but you have to find the solution to your problem and not those of other people.

Think about each area that could present a pain of action. Do you fear emotional pain? Physical pain? Mental pain? Financial pain? The more information you can discover now, the faster your desire will be achieved later.

It is also helpful to consider a stretch of time. What you fear about taking action today is one thing, but there are also fears about future pains. What possible future events that involve your desire do you associate with pain? An example of this is speaking in public. You may not associate much pain with putting together a talk, but the future event of speaking in front of a group may hold a great deal perceived pain.

The act of recognizing and accepting each of your fears is enough to create a positive change. It gives you a sense of control over your life and hope for a better future. Listing each of your pains of action is only the first step you'll take to overcome your fears. You now have to analyze each fear to discover its type and corresponding solution.

2. Analyze. Every fear has a source. It doesn't matter if the cause is rational or not; if you are afraid you have to do something about it. Some fears are logical. Jumping out of an airplane is a reasonable fear due to the dangers inherent in the activity. Others, however, are unsubstantiated and need to be recognized as such.

Being afraid to meet new people because you believe they will hate you is most likely an irrational fear. Taking a look at the facts of the situation along with your history of successful friendships would help you see that you have little to worry about. By examining the source of each of your fears, you will be able to weed out the irrational pains and work to overcome the ones that have a possibility of actually happening.

Let's begin with irrational fears. These are fears that will never happen or have an extremely low probability of ever occurring. The solution to ridding yourself of these obstacles is simple. You have to take an objective look at the pain and measure it by factual standards.

Flying is a perfect example. If you have a debilitating fear of flying, you need only look at the facts to put your fears to rest. The chance of being killed in a commercial airplane is one in eight million. You are twenty-one times safer flying than driving, and your chances of being killed by a donkey are greater than those in an airplane. Knowing the facts sheds new light on your pain of action. When you know the truth and measure your fears by objective standards, you can safely put them to rest.

Reviewing your past experiences may also provide the information you need to overcome your irrational fears. For instance, if you are afraid to learn something new because others may laugh at you, recall a previous time in your life when you learned a new skill. Did people actually laugh at you? Was the pain unbearable? This method will help to decrease or eliminate the fear altogether.

Knowing the difference between an irrational fear and a logical one is not always easy to do. You have step outside yourself and take an honest, unbiased look at the situation. If you truly believe the things you fear will happen, they deserve further attention. However, if you are merely making something out to be more than it really is, it's time to check the fear by objective facts and put it behind you.

We'll now examine fears that have a rational explanation. To begin, I want you to finish the following sentence with each of your desires:

I am afraid to _____ because _____.
               (action)   (painful outcome)

Examples:

- I am afraid to stop smoking because I will gain weight.
- I am afraid to travel because I don't feel safe outside of my hometown.
- I am afraid to audition for roles because people may reject me.

The cause of your fear (painful outcome) is where the progress will be made. You can't do anything with the pain of action until you know what causes it. If you tell me, "I'm afraid to quit my job," I won't know where to begin. There are thousands of reasons you may associate pain with quitting, and until you tell me what the reasons are, improvement can't be made.

Once you tell me, "I am afraid to quit my job because I don't know if I'll find another one," we have something to work on. You can take steps to learn what you want to do with your life and overcome the fear that holds you back.

When you have located the cause of your fear, you have to take steps to minimize the probability that it will occur. Learn all there is to know about your desire and how to avoid the pains of action that keep you from what you want. What steps can you take to prepare yourself for success? What can you do to ensure the things you fear never happen? You'd be amazed at how easily a fear can be reduced or eliminated when you fight it with facts.

Most people never examine their fears. They feel afraid and that's where it ends. They turn from their authentic desires and run away without ever turning back—an unnecessary and unfortunate reaction. You can beat your fears and do the things you have always wanted to do. It simply takes honesty and information.

If you are afraid to fail, learn how to succeed. One of the most useful tips given to aspiring professional speakers is to prepare, prepare, prepare. When you know your information inside and out, the fear that is associated with public speaking subsides. Instead of letting the pain become an overwhelming force, steps can be taken to improve the situation. Use this advice with your own desires.

Using the previous examples, let's take a look at some possible solutions to reduce the pain of action.

Fear:

I am afraid to stop smoking because I will gain weight.

Solutions:

Learn how other ex-smokers have quit without gaining weight.

Create a complete lifestyle plan that includes quitting smoking, exercising, and healthy eating.

Replace smoking with a positive habit.

Join a support group for ex-smokers.

Fear:

I am afraid to travel because I don't feel safe outside of my hometown.

Solutions:

Learn the facts about the probability of being harmed while traveling.

Learn how to keep yourself and your belongings safe while traveling.

Travel with someone who has traveled safely in the past.

Fear:

I am afraid to audition for roles because people may reject me.

Solutions:

Study the path of experienced actors.

Enroll in a course to learn the ins and outs of a successful acting career.

Accept the risk and carry out the desired action.

After reducing the probability that your fears will occur, you need to take steps to minimize their impact should they come to pass. An example is someone who fears heights wearing a hardhat as he climbs a ladder. The painful outcome he wishes to avoid is falling to the ground. If the pain of action occurs, it will not be as intense had he climbed without protection. This may be a little simplistic, but the point should be clear: If you are afraid that something painful will happen to you (emotional, physical, mental, financial, etc.), take steps to reduce the intensity and duration of the pain should it ever take place.

You can also look to past experiences with the pain to help you overcome your fears. If you have already lived through the pain you wish to avoid, examine your experience. How bad was it? Were you able to get over it? What preventative steps could have been taken to reduce its occurrence and duration? When the fear is an old friend, you will realize that you were able to overcome it once and you can do it again.

Every rational fear has a set of solutions to reduce its probability and impact. Your job is to find the solutions and put them to use. Fortunately, you live in a world that is bursting with information and resources to help you do just that.

Recalling the final solution for our hopeful actor, "Accept the risk and carry out the desired action," leads us to a very important aspect of overcoming the pain of action. Some fears cannot be completely eliminated. Regardless of how prepared you may be, success can never be an absolute guarantee. The risk of failure will always be present. When this is the case, you have a decision to make: Is it more important to remain in your comfort zone or take a chance at a life of meaning, success, and unparalleled happiness. The choice should be clear.

3. Implement. Once you have identified the fear, the cause, and the solution, it's time to implement your plan. Every step you take to neutralize or eliminate the things you fear will lesson the negative weights upon your scales. With your fears quickly diminishing, you will shift the balance of power and achieve the all-important tipping point.

Your typical reaction to fear may have been hesitation, but using this method will help you confront your fears head-on. Instead of putting your desires on hold while you wait for the fear to pass, you will know how to take the wind out of its sails and proceed in your chosen direction.

You now have the tools to take an authentic desire and build it to an overpowering strength. Plug a new desire into the matrix and you will be driven to act every single day until you reach your goal. Take an old desire and plug it into the matrix and you'll have a renewed passion to stay the course and achieve your objective. If you find that action doesn't result, it only means that you haven't reached the tipping point. You simply need to develop your positive motivators and further reduce the impact of your negative influences to solve the problem.

It doesn't matter what you want, the matrix will help you get it. Your old patterns of thinking focused on the pleasure of inaction and the pain of action, keeping you from the things you wanted. By recognizing these limiting patterns and replacing them with a focus on the pleasure of action and the pain of inaction you will begin to make drastic changes in your life.

You can also use the matrix to inspire others to action. Because motivation is a constant force, you cannot motivate others, but you can definitely direct their motivation. The matrix is the ideal tool to get the maximum results from athletes, employees, students, and children, among many others.

Figure 11 is the completed pleasure/pain matrix. Work and rework your desires through each quadrant to give them the power they need to create positive motivation and change your life.

You have completed the second pillar. You know how to discover an authentic desire, have six lists of goals that will enrich your life, and understand how to send each of them straight to

Pleasure/Pain Matrix

I Pleasure of Action	II Pain of Inaction
Stage 1: Identify a. stored	Stage 1: Identify a. stored
Stage 2: Discover a. observed b. experienced Stage 3: Develop	Stage 2: Discover a. observed b. experienced c. created (bridge burning) Stage 3: Develop
III Pleasure of Inaction	IV Pain of Action
Stage 1: Identify	Stage 1: Identify
Stage 2: Analyze	Stage 2: Analyze
Stage 3: Implement Strategy a. replace - or - b. compromise - or - c. eliminate	Stage 3: Implement Strategy a. eliminate (irrational) - or - b. reduce probability reduce impact accept the risk

FIGURE 11

the tipping point. Making it this far into the program is enough to positively impact your life forever. But we can't stop there. Successful action requires that each pillar be in its place, keeping the path to your desires free and clear of insurmountable obstacles. Only after making the entire program a part of your life can the truly remarkable results occur.

It doesn't matter how powerful a desire is if you don't believe you can achieve it. I may know that you can get what you want, but you are the one who must believe it. Success requires an absolute confidence in your ability to create the changes you desire. The next pillar will offer you the information you need to work toward your desires free of worry and doubt, with an unshakable confidence in your ability to create the life you want to live.

NOTES & IDEAS

Pillar III
Believe

Chapter 6

The Secrets to Gaining
Unstoppable Confidence

As is our confidence, so is our capacity.
—William Hazlitt

"C AN I REALLY GET WHAT I WANT? Is it possible?" Emphati-
cally, yes! I not only believe that you can achieve your desires, but have the facts to prove it. It doesn't matter how smart
you are, the people you know, or what you do for a living if you
don't believe you can do it. Belief is exactly like desire in that
you cannot replace it. If you want to succeed at anything, a belief in your ability to accomplish the goal is a must.

If I asked you to squeeze a piece of coal in your hand in order
to change it into a diamond, how long would you do it? My guess
is that you wouldn't even begin. This same thing happens in the
minds of millions when they choose a goal that they believe is
out of their reach. Why put time and effort into an impossible
task? Why risk the failure and humiliation? This mindset keeps
most people from getting what they want.

It doesn't have to be that way. You can take the desires you
have in your mind and work to create them in your life. It has
happened before and it will happen again. But there is a setback
we must first overcome. You have probably been told time and
again that you can succeed, but you were never told the second
half of the story.

I can't tell you how many times I have seen or heard the four-word phrase, "You can do it!" Speakers and authors galore cover the subject of confidence without ever giving concrete reasons as to why this is true. This wasn't enough for me, and I assume it isn't enough for you. I need to know the reason why I should believe in something. I often find myself asking, "How do you know I can do it?" Without the answer to this question, it didn't matter how much someone else screams those four little words.

That is why I feel so strongly about this chapter and its purpose. Yes, I agree that you can do most anything you set your mind to, but I have reasons to back up my belief. Filling you with positive feelings won't do much if they aren't based on unshakable facts. Motivational rah-rah sessions are short-term solutions to a long-term challenge. When you have the facts of success locked in your mind, you will move toward your desire with unstoppable force.

Confidence in your ability to succeed will inspire you to take action and overcome your fears of failure. It will drive you to keep trying in the face of obstacles and setbacks. I hold a set of beliefs that convinces me of the possibility of creating my ideal life. Those beliefs are the energy behind my authentic desires, and are now available to you.

A History of Success

Whether you realize it or not, you are your own best proof that success is possible. You have to look no further than your own past to find examples of setting and achieving countless goals. By the very act of reading these words, I can tell that you have already accomplished a great deal, and the pattern can continue if you recognize this fact.

When the expectations called for learning how to read, write, and speak, you did not fail. Although you may have stumbled along the way, you never gave up. When I was younger, I considered the act of reading an insignificant accomplishment. Everyone around me could read, so what was the big deal? I now realize it is a huge deal. For any young child to recognize and recall thousands of words and rules to communicate with others is no small feat—it's simply an expected feat. This expectation lowers the perceived value of the skill, but reading, writing, and speaking are among the most difficult processes to master.

The skills and abilities you have learned in the past prove that you are capable of amazing things in the future. It's not that you can't reach your goals and achieve your dreams; it is that you have accepted the standards of the masses. As your expectations decrease, so too does your confidence.

Do you have a high school diploma? If so, then I want you to consider the following requirements that you were able to meet and complete successfully. The little piece of paper hanging on your wall or tucked away in some closet is all the proof you need that your current desires will be achieved in time.

The typical high school graduate has experienced the following:

1. A thirteen-year commitment to a single outcome.
2. More than 18,000 hours of on-site training.
3. An additional 5,000 hours of at-home work.
4. Thousands of assignments, papers, and projects.
5. A mandatory standard that had to be met every quarter in order for you to successfully complete your goal (report card).
6. Working with approximately 2,500 peers.
7. Working for approximately fifty different supervisors.
8. A final report that critically affected your future opportunities for happiness and success.

When you view school from this perspective, it takes on a new light. It's really exciting to know that thousands of children are able to accomplish this feat generation after generation. Just imagine what they could achieve should these high expectations extend into adulthood.

The history of your success doesn't end with the basic tenants of education. If asked, I have no doubt that you could list many things that you have accomplished from career objectives to raising a family. The problem is that we have become so accustomed to these worthy successes that they lose their ability to inspire confidence. I want you to take another look at the things you have already done in your life to fully realize the significance of your accomplishments and how continuing the cycle is easily within your ability.

If you did it once, you can do it again. You have already shown that you can handle an enormous goal that extends for many years and thousands of hours. When you think about your desire or speak the words out loud, remember your past. When doubt begins to enter into your mind, you have to fight it with fact. It is a fact that you have already achieved many successes, and it is a fact that you are capable of many more.

Take the desire of physical health and vitality. Studies have shown that 30 minutes of exercise at least three times per week can seriously decrease your risk of illness and disease. This amounts to only an hour and a half of effort per week. While in school, you were able to show up and fulfill your responsibilities at least seven hours a day, five days a week. This comparison demonstrates how easily you could attain your goals if you only took the necessary actions.

Your personal history of success presents us with only the first proof of possibility. With a thorough review of your past accomplishments, this single idea could be enough to inspire you to take positive action. You don't have to rely on this idea alone. There are many more principles to come. With enough proof behind your desire, you will have an unwavering belief in your ability to get what you want.

Breaking Down the Goal

Can you take a single step forward with your right foot? How about your left? Can you write a single word on a piece of paper? How about make a phone call? If you can do these simple things, you can do most anything.

Most changes you will be working to create in your life do not happen overnight. I say *most* because the change in mindset can happen in an instant. Deciding you want a better life happens in a moment. The manifestation of this decision, however, does not always come in a flash.

Every desire you have consists of small steps. Starting a business may sound like an overwhelming task, but if you listed every action taken you would find a list containing activities such as making phone calls, writing letters, talking with people, and returning e-mail. Yes, it is difficult to start a business, but it isn't impossible. It's just a matter of doing the right small steps in the right order.

Nearly every goal you have can be broken down into bite-sized pieces. The challenge is not in accomplishing the small tasks, but in getting yourself to stick with it. This is what success is made of. It isn't in taking one massive leap over the mountain; it's in taking hundreds of small, calculated steps toward the peak.

A few years ago, I visited an old friend back in my hometown. When we last met, his wife had just given birth to a beautiful baby girl, Elizabeth. They had wanted a child for some time and were ecstatic about the addition to their family. After a pleasant evening of dinner and playing with Elizabeth, I said what would be my last goodbye for several years.

When the opportunity to reunite arose, I jumped at the chance. I had a conference near their home and had a few hours to spare in the afternoon. As I walked up to the front door, I saw the three of them standing there waiting for me. I had to do a double take when I saw Elizabeth. What had been a newborn baby was now a walking, talking little girl.

I was shocked at how much she had grown. I'm sure you've had the experience when you see an old friend's son or daughter and are amazed how much they've changed. There is a very important lesson to be learned here. Because of my absence, I had the image of Elizabeth changing overnight. I wasn't there to see her learn how to crawl, walk, and talk. It all seemed so sudden.

My friends had a completely different perspective. To them, the changes took place over many days, months, and years. It was a work in progress that had its ups and downs. When you add all of the small improvements together, you get an astonishing transformation.

This principle of change inspires confidence. Success takes time and is built upon a sequence of small steps that are easily within your capability. It's not hard to understand why people have such a distorted view of change and improvement. All they

see in front of them are finished products that seem to materialize out of nowhere.

When you walk through a bookstore, you see the finished
product. You see the books all stacked nicely together on the
shelves. What you don't see are the authors toiling over their
manuscripts, struggling each night to find just the right word to
bring an idea together. When you go to the theater, you see the
finished product. Two hours of action, comedy, drama, or horror
and you're out the door. What you miss are the years of time,
effort, and thousands of steps that went into making the experience possible.

Most of what you see around you resulted from a process.
Think about the pyramids in Egypt. Do you think that all of the
stones were dropped into place at once? It took years to move
all of the blocks to their final destination until the structure
we marvel at today was complete. Small steps lead to massive
change.

It's extremely important that you grasp this concept because
the distorted view of change can be overwhelming. I know of
many people who have some level of desire to change, but believe it is too much to handle. Their view of the overnight success scares them away from even beginning the process. These
individuals are running away from a monster that doesn't even
exist.

For proof of this principle, we can look to examples of so-
called "overnight success":

- Dave Thomas, of Wendy's fame, took nearly twenty-nine
  years to finally realize his dream.
- Sam Walton, the founder of Wal-Mart, worked tirelessly for
  forty years until he reached the pinnacle of his success.
- Starbucks founder, Howard Schultz, invested ten years of
  early mornings and late nights to create the organization
  you see today.

Nearly every man, woman, and organization follows a similar story. Everything is built upon smaller units that combine
together to form the finished product. Aside from creating over-

whelming feelings, the overnight success myth tends to cause people to think that achievement is built upon luck. They believe that some people go to sleep poor and wake up rich without lifting a finger. It's reassuring to know that it isn't based on luck or "the breaks." It's based on the same actions that you and I can take. Success is available to anyone who is willing to put together a string of positive steps.

You can only do one thing at any given time. Successful people don't have two brains or four arms. They simply use every moment in their lives to do the right things. If you can take a single step, you can run a marathon. If you can write a single word, you can write a novel. If you can clean a single room, you can keep your entire home spotless. If you can get along with one person, you can get along with most anyone. If you can take one step toward your desires, you can and will achieve them all.

Proof of Possibility

There is undeniable proof that reaching your goals is possible. It's a formula that has helped countless individuals believe in themselves and to hope and work toward a better life. It serves as a constant source of assurance that you can create the life you have always wanted to experience. I have been looking forward to sharing this formula with you because it has done so much for me in the past and continues to do so on a daily basis.

The formula consists of four stages: 1. Someone else has done it. 2. You possess the essentials of success. 3. Success resulted from a specific set of reasons. 4. The cause and effect relationships remain. By taking a focused look at each stage, you will realize that the power to change is within you. You will have the only proof you'll ever need to instantly and forever eliminate the fear and doubt that stands in your way.

1. Someone Else Has Done It. If I filled a room with 1,000 people and asked them each to write down ten goals, you would find that each of the desires listed has, at one time or another, already been achieved in one way or another. I could multiply the number of participants by ten and you'd get the same results. People desire things that have been proven to be accessible. The

fact that someone else accomplished a goal is undeniable proof
that it is possible and can be repeated.

In some form, each one of your desires has already been
achieved. It may not have contained every detail and intricacy
of your goal, but the basic idea has already been desired, acted
upon, and accomplished. Let's say you desire to lose seven and
two-thirds pounds. Someone may not have desired to lose that
exact amount of weight, but you know that others have wanted
to lose some weight and have achieved the goal. The exact number doesn't matter as much as the basic desire underlying the
specifics.

Could a hopeful inventor look to this formula for proof that
his dream is possible? As an inventor, your purpose is to introduce to the world something that has never been seen before.
No one has ever done what you are trying to do. Again, the specifics don't matter as much as the basic desire. Because inventors
in general have succeeded in the past, it is proof that another invention can succeed in the future. You can use this fact as proof
that inventing something is possible.

In the end, we can safely say that someone else has already
achieved every one of your desires. If someone has done it in the
past, you can do it in the future. You no longer have to question
whether or not it is possible. You know it is. The question becomes whether or not you can repeat the process of success.

2. You Possess the Essentials of Success. If you gathered together every successful person throughout history, you would
find millions of unique traits, abilities, and talents. Some people
are artistically gifted and others have a knack for athletics. Some
were born with the innate ability to paint and play music while
others are genetically predisposed to high-level mathematics.
Every past and present success may have possessed distinct
characteristics, but at the core were the same essentials for success—the same essentials you have within you.

People have been around long enough to prove that most anyone in any situation can achieve anything. People without arms
have scaled mountains. People without legs have run marathons.
People without sight or hearing have taught others how to com-

municate with the world. Individuals with every setback and disadvantage imaginable have accomplished unbelievable feats. What they all have in common is the desire to change and the ability to communicate that sentiment to themselves and others. These two characteristics are behind every accomplishment you see around you. If you desire change and can communicate that fact internally or externally, you share the fundamentals that fueled so many others before you.

I differentiate between communicating internally and externally because certain goals don't require the assistance of others. If you want to exercise, you need only communicate that thought to yourself. Jogging around the neighborhood each morning has nothing to do with other people and therefore only needs to be felt inside. On the other hand, desires such as improving relationships or working toward a promotion need to be communicated to the outside world.

In the end, desire and communication are all it takes to create change. It doesn't matter what your particular situation is, or how many obstacles you will face along the way, it can be done. Amazing individuals like Christopher Reeve and Stephen Hawking may lack the ability to move freely, but through desire and communication alone they are changing the world in which we live.

Combining the first and second stages of the process, we reach a simple truth: someone else has already achieved what you now desire, and you possess the same essential characteristics that were necessary for success. Every possible excuse for inaction has been erased by history. Individuals in far worse circumstances have proven that desire and communication are the only requirements for transforming a dream into its tangible counterpart.

However, in order for the first two stages to provide confidence, a third element is needed. If the individuals who share your desires succeeded by merely snapping their fingers, you would have no way to learn from their example. Believing luck played the major role would give you nothing from which to build. There has to be something for you to model and apply to your own life.

3. Success Resulted from a Specific Set of Reasons. Luck—one of the most destructive beliefs surrounding success. If you think that happiness and achievement simply fall into someone's lap, you will face a hopeless situation. Instead of feeling that you can make improvements in your life, you will have to wait around for "luck" to come your way.

As we talked about before, if luck was the only reason other people succeeded in the past, you couldn't use it to increase your confidence. You can't control luck. If it was the reason for your neighbor's newfound passion in life, you would think, "He's just lucky. I'll never find what I'm looking for." Where do you go from there? What tools or resources can you pick up from your neighbor's example? You cannot learn or benefit from past successes if you believe in luck because you give up your control to chance.

Before we can get anywhere with our formula, we have to dispel luck. You have to realize that success happens for a set of reasons that can be repeated. Imagine that you walked around the corner and bumped heads with a woman who has the power to change your life forever. After regaining your senses and balance, she apologizes and offers you the opportunity of a lifetime. You accept on the spot and live happily ever after.

Were you lucky? Most would say so, but they would be wrong. The experience happened for a reason. First of all, you made the decision to wake up at a certain time and walk down a particular street. You also made the decision to turn at the exact moment someone else did. All you can say about the situation is that it happened. It wasn't luck; it was simply the conclusion of a set of specific and deliberate steps set in motion. If you turned left instead of right that wouldn't make you any unluckier than before.

More importantly, if you weren't prepared to take the offer, the meeting wouldn't have amounted to much. You may encounter fortunate circumstances, but nothing will come of it if you fail to take action. You have to be prepared to take advantage of opportunity when it presents itself. This removes the factor of luck from the equation. When you speak of luck, you are actually referring to a match between preparation and opportunity.

Let's get a little more involved with our story. Let's imagine that the person you bump into is a famous record executive. After mutual apologies are exchanged, she offers to help you in any way she can. You thank her for the offer, but decline and continue on your way. The opportunity was not acted upon and therefore nothing came of the meeting.

Now imagine that you are a struggling musician looking for a way to break into the industry. After she extends the offer to help, you seize the opportunity. Because of your practice and dedication to your craft you are able to make it to the top and live the rest of your life as a successful and fulfilled performer.

You later tell the story to a friend and he responds, "Wow! You sure were lucky!" Luck? Luck had nothing to do with it. Yes, it was a coincidental meeting, but no one touched you on the head with a magic wand and deemed you lucky while the rest of the world was dubbed "unlucky." Success was achieved because of the countless nights spent perfecting your talent and the guts to make the most of the opportunity. Luck would take away from your accomplishments. Fortunate? Yes. Lucky? Impossible.

Believing in luck has the potential to cause a great deal of damage and depression. If luck is the only reason behind success, then you have no control over your life or your future. You have to sit on your hands and hope it comes knocking at your door. It never will. You are in control of your life, and until you recognize that control you cannot improve by choice.

Now that luck is out of the way, let's consider the most common success story. The number of individuals who owe their success to rare coincidences pales in comparison to the number of successes who took very specific and deliberate steps to get what they wanted. These are the examples you should look to for your proof of possibility.

Any outcome, both favorable and unfavorable, results from a specific set of reasons. If I wake up late for work, finish projects past their deadlines, and constantly argue with my superiors, getting fired will not be a sign of bad luck. My choices created the negative outcome. It is all about cause and effect. Negative choices on my part equaled a negative outcome. The same is true with positive outcomes.

When someone succeeds, it is because they took certain actions to create a particular result. They did things in a certain way and order that produced the results they wanted. If someone you know seems to get along with everyone, it is because he does certain things that attract other people. Your charismatic friend may not even recognize what he does to create the positive effect, but that doesn't matter. It's there. He is doing very specific things that make him more likeable to others. If you could match his strategy exactly, you would get the same results.

There are instances when the original environment cannot be recreated. If you tried to come out with the pet rock exactly as it had been done before, you would most likely have a business disaster on your hands. You also may not be able to recreate the physical features of your charismatic friend. This is because certain external aspects are not under your control. What you can always control are your choices and actions. These are the things that will get you to where you want to be.

We have covered a lot of information here, but it all comes down to a simple principle: Success happens for a reason. It is a cause and effect relationship. If you can repeat the causes, you will get the corresponding effect. This principle proves that it is possible to do something that someone else has already achieved. Because every desire you have, in some way or another, has already been done, you can do it, too. That is, of course, if the fourth and final element of the formula is in place.

4. The Cause and Effect Relationships Remain. If I pushed the "A" key on a keyboard, and you saw it appear on the screen, you would think that you could do the same. But what if hitting the same key produced a different letter? What if the cause and effect relationship changed without notice or pattern? If this were the case, it wouldn't matter how many people succeeded in the past because you wouldn't be able to reproduce their steps with any assurance that they would create the same outcome. Every step you took would be a guess.

In order for there to be proof of possibility, the reasons other people succeeded have to hold. If your friend gets in shape by exercising and eating well, and you repeat the same process (with the same body type and chemistry) and you end up gaining more weight and developing health concerns, you would be at the mercy of a random pattern of cause and effect. You would have no idea how to actually get in shape because the causes are constantly changing.

Fortunately, the cause and effect relationships remain the same. Recreating the exact, with emphasis on exact, circumstances will create the same outcome each and every time. If you drop a ball, it will fall to the ground. If I drop the same ball, it will fall to the ground. If you model someone's strategy and get different results, it only demonstrates that you didn't recreate the exact environment.

This brings us to a very exciting conclusion: If someone has already achieved the goal you desire, and they did so because of a specific set of causes and effects that remain the same, then those reasons, the cause and effect relationships, will work for you as well.

For most desires, the cause and effect relationships are not hidden. The specific steps required for success have been written and recorded for anyone to learn. There is a system for everything and your job is to find the right one. When you do, your desire will be achieved.

Desire Will Find a Way

There is little that can hold back an authentic desire. If you want something enough, you will find a way to get it. Your own deeply rooted desire to change and achieve is the last evidence I offer to convince you of the possibility of success.

An unshakable desire was the key to Mahatma Gandhi's success in transforming the nation of India. It was the driving force behind Martin Luther King Jr. and his dream for equality. Desire was at the core of history's greatest inventions such as the telephone, electric light, automobile, and personal computer. Every visionary, inventor, scientist, statesman, peacemaker, mother, father, son, daughter, and friend that has enjoyed success relied on a burning desire to provide the energy and dedication necessary to succeed. It is the heart of change and improvement, and you have it within you.

This feeling is available to all who seek it. There are no rules or regulations to acquiring a deep desire to change. It costs nothing and lasts for as long as you choose to keep it. There are no prerequisites required to possess the desire to achieve more. Everyone, from the poorest of poor to the richest of rich, is given the gift of desire. Not everyone uses it to the same degree. How far your desire can take you is up to you.

After a late night at the office, I packed my things up and walked to my car. The light that usually lit up the parking lot wasn't working, and the entire area was pitch black. It was so dark that it took me a while just to find my own car. When I finally found the right one, I pulled out my keys to unlock the door. I really had my work cut out for me. Without any light, I couldn't make out the right key or the keyhole.

What do you think my chances were of unlocking the door? Do you think that I made it home by car, or by foot? "Of course you unlocked the door," you are probably thinking to yourself. "You have the key, and the keyhole is there, you just have to keep trying to unlock the door." This experience symbolizes the power of an authentic desire.

I had the desire to get home by car. Because of that desire, I didn't give up when I chose the wrong key or couldn't find the keyhole. I knew it was there, and I knew the right key was in my hand. It was simply a matter of time before I succeeded.

This is true of your desire. The answers you are looking for are there. If you have a strong enough desire you will find them. If you are willing to read the books, learn the techniques, talk to the experts, try, try, and try again, you will find a way to succeed. If your dream takes money, you will find a way to get it. If your goal relies on the help of others, you will find the help. If your desire requires taking a chance every day and risking rejection, you will take the chances. If you are willing to do what you have to do, and make the choices you have to make, you will succeed. You may pick the wrong key occasionally, but the right one is sitting in your hand.

It all has to do with the strength of your desire. True confidence will only come when you have a desire that doesn't quit. Imagine two men standing on a basketball court. Each one holds a ball and lines up at the free throw line. Both shoot the ball and miss. One of the men gives up and walks away without succeeding. The other shoots seventeen times until he finally succeeds.

The difference was not possibility. Both men could have made a basket. The difference was the strength of desire. Where one lacked the drive to keep trying, the other knew he could succeed. This explains why two people who desire the same thing don't necessarily reach the same outcome.

You may miss on your first attempt, but that doesn't mean that you will never make a shot. It all depends on how badly you want to make it. If your desire to succeed is strong enough, there is nothing that can stop you from getting what you want in the end.

There is an important distinction to be made about our two players. One could have natural talent while the other is uncoordinated. This only changes the amount of time and attempts, not the possibility. It may take you more time to reach your goals than someone who has more talent, training, or experiences, but that doesn't change the fact that it is possible.

You can do it, but not because I or anyone else says it to you. You can do it because of the proof of possibility. You have the proof to proceed with confidence toward your desires. You can have all of the things you think about during the morning, afternoon, and night. The dreams you had when you were young can be achieved today. The desires to improve physically, mentally, emotionally, and financially are within your reach. If your desire is strong enough, you will find a way to make it happen.

You know what I'm saying it true. You know that you've succeeded in the past. You know that you can easily complete the small steps that are part of every goal. You know that someone else has done what you are now wishing to do, and that you can repeat their success. You know that a strong enough desire will find a way around, under, or through any obstacle you confront.

Confidence is the first mental resource you will need as you begin the process of change, but it isn't the last. If you are confident that life can improve, but wait around for someone else to make it happen, you will end up just as unhappy as someone who has no confidence at all. It takes two more elements to complete the package. Responsibility and the right attitude are vital to your success. With these three mental resources in place you will have the mindset necessary to create positive motivation.

Without a healthy responsibility for your actions and the corresponding outcomes, you cannot begin to change or improve. You must believe in your ability to get what you want, but just as important is the belief that you are the one to make it happen.

NOTES & IDEAS

Chapter 7

Taking Control of Your Life

The sower may mistake and sow his peas crookedly;
the peas make no mistake, but come up and show his line.
—Ralph Waldo Emerson

HAVE YOU EVER FELT OUT OF CONTROL? If so, then you know it's not a pleasant feeling. It is a feeling that creates stress, worry, and fear. It eats away at your desires, and breaks down the spirit until there is nothing left. The life you want to live can be found only through a firm control over how things are and where they are heading.

The feelings of helplessness and fear invade every area of life. Feeling out of control can affect you physically, causing stress-related illness and fatigue. It can damage your relationships, creating tension and anger toward the ones you love. Most importantly, a lack of control creates unhappiness. When you can't seem to find a way to feel good anymore, nothing else matters. That is why this subject is so vital to your success.

The feeling you get when you discover just how much control you have over your life is beyond words. It's like a whole new world appeared out of nowhere, and you are free to go where you please. It is a freedom rarely experienced in day-to-day living. Recognizing the control you have over your life will free you from fear. It will give you back your spirit, or develop the one you have now to a whole new level.

Positive motivation cannot exist without accepting control

and taking ownership of your life. This principle, like all others, serves as a supporting pillar carrying a share of the weight of positive motivation. Without taking control, the structure will fall, and your hopes of success will fall with it.

As you enter this chapter, I must ask you to be open and honest with yourself. I know this isn't always an easy thing to do, but it's essential to your success. You have to be able to look at a situation without bias and accept partial or complete responsibility for its outcome.

Taking responsibility is not a negative thing. It isn't about accepting the blame for everything that happens in the world, nor is it about feeling guilty for the rest of your life. Taking control is about being honest with yourself, perhaps more so than ever before, and taking possession of this immensely powerful gift.

If you are completely satisfied with every aspect of your life, you may not need a shift in belief. However, if your life could use a little tweaking, or perhaps a total transformation, you must understand that the change has to start within you. Something isn't working, and the first place to look for causes is in the mirror. You can only blame other people for your misfortunes for so long. There will come a time, hopefully sooner than later, when you realize the control to change is in your hands. If you are to enjoy the process and achievement of success it will come about because of the choices you made, and not because someone else stepped in and did it for you.

The feeling of being in total control of your life and future makes every experience that much better. It adds a sense of energy and enthusiasm to everything you do, as well as puts you in a position to say what you want and make it happen.

As with confidence, it is available to everyone. That is the amazing and tragic thing about positive motivation—all of these powerful tools are there for anyone to claim, but very few recognize and benefit from them. Slowly but surely, you and I can help to change this unnecessary condition.

No Responsibility, No Change

Not long ago, I watched a movie that documented the life of an aspiring comedian. From the beginning, he was a little abrasive, and I could tell that rough times were ahead. And I was right. At certain points in the movie, his act failed to create even a single chuckle. The comedian simply failed to make the people laugh. At least that's what I thought.

I soon learned from our documented comedy pro that the audience didn't laugh because they were a terrible group of people. Granted, some audiences are not primed for laughter. Holding a show at certain times of the day is not as good as others, but his act failed several different times in front of very different audiences. He was convinced and even furious about the fact that the audience had failed to respond correctly to his routine.

He was blaming the audience because his jokes weren't funny! The comedian would not accept any responsibility for the crowd's response and in doing so gave up all control. Because he didn't see anything wrong with his routine, he continued with the same act, thinking it was the audience who needed to change.

You know just as well as I do that the comedian would never get what he wanted until he took responsibility for the situation. Instead, he sat back waiting for others to fix the problem that actually belonged to him. His desire was to make people laugh, but blaming the listener instead of the speaker pushed his desire further and further away. You can't blame the audience if you aren't getting what you want.

Nowhere in this book will I suggest that you sit back and wait for better things to come to you because I am convinced this is not the way to success. There is only one way to get what you want: Accept a healthy responsibility for the circumstances in your life and take action to change them. You are not a victim, and the sooner you realize this fact, the sooner you'll enjoy improved results.

What if I told you that your level of success and happiness depended solely on the temperature in London? What could you do to improve your chances of getting what you wanted? You could wait patiently in your house sitting on the couch watching the weather channel. In other words, you couldn't do a single thing. You would have to wait and see what London handed you. It wouldn't matter if you worked harder or smarter. Nothing that you did would matter.

There is no difference between this example and the real-life examples of people blaming others for their station in life. "It's not my fault I can't find better work. It's the economy!" "It's not my fault I can't lose weight. It's the food industry!" "It's not my fault I failed the test! It's the teacher." "It's not my fault ... it's your fault!"

Initially, the role of a victim creates pleasure. If it's not their fault, they have nothing to worry about. It feels better, in the short-term, to place the blame on someone else. What most people don't understand is that giving up responsibility is synonymous with giving up control. If it is someone else's fault, you have to wait for them to fix it. You have no control over the situation. As we have seen, instant gratification always creates more problems in the long-term.

In the beginning of this chapter, I talked briefly about the pain of feeling out of control. Being powerless is something that people will work to avoid like the plague. If only people understood that blaming others is welcoming in the feelings of helplessness.

When I was in sixth grade, I confronted this issue head on. After the first few weeks of the new semester I was handed my first math test. Next to my name was a dark red "F." In an instant I was upset. It wasn't fair. I glanced over at my friends only to see them smiling at their above average grades. I glared to the front of the room at Mrs. Sidlock and knew she was the reason I failed the test.

Weeks later, we were handed back our second test, and once again I saw the same letter at the top of the page. "It's not fair! It's not my fault she doesn't like me. Everyone else gets better grades, and I work just as hard as they do!" I told my parents. "It isn't my fault."

After seeing the results of my first test, I blamed my teacher without ever considering what role I played in the outcome. It was obviously something she did, and so I kept doing what I had always been doing. When a test rolled around, I would check over my notes for a few minutes and leave it at that. Why should I change if it's her fault in the first place?

The second test showed what helpless thinking leads to. Looking back, I now realize that I didn't study half as much as my "lucky" friends and never took the necessary steps to understand the concepts that confused me. The moment I blamed Mrs. Sidlock, I gave up all control. Until I accepted responsibility for my actions, my grades continued to suffer. Fortunately, I soon improved my outlook and in turn my performance.

You have to control a situation in order to improve it. You have to be responsible for your fair share of things. When you take an honest look at your situation, and take control of the things that are within your realm of responsibility, you put yourself in the perfect situation to get what you want. You have to bypass the short-term payoff of blame and look to the long-term reward of taking ownership of your life.

You are not 100% responsible for every event that happens in and around your life. There are circumstances that you have played a major, minor, or nonexistent role in creating. I am not asking you to take the blame for the world's problems. This would do just as much harm as not taking any at all. The thing you should be shooting for is a healthy responsibility.

A Healthy Responsibility

A feeling of being out of control will create many mental, physical, and emotional problems, but the same is true of feeling responsible for everyone's setbacks and heartaches. Neither extreme is beneficial. The goal is to feel responsible and take control for the things for which you are responsible. You should aim to match reality.

There are three levels of responsibility and control that you have available. The three levels of responsibility are taking on too much, too little, and a healthy ownership of the things you play a major role in creating.

1. Maximum Responsibility. Every problem in the world and in your life is not your fault. There are some situations that are simply out of your hands. If you fail to realize this, and feel accountable for every negative thing that happens, you will feel overwhelmed and remorseful. Allowing these emotions to monopolize your life will create a situation in which positive motivation can't exist.

The guilt that is created from taking on too much responsibility can literally tear a life and family apart. I remember receiving a letter from a woman, Stacy Nelson, who had always felt responsible for her father's drinking problem. She knew that it was the things she did or didn't do that drove her father to alcohol. When her father passed away at a very early age, Stacy had a meltdown. She was convinced that he would still be alive and well if only she had been a better daughter. It had always taken its toll on her personally, but it began to create problems in her relationships with others.

Stacy began to take it out on her daughter and husband. The pain she felt inside made her constantly irritable, resentful, and unable to be there emotionally for her family. Eventually the situation reached a breaking point and Stacy received professional help. She was able to let go of the responsibility of her father's disease and move on with her life. The real Stacy had come back to the surface and her relationships improved dramatically. Had she not realized the truth, there's no telling where she would be today.

I'm sure you can see how being in this state makes personal and professional growth and success impossible. Positive motivation is a process that works from the inside out. You cannot feel guilty and shameful on the inside and work to improve your life on the outside.

In most cases, the extremes should be avoided. Moderation is usually the key. Responsibility is no different. While you should avoid feeling accountable for everything that happens, you must also avoid refusing responsibility for anything at all.

2. Minimum Responsibility. This level of responsibility was the focus of our earlier topic. If you refuse to take responsibility for the things with which you are unhappy, you will never do what it takes to change the situation. Passing the buck is as prevalent as it is in our society because fault is too difficult to accept. No one wants to admit they did something wrong. This resistance to reality only serves to create more of the feelings you were hoping to eliminate. The cure to the victim's cries from the earlier examples is reality.

"It's not my fault I don't have a job. It's the economy." Wrong. Millions of others have found work within the same job market. While you sat around the house blaming the world for your problems, the rest of the working world was busy securing and maintaining employment.

"It's not my fault I can't lose weight. It's the food industry." Wrong. You were never forced to eat anything. You are over-weight because you drove to the store, you purchased un-healthy foods, and you ate them. Exercising and eating right were pushed to the side for fast food and late night snacks.

"It's not my fault I failed the test. It's the teacher." Wrong. You received a low grade because you gave the wrong answers on the test. Instead of asking questions, reading, and studying, you chose to watch television and talk on the phone.

As we talked about in the previous chapter, there is a reason for everything. Ignoring the actual causes and focusing solely on excuses will never get you what you want. There is an answer to each problem you face. Spend your time seeking out the solu-tion instead of blaming, rationalizing, and refusing to take own-ership of your troubles.

The flipside of this point is taking responsibility for your suc-cess. When you do something right, claim it. You don't have to dance around the office or shove it in your family's face; you simply have to know it on the inside. Constantly giving credit to others without recognizing your contribution can dissolve confi-dence and control just as quickly as playing the victim. Owner-ship of victory is just as important as ownership of defeat.

If you're ready to change and achieve the things you desire, it's time to take an honest look at reality. This is the secret to gaining control over your life. A healthy responsibility will place the power back into your able hands, allowing change to happen on your schedule.

3. A Healthy Responsibility. After visiting both extremes, we find ourselves in the middle of the road. There are two aspects that combine to create a healthy responsibility and equip you with the tools to correctly analyze a situation and choose the best response—your external and internal environments.

Your External Environment

Your external environment can be defined as things that happen to and around you. This excludes action and thoughts that originate within you. Being promoted is an example of something happening to you and would therefore fit into your external environment. Likewise, a rainy day is something that happens around you and would fit into the same category.

The two examples just used, a promotion and rain, were chosen because they represent the main point of this subject. The promotion may have happened to you, but it is highly likely that you did something to be promoted. Your work ethic, past success, and personal relationships all may have played a part in your success. This is an example of an external event that you had some control over.

The rainy day has nothing to do with you. It would have rained on that day had you been out of the country. This type of external event is completely out of your hands and cannot be personally influenced or manipulated.

The skill I want you to develop is how to accurately differentiate between those things that you can control and those things that are out of your hands completely. This skill will allow you to focus your time and energy in the right places. If you spend years banging your head against the wall trying to change something that is completely out of your hands, you will have wasted precious time that you can never get back.

Along with helping you recognize controllable factors in your environment, it will add to your growing understanding of responsibility—where it should be placed and how to take advantage of it. What you will find in the external environment are many examples of shared accountability. That is why it falls under the category of a healthy responsibility.

Have you ever seen a witness to a crime being interviewed after the incident? "This place is so unsafe. I worry about my children getting hurt. I worry about myself getting hurt." This is an example of shared, although unrecognized, responsibility.

The witness did not commit the crime. He also didn't have any direct influence over the criminal. Most people would say that he was not at all responsible for the action, and they would be right. However, by choosing to move into a dangerous ncighborhood and continuing to live there after a crime has occurred, the witness is partially responsible for any harm that comes his way.

Another example of partial responsibility for an external event is not being invited to a party. I know it isn't an uplifting illustration, but it explains the point nicely. Most people, if not invited to a party comprised of their friends, would be upset and blame the group for being cruel and hurtful. Yes, the move may not be nice, but the fact that you weren't invited happened for a reason. Because of the person you are, including your appearance, personality, and other elements that create your identity, you were not chosen. You are responsible for who you are and in turn for the way others treat you.

I am not advocating the changing of your personality to fit in better with others. It may be that you simply didn't fit well with that particular group of people. My purpose is to shift the focus from, "My friends are jerks. Just wait until I tell them what I think about their little party," to, "I wasn't invited because they didn't want to invite me. A different group of friends will accept me for who I am."

If someone treats you poorly, it is because you have taught them that you are someone to be treated poorly. If someone treats you kindly, it is because your identity communicates the right messages to be treated kindly by that particular person. Although your control is limited with respect to how someone else thinks or behaves, you still play a role in their behavior.

I want you to practice looking at your life and picking out pieces of external events in which you share the responsibility. You will be gaining more control over your life each time you discover a situation in which you are partially accountable for the outcome. This skill is another way to avoid refusing ownership and blaming others for what rightly belongs to you.

Think back to a failure that occurred in the past. Did you play a role in the external event? Imagine submitting a manuscript to ten publishers and having each one decline your work. You could rant and rave about the industry and the injustice of it all, or you could view the situation with a healthy responsibility.

If some books are being accepted, and your book wasn't, that means that your book didn't fit the publisher's qualifications. That is your fault. It is at this point that you have a choice to make: Do you complain and take no responsibility for the outcome, or do you respond to the situation with a sense of control and power?

The answer leads us to the second element of a healthy responsibility. The real power is not in what happens to you but how you respond to the situation. Once you have examined your external environment and located areas of shared responsibility, it's time to turn to your internal environment.

Your Internal Environment

Your internal environment consists of every thought and action that originates within you. It is the vehicle you use to respond to your external environment. The two spheres may work with one another, but they differ in one key respect. Where your external event contains shared responsibility, or some control, your internal environment is 100% within your hands. You decide what meaning to give the experiences and circumstances in your life.

Your internal environment centers around two choices—to react or to respond. To be more exact, the goal is to replace negative reactions with positive responses. If someone pushes you, a negative reaction would be to whip around and push them back without asking questions. A positive response would be to assess the situation and find the cause of the problem. As you know all too well, we live in a world of quick reactors with a few responders sprinkled in here and there.

Let's take a quick look back at the example of the witness to a crime. The external event was a crime that occurred near the man's home. As we have already discussed, he shared responsibility because he chose to live in an unsafe place. After the crime, the internal environment kicks in. A positive response would be to move to a safer area. A negative reaction would be to blame the police for not protecting the streets and stay put. Either way, the response to the event is internal and completely in the hands of the witness.

The bottom line is simply this—you can't control everything that happens to and around you, but you can always, no matter what the situation, control how you respond to it. The important piece of the puzzle, how you act in response to your external environment, is always in your hands.

This creates a very advantageous situation for you. If something negative happens, you are in the position to change it. Complaining about it won't help. Blaming someone else won't help. Only responding with positive action will fix the problem.

Two women, Julie and Jenny, are talking at the water cooler about a common problem they are facing. Living in the same neighborhood, they are getting stuck in the worst traffic jams imaginable, and arriving late for work because of it. This represents the external environment. They have no control over the traffic patterns in their town. The problem may be the same, but the meanings they give it are completely different.

"It's a pain in the neck," Julie says to Jenny. "The city should do something about this. I'm not about to get up an hour earlier just to make it through that mess and get to work on time." Julie's internal choice is to react. She decided to complain and blame. In the end, Julie will end up stuck in traffic, late for work, and blaming the world for her troubles.

Jenny sees the situation in a completely different light. She nods along with Julie and tells her, "I know what you mean. It's not a fun situation to deal with in the morning." However, internally she is making a decision to respond to the situation. Jenny knows of a different route that will only add an extra five minutes to the office, but will bypass the entire traffic jam. She mentions it as a solution to Julie, but she isn't interested. "I shouldn't have to change," is her sharp reply.

Two women, same external environments, very different internal choices. Jenny will be happy each morning and accomplish all of her duties without stress or worry. Julie will be angry before she even sets foot inside the office, and be in a constant state of chaos as she tries to make up for lost time. Both women are in total control of how they respond to the situation, but only Jenny uses this power to her advantage.

If you don't like a particular aspect of your life, you are in a position to change it. When a problem comes along, consider how you can positively respond to the event. You may not have caused the issue, but shaking your fists won't improve the situation. Take control and seek out a solution. You may not be responsible for everything that happens to you, but you are completely responsible for the meaning you give to it.

The Power of Choice

One choice—that's all it takes to completely change the course of your future. There are certain decision points in life that hold the power to lead you in a new direction or solidify your path indefinitely. These vital points, such as getting married, relocating, and having a family, only make up a portion of the impact and influence of choice. The seemingly less important decisions you make on a daily basis also work to shape the content and quality of your life.

You are making decisions every second. The choices you make throughout the day either bring you closer to the things you desire or further from them. These minor decision points are building blocks whereas major ones are springboards. The decision to smoke is a major decision point, while the decision to continue smoking a cigarette every day is a minor decision point. One introduced you to the habit while the other served to reinforce it on a daily basis.

Realizing the power of both major and minor decision points is key to taking control of your life. It aids the process of ownership. If you can pinpoint certain choices in your life that have led you to your current situation, you will be able to say to yourself, "I am where I am because of the choices I made in the past." This will give you control over your future. By taking responsibility for the choices you have made, and their corresponding outcomes, you can begin to make decisions that bring you closer to what you really want.

Two of my close friends from high school, we'll call them Matt and Sam, offer a prime example of the power of choice. Although close in friendship, their personality and style were as different as you could get. While Sam spent his time hitting the books, Matt was busy skipping class, going out every night, and pushing the books as far away as possible. After four years of this cycle, it wasn't hard to see where their two paths were heading.

Surprisingly, both of my friends wanted to go to college. While Matt was never one for studying, he desired the perks that a college degree offered. He wanted a prestigious position and its prestigious salary. When the time came to send in college applications, Matt and Sam sent out an equal amount. Sam received three acceptance letters. Matt, on the other hand, received only rejections.

"It's not fair," I remember Matt saying. "The system stinks." Blame the "system" all he wanted, it didn't help him achieve the goal. Matt quickly gave up on the idea of college and settled for part-time work instead. Meanwhile, Sam had his pick of top schools, and finally decided on Stanford.

Years later, after their respective choices created very distinct paths, the three of us got together for dinner in Sam's new home. It was great catching up on new experiences and reminiscing about the old. It turned out that Matt had struggled over the years to find the high-paying career he had his heart set on, and instead jumped from job to job without finding satisfaction or enjoyment. Sam, on the other hand, looked happier than I had ever seen him. It wasn't just the income; it was the way in which he lived his life. He was fulfilled in every way, and you could see it in his face. At one point during the evening, Matt leaned over to Sam and said something that explained why things had been so difficult for him.

"You're so lucky, Sam," he began. "You've got it all. An amazing home, a promising career, and you seem to be on top of the world. I don't know how you did it. Some people are just born with a gift, I guess."

Everyone is born with the potential, but it is up to us to utilize that power. Matt failed to recognize the truth, at least that's the impression he gave. Perhaps he knew the error of his ways and words and chose to ignore them rather than take responsibility for the decisions he made in the past. It wasn't luck that led to Sam's lifestyle; it was making the right choices. By consciously choosing to study each and every night, and fully prepare himself for higher education, Sam succeeded. It was the pattern of choices that created Matt's unhappiness.

This story represents the power of choice, and the need to live up to the ones you make. You can't improve until you take ownership and responsibility for the problem. If you are a smoker, you made the major decision to start and the daily decisions to continue. If you are overweight, you made the major decision to accept your size and the daily decisions to intensify the problem. If you don't enjoy your job, it's because you made the major decision to join the company along with the daily decisions to stay.

You are where you are because of the choices you have made in the past. Your future will be a result of the choices you make tomorrow. You may be thinking to yourself, "But I didn't know the choices I made would lead to the life I have." That may be true, but it doesn't matter. You have to live up to your choices even if you weren't fully aware of their consequences.

Whose fault is it if you become ill from eating a berry you found in the woods? Who would be to blame if you had no clue what you were eating or what it would do to you? Is it the berry's fault? The woods? You are obviously the one responsible for the outcome. You can only blame yourself for not knowing what you were doing. The cause and effect relationship remains in place whether or not you understand their full impact.

The major and minor decision points you meet with every day are yours to control. Own up to the choices of the past and direct the decisions of the future.

Life by Design

Out of everything we have covered in this chapter, the following principle stands out as the most exciting. We have talked about taking responsibility for your problems and successes, and realizing that you are in control of your life. If you take the ideas we have discussed and combine them, you are left with one overriding principle: You can live life by your design.

You can have things exactly as you want them, without having to "deal" with any aspects you don't enjoy. Whatever your picture of an ideal life looks like, you can make it happen. You have the power within you to choose a desire and achieve it.

Settling is a way of life for most people. "I hate my job, but what can I do about it?" "I'm not in the best shape, but I guess that's life." "The weather is horrible here, and the neighborhood isn't that safe, but that's just the way it goes." "My life isn't perfect, but I can't complain."

It's hard for many to even comprehend this idea. They are conditioned to see a problem and merely deal with it. They don't like what they do, where they live, how they feel, how they look, and where they're heading, but that's life. No, that's not life. That's only one example of a life lived far below what is possible.

You don't have to settle for anything you don't enjoy. Imagine waking up in the home of your dreams, with the man or woman of your dreams, in the neighborhood of your dreams, getting ready to go to the job of your dreams, spending time with the friends of your dreams, and bringing to life everything you have ever wanted to have, do, or be. Just imagine how that would feel. Imagine living your ideal life.

If your desire is strong enough, you can choose:

- What you do for a living
- Where you live
- With whom you spend your life
- Who your friends are
- What you do to relax
- Where you spend your vacation
- The skills and abilities you have
- The things you eat
- The hobbies you enjoy
- The time you wake up
- The time you go to sleep
- The health and shape of your body
- The amount of money you make
- What you do each and every hour of the day

The list is endless, but the point should be clear—anything you want, if you want it enough, can be yours. Every moment you are alive is under your control. If you realize that you don't like where you work or what you do, pursue a new career. If you realize that you don't enjoy spending time with people who make you feel inferior, seek out accepting and caring friends. If you realize that you hate to get up early in the morning, find a job that allows you to head in late or start your own business and set your own hours.

You can design your ideal life and put the plan into action. You can do what you want, when you want to do it, and exactly how you want it to be done. If you put in the time and effort, you can spend the rest of your life living on your terms.

A healthy responsibility makes all of this possible. If success or failure depended solely on the whims of an uncontrollable force, you couldn't actively create the life you desire. You couldn't improve or control anything. This is the dilemma faced by the many who give up ownership of their success and failures. Accept what is rightfully yours and live your life by design.

The last mental resource to complete the package is attitude. With the right attitude in place, you will be able to handle what life throws your way and benefit from your negative and positive experiences. We all agree that a negative attitude is something to avoid, but the same is true of positive thinking. As you will soon see, neither of these attitudes will give you the same advantages of the third and final option.

NOTES & IDEAS

Chapter 8

The New Attitude of Success

Common sense is the knack of seeing things as they are,
and doing things as they ought to be done.
—Josh Billings

HIS NAME WAS BRIAN REEBER, and he was the model of positive thinking. Always an optimistic message on his mind, he never let failures get him down. People were constantly complimenting Brian about his attitude, and he, with a quick grin, would reply, "It doesn't matter how bad things get. They will always get better."

As I learned more about Brian, I soon discovered that his life wasn't the picture of happiness and success I had imagined. With such an upbeat attitude, I assumed that things were right where he wanted them. Positive thinking was his secret to success, or so I thought, and he was a master of the craft. Behind the scenes, however, I realized Brian's outside attitude didn't match his internal feelings

Despite his positive ways, Brian was struggling through life. He didn't really enjoy what he did for a living, and seemed to always have more bills than income. He had several health problems, caused by an unhealthy diet and a lack of exercise. All in all, the man to whom everyone looked for a positive pick-me-up was actually quite unhappy. The positive thinker was living a life of negatives.

This experience taught me a very valuable lesson in life—a positive attitude can cause just as much damage as a negative one. Neither way of viewing the world will get you what you really want. They lack the main ingredient to creating successful outcomes, and should be put aside. Without a negative or positive attitude, where do you go? There is a third option, and one that I guarantee will equip you with the mindset to make the quickest progress with the least amount of pain.

Before we get into the details of each option, we need to come to an agreement. If you believe that every situation can be seen in only one way, we will have a very hard time implementing change. Before any real progress can be made, you have to realize that what you see around you, and the meaning you give it, is not necessarily the only way to view the situation. There are shades of gray to everything.

Shades of Gray

"I'm really sorry to have to say this, but we're going to have to let you go." As the two men sat stone-faced listening to the news, their minds were spinning with conclusions. Mike and Robert had been with the company for nearly ten years, and its poor performance and need to downsize were taking their toll. The two men left the office with the same facts, but completely different attitudes.

Robert was devastated. The news came as a shock. He reached his office door and with a jittery hand turned the knob. While cleaning out his desk, Robert fell into his chair and dropped his head into his hands.

"What am I going to do?" he thought to himself. "How could this happen to me? What am I going to tell Amy and the kids?" Robert was angry with the company for betraying him. He was worried and fearful of the future. Being fired was the worst news of his life, and as far as he was concerned, the best years were behind him.

Mike, who sat in the same office and heard the same news, saw the situation in a completely different light. Being let go was unexpected, but he didn't focus on what he was losing. Instead, he thought about the new opportunities that were ahead. Rebounding may be difficult, but Mike knew he could do it. He found a job that he enjoyed once, and the process could be repeated.

While he was sorry to leave the company, Mike felt it wasn't the end of the world. Perhaps he could find an even more rewarding career in the future. The change may have come out of nowhere, but he wasn't about to let his life suffer for it.

While Mike finished packing up his things, he paused for a moment to take a look around the office. Instead of fearing the future, he imagined what it would be like to work in a position that really challenged him. Mike believed he was capable of more, but was never given the chance to show what he could do. He looked forward to the road ahead, and left the building confident that better things were to come.

Mike eventually found the position he was looking for, and things turned out better than he had hoped. Robert struggled to find work and settled for a lower-paying position with a competitor to his old company. An identical set of facts created two completely different results. Both men thought they were dealing with the reality of the situation when they were actually dealing with their own version of it.

You have a choice about what things mean to you. Nothing has meaning until you give it that meaning. When you face a situation, your mind takes in the facts and attaches feelings to what you see. Some people choose to give negative meanings to the things that happen in their lives, while others choose to give a positive spin on things. A smaller, more successful group deals with life in a very different manner. We can't move on to the secret just yet. Before you can utilize the solution, you have to fully understand the problem.

The Negative Attitude

"I can't do it." "I always mess things up." "It's impossible." Have you ever heard someone say these things? Perhaps even you? I know I have at times, and I also know that if I continued on the path of thinking negatively, I would never be able to get positively motivated to achieve anything.

There are two ways to spend your time—thinking of every reason why something can't be done or thinking about the solutions to problems. A negative attitude focuses on the former, and wastes time, energy, and ultimately, your life. It is synonymous with negative motivation in that it's easier in the short-term to throw your hands up in defeat and cry in the corner, but this will only serve to create more misery in the end. The solution to every problem is at the top of the staircase. While the successful people of the world rise to the top, the negative thinker is too busy complaining to take a single step up.

A negative attitude creates a false sense of despair. It looks for every possible reason for failure and sadness and blows it out of proportion. "I'm horrible at everything!" Are you really horrible at every single thing you have ever done? Do you really believe that there isn't one good thing about you? "Well, I guess I'm alright at some things." That is where the focus should be.

Whatever you focus on you get. If you focus on the reasons why something won't work, you'll make sure it doesn't. Your mind develops what you give it, and a negative attitude fills your head with fear, failure, and frustration.

The principles of positive motivation are intertwined and build on one another. Attitude and control are great examples of this interdependence of ideas. As you recall, you have the choice to respond with reason or react irrationally to the situations in your life. A negative attitude is the perfect example of this type of irrational reaction. Without reasoning your way through the situation, you only intensify your problems.

You know you can find a solution to the things that don't go exactly as you had wished. It's not that you can't think of answers. The problem with a negative attitude is that it blocks the answers while it busily works to create more obstacles and setbacks. You have the right information in your mind, but it can't get through if you focus on the reasons why something can't or won't work out.

We all fall into the trap of negative thinking. The secret is in paying a visit only, not living there. The answer isn't to be Mr. Positive twenty-four hours a day. This would cause just as many problems, as we saw with Brian Reeber. Everyone gets down on themselves now and then, but the real damage is done when you can't bring yourself back up.

Imagine that you just graduated from college. You head off to your first interview, and after waiting several days, you get a call from the company. "We're sorry, but we don't have anything for you right now."

With a negative outlook, you begin to blame the interviewer for doing a poor job and eventually turn to your own shortcomings and weaknesses. "Why can't I do anything right? It's just like me to screw up my first chance at getting a job," you say to yourself. "I'll never find work."

If you thought like this, you'd be right. You never would find a job because you wouldn't give your mind the chance to think of a solution. Spending your time dwelling on the terrible person you have become would only lead to more reasons why you can't succeed. Sounds like a positive attitude is desperately needed—think again.

The Positive Attitude

I know what you have probably been thinking to yourself from the start of this chapter: "Positive thinking is a bad thing?" From birth, you have been told that a positive attitude is the key to success. Thousands of books have been written on the subject, with many more to come. So why, after all of these writers, speakers, and consultants have been advising a positive attitude, would I warn against it? Distortion.

When you're thinking negatively, you are distorting the truth. If you say that you are horrible at everything, you are not being honest. Obviously, you are good at something. This distortion creates a rift between what actually happens and what you think happens.

The problem of distortion is not unique to a negative attitude. While negative thinking creates a false sense of despair, a positive attitude can create a false sense of hope. Please don't misunderstand, hope is a good thing, but it doesn't come from distorting reality. The real power of hope comes from the third attitude.

A positive thinker will scream, "I can do it!" When asked, "Why do you think so?" they will answer, "Because I think I can!" Unfortunately, that isn't enough. Positive thinking can lure people into believing that all you have to do is stay positive and everything turns out perfectly. It's a quick and easy fix that takes little time and effort. Tell people all they have to do is think positive thoughts and you'll have millions listening.

Positive attitudes of this sort are some of the biggest culprits of inaction. If a positive attitude solves all your problems, then you don't have to actually get up and do anything. You can wait for better things to fall into your lap, and all you have to do is think good thoughts. This is where positive thinking gets the negative image of thousands of people saying, "You're good enough," into the mirror, believing that's all it takes to improve.

This attitude poses such a danger because success depends on action. You have to get out there and create the changes you want to see. Positive thinking is like a warm, inviting bed that soothes you to sleep. If at first you don't succeed, thinking positive thoughts won't do a thing. You'll fail a second time if you don't change the process. The secret is not in thinking positive thoughts. It's in making positive changes. A positive attitude is thinking positively and acting repetitively.

Think back to the example of being turned down for your first job. Instead of a negative attitude, this time you think positive thoughts. The call comes in and you hear the bad news. You walk over to your bathroom mirror and proudly state, "I'll get it next time! I can do it and won't give up!"

The outcome is much like that of a negative attitude. You don't get your next job, or the one after that, because you keep doing the same things wrong. Positive thoughts didn't help you create positive changes, and although you never give up, you also never win. Thinking coupled with a pro-active approach is better than thinking alone.

Here's the exciting news: There is one more option that gives you the energy and inspiration of a positive attitude along with the goods to back it up. Every helpful aspect you have attributed to a positive attitude (refusing to give up, seeking out the opportunity in every situation, hoping for a better future) is part of a third mindset that avoids the drawback of distortion.

Reality-Based Thinking

Has anyone ever told you to get real or to be realistic? Perhaps you told a friend about a personal desire and he just shook his head saying, "You're dreaming. Come back to reality." In this case, being real or dealing with reality meant lowering your standards and giving up the desire to achieve more. A realistic attitude was one that accepted the status quo and didn't aim too high.

That has all changed. From what you have learned in this book, and what you will learn in the upcoming chapters, the reality you face is one of endless possibility. I do believe the attitude of success is based in reality, but not in the terms mentioned above. As we work through this segment, think of a reality-based attitude as an empowered mindset that recognizes the limitless opportunity in life, and erase the thought that it means letting go of the things you once dreamed of achieving.

In reality, you can have everything you want. You can work to create the physical body you have always desired. You can learn how to do the things you have always wanted to do. You can live where you want to live, be what you want to be, and spend the rest of your life enjoying each moment like never before. This is the reality of life. This is being realistic.

As we have discussed, distortion is the problem with a positive and negative attitude. One cries, "You'll never succeed!" and the other, "You'll never fail!" Neither outlook is true nor are they beneficial. The truth of the matter is, you will succeed and fail in the short-term. Reality-based thinking will ensure you meet not only with short-term success but also long-term fulfillment.

Let me explain exactly what I mean by reality-based thinking. It takes viewing the facts of the situations you face without assigning distorted meanings to the events. You don't fail because you are a bad person and you don't succeed because you think good thoughts; you fail or succeed because of what you do. If you dial the wrong phone number, it has nothing to do with a negative or positive attitude. The reality of the situation is that you dialed the wrong number.

This may sound simplistic, but most powerful concepts sound simple until they are applied to real-life situations. Never giving up is a relatively uncomplicated idea, but just imagine what could be accomplished in the world if individuals with positive desires actually followed this simple advice. The world would be transformed overnight. So you see, a simple idea, when faithfully applied, can change everything.

Every situation you face can be scrutinized for the facts. This cuts away the negative feelings that are too often associated with short-term setbacks and failures. It also cuts away the tendency to sit around and think good thoughts while the situation actually becomes worse. Whenever something happens to you, either good or bad, look immediately to the reality of the situation and deal with what you know to be true.

If you are deeply in debt, you can look at the situation in three different ways. First, you can believe that you will never free yourself of the burden and be doomed to a life of debt-collectors and depression. Second, you can believe that everything will get better with time, and end up dealing with the burden of debt-collectors and depression. Finally, you can be realistic. You can discover exactly the source and amount of income and the source and amount of expenses. From here, you can spend your time evening out the equation.

Reality-based thinking provides you something with which to work. The problem is laid out before you and you can take informed steps to solve it. Negative and positive mindsets add complexity and distortion to situations that are actually quite simple to understand and improve.

If you are overweight, it is because you take in more than you burn off. Those are the facts. This gives you the foundation to take action. You'll know where to focus your time and energy without feeling depressed or worthless. It is a direct path to empowerment.

Consider the reach of reality. Every problem in your life is happening for a reason. Choose a negative or positive attitude, and you choose to overlook those facts. Follow the attitude of reality, and you will quickly discover the causes behind your problems and work to bring about a successful resolution. Where reality-based thinking really gives you an edge is failing. It only takes one failure to derail a positive change, making it vital that you have the ability to maintain action in the face of short-term setbacks.

If at first you don't succeed, there is a reason for the failure. This is what I want you to focus on when things don't go your way. Imagine that you are a writer for your local newspaper. Your latest column receives poor reviews and the readers aren't pleased. With your reality-based attitude, you know there is a reason for the short-term failure. You look into the problem and discover that you wrote about something to which no one could relate. The mistake is corrected and the next issue receives rave reviews.

This simple story represents the possibilities of reality-based thinking. When you stumble along the way to your desires, you don't have to fall into a trap of self-hatred. You will realize that a problem happened because of something you did, not because of the person you are.

Anger and frustration are a result of being out of control. If you don't know why you are failing and have no way to fix the problem, you will experience feelings of helplessness that break down your positive motivation. Taking a closer look at the facts of the matter will put the power of change back where it belongs—with you.

Action, as you already know, is the key to success. Thinking about what you want is only the first stage. It serves no purpose without the addition of intelligent action. Where the extremes rely on thoughts alone, reality-based thinking depends on action backed by positive thought.

Again, think back to the example of finding work after graduation. You are excited about the prospects that are ahead of you, and wait eagerly by the phone. You receive the news and hang up the phone with the same feelings. Instead of dwelling on your short-term setback, you see an opportunity to learn something important.

You call the human resources department at the company and ask to speak with the woman who conducted your interview. After a brief conversation, you learn the exact reasons why you were turned down for the job. You make the necessary changes in your approach and are successful on your next attempt.

With a negative attitude, you blamed it on the interviewer and then gave up any hope for the future. With a positive attitude, you shrugged your shoulders and looked forward to the next interview. With a reality-based attitude, you found the reason for the turn down, took action to correct it, and succeeded in the future.

Think of it this way: The negative thinker says the glass is half empty, the positive thinker says the glass is half full, and the reality-based thinker drinks when he's thirsty.

With the confidence that success is possible, the responsibility to know that it's up to you to make it happen, and the attitude of success, you have the three mental resources necessary to create a strong belief in your ability to get exactly what you want.

You have completed the third pillar of positive motivation. You have the principles necessary to proceed in the direction of your desires free of doubt and fear, believing in your heart that achieving success is only a matter of time. From here, you must plan. In the next section, we will transform your desire into a step-by-step, workable strategy. Creating a plan for your goal will give it the vehicle it needs to become more than just a great idea; it will become a living, breathing thing that can begin to take form.

NOTES & IDEAS

Pillar IV
Plan

Chapter 9

Transforming Your Desires into Realities

I have always thought that one man of tolerable abilities may work great changes and accomplish great affairs among mankind, if he first forms a good plan ...
—Benjamin Franklin

YOUR TASK IS SIMPLE. Standing approximately twenty feet away is a ten-foot by ten-foot target that you must pierce with an arrow. Six arrows sit on a table at your side. It seems like an easy enough challenge as you ready yourself and take aim. There's just one small problem with this scenario—there's no bow.

Your chances for success have become impossible. The destination is clear, but you lack the means to make it happen. It doesn't matter how much you think about hitting the target if you don't have the instrument to shoot the arrows. You will never hit it.

The frustration that results from not having the tools to get what you want is the same situation that millions of dreamers face every day. I have yet to meet an individual who did not desire something, but the majority of people haven't the slightest clue how they are going to get it. Hitting the target is their desire, and the bow is the strategy that makes success possible. Without a bow, there can be no success.

Creating a strategy is critical to achieving your desire. Although it is true that a few successes may come your way by chance, enhancing the quality of your life on a consistent basis requires a plan. If you fail to create a plan of action, you'll be no better off than a man who has a target but no bow.

Jumping into the process of planning without fully knowing what it is you're dealing with will only lead to trouble and an uncertain future for your desires. If a strategy is to be of any use to you, it is important that you know exactly what it can and cannot do. After gaining a complete understanding of the process and importance of this pillar, the upcoming chapters will teach you the specific elements of an effective strategy along with how to create your own plan of action.

Breathing Life into Your Desires

Thinking makes the world go round. Every invention, discovery, luxury, necessity, innovation, and breakthrough in science, mathematics, arts and literature, engineering, and business began as a thought in someone's mind. But thought was only the first stage. It was the beginning of the things you see around you.

You cannot think your way to a better medicine to treat disease. You cannot think your way to building the first airplane or automobile. A thought is not enough to produce change and improvement in the world. Thoughts and desires require something more to give them shape.

Imagine what the world would be like had the Wright brothers or Ford only thought about what they wanted to do without giving their ideas the resources necessary to materialize. There's no doubt that millions of potential discoveries and advancements have been lost because the thinkers and dreamers of history never took the next step. You have a list of desires that you want to achieve to make your life more than it is now. It would be an unfortunate loss should you choose to leave them hidden in your mind.

The next stage is giving shape and force to desire. Extracting the ideas from the clutter in your head and giving them a tangible, concrete strategy will give your goals the vehicle they need to become more than just a passing thought.

If you take two people with identical desires, and one has a detailed strategy outlining what has to be done, and the other has nothing from which to work, which do you think has a better chance of success? It's that simple. A strategy gives you a fighting chance at getting what you really want. It's the difference between having an airplane to fly you across the ocean and having a rowboat to carry you there.

When you get past all of the excuses and stories you tell yourself, you know just as well as I do that accidentally bumping into everything you want will never happen. You are not going to wake up tomorrow to find each and every goal realized because you dreamt about them. The need for a strategy sounds logical, but the reality we see every day is overcrowded with dreamers who lack a plan, and a rare few who dream, plan, and succeed. You have to create a strategy if you want to be part of the minority who actually achieve what they want.

Your own life is the best proof available. Think back to the things you have accomplished in the past. I guarantee that nearly every success came about because you had some type of strategy to make it happen. This doesn't mean that you had a step-by-step plan that outlined every stage of your goal. Strategies are built in many different ways, and not all of them include a piece of paper and a prioritized to-do list. In some way or another, each success you enjoyed in the past was made possible because of a plan. Your current and future desires will be no different.

If you're still not certain about the need for a strategy, spend a few days researching successful and fulfilled individuals. You will find that each and every one of them had the desire to succeed, the belief that it was possible, and a strategy to make it happen. Books, magazines, newspapers, and newsletters are filled with stories of successful people who took a goal and ran with it. The only reason they knew where and how far to run was because of a strategy.

One of the most important reasons behind creating a strategy is how much it helps to develop your desires to the tipping point. I know how exciting the process of forming a strategy can be, and I want you to experience the same thrill. Thinking about your goal is one thing, but nothing can compare to the exhilaration you'll experience when you hold a plan in your hands that will bring your desire to life.

A close friend of mine had always talked about writing a book. Her ideas were fantastic, but they never made it past her mind. Finally, after realizing the power of creating a strategy, she sat down and formed a plan around her desire. It was amazing what a few words could do in such a short amount of time. She had been a little excited about the idea in the past, but everything changed the moment she wrote out a strategy on paper. Her goal became a real thing, something she could actually do. Putting together a strategy gave life to her desire.

When you see your goals and dreams taking shape, the scales begin to shift. The pleasure of action increases in strength as your confidence, excitement, and anticipation grow. The pleasure of inaction and the pain of action diminish as you focus on how remarkable your life will be once you have achieved your ambitions. Creating a detailed strategy will give you the leverage necessary to inspire action on a daily basis.

Your desires are like seeds. They require certain resources to live and grow into their ultimate form. If you fail to plant or water the seed, it will never become what it could be. It will always represent the potential of something beautiful, but will never be able to fulfill that possibility. You have to plant your desire within an effective and efficient strategy and water it with consistent action.

A strategy is the vehicle you will use to get what you want. It will inspire you to take action toward a desire that has only been thought about in the past. I have wanted a lot of things in my life, but it wasn't until I plugged the desires into a plan that I really got excited about taking action. You'll begin to think, "I'm actually going to do it!" My heart still pounds a little bit faster from the thrill of seeing my dreams in concrete form.

The ability of a strategy to give shape and inspiration to a desire is not the last of it. Creating a plan also allows you to break free from one of the most deadly conditions in the world. This affliction is the reason many well-intentioned individuals never achieve a great deal of success or enjoy happiness on a consistent basis. Take steps to put together a strategy and you will be taking a major step toward ridding yourself of this self-destructive force.

Disengaging Autopilot

You can see it on the faces of people passing by you on the street. It's easily noticeable at work, and may have already found its way into your home. If you take a minute to look for it, you can see the blank stare and zombie-like trance that people are in as they go through the motions of living. For a large portion of the world, autopilot is running the show.

Another name for this condition is routine. It means doing today what you did yesterday merely because it's what you did two days before. It's being stuck in a rut without realizing it. Autopilot is getting up, going to work, working, coming home, eating, sleeping—repeat. There is no room for real living because the ingrained routine has taken over completely.

If you stopped one of these people on the street and asked, "Why are you doing what you are doing?" the answer, after a confused pause, would most likely be, "I have always done it." That's the justification for letting the routine run life instead of waking up and taking control.

You have to be honest with yourself and ask whether or not routine has found its way into your daily life. Do hours pass by without notice as you go through the pattern? Do you flip on the autopilot and go through the motions without thinking or choosing a better way? It happens to the best of us. Habit and patterned behavior are quick to take hold, and can only be eliminated with conscious effort.

A negative routine is such a dangerous force because it enters without detection. You fall into a pattern and begin to rely less on thought and more on habit. The affliction doesn't tap you on the shoulder and say, "Hi. I'm routine and you're stuck with me." Instead, it eats away at your desires and pushes them further and further to the back of your mind until they become distant memories. One day, after years of potential happiness and success have been lost, you'll think back to the goals and dreams you once had, scratching your head in confusion over what happened to them.

Autopilot leaves no room for thought or planning for the future. You are too busy being busy. If you happen to fall into the trap, and no one is there to help you out, the routine can run throughout the remainder of your life. You know I'm not exaggerating. Many people have spent thirty, forty, or even fifty years of their life doing the same thing every day without a single thought as to breaking free and reaching for more than what habit has offered.

Desire and change are synonymous whereas routine and progress are opposites. Change requires that you break free of habit and negative patterns, which leads to the next benefit of creating a strategy. By taking steps to plan a change in your life, you are forced to break the cycle. You cannot live by habit and patterned behavior when the goal is to create a change.

I've mentioned negative routine several times to differentiate between that and a positive routine. If your routine is to get up early to read a few chapters in your favorite book or to jog after work, there is nothing negative about that. Routine, if thought through and properly planned, can be very beneficial. It is only when you stop thinking and start losing control that the pattern becomes negative.

The percentage of nonplanners boggles my mind. Asking 1,000 well-intentioned individuals whether or not they had a detailed plan in place to achieve their desire would leave you with 999 negatives. It's the allure of short-term thinking again. Taking the time to create a plan for the future is too painful for most people. It's easier to wish than write. If only they saw the amazing rewards that come from creating a strategy, they might be saved from the edge of the waterfall toward which they are heading.

In 1953, Yale University conducted a study on their graduating class. Upon exiting, only 3% of the class had clearly defined goals, while the remaining 97% had little to no plan for the future. After twenty years of living in the real world, the students were revisited, and the results were striking.

The 3% that had goals were happier, healthier, and in higher positions within their career. However, that is to be expected of goal-oriented individuals. The amazing part is that the 3% who believed in planning for the future earned more each year than the remaining 97% combined. The moral of the story: Break free of the autopilot dilemma and enjoy amazing success now and in the future.

Decisions, Decisions, Decisions

As you already know, the decisions you make each day create the life you live. Both major and minor decision points are of the utmost importance, and are guaranteed to change your life. The question is in which direction each decision will take you. With the use of a strategy you can ensure that the choices you make bring you closer to the things you want. It gives you a basis for all future decisions. Instead of habit or emotion taking control, you can pinpoint the option that best serves your needs. A simple walk around the neighborhood can help demonstrate the point. Let's look at the situation from two perspectives—with and without a strategy.

If you have no plan in mind, coming to an intersection while walking down the street calls for an emotion-based decision. "Do I feel like going right? How about left?" If you continued this way for several turns, there is no telling where you would end up.

If you have a plan in place to get you home as quickly as possible, each intersection will be treated much differently. Instead of a making an uninformed guess about which way feels better, you will know exactly which turns to make and when to make them. Your strategy serves as a guide to your decision making.

The first method is perfectly acceptable for a leisurely walk, but most people use it for the entirety of their lives. There are times when acting from emotion is more than necessary, but achieving success on your schedule calls for an element of strategy and reason. The following are examples of how emotion-based and strategy-based decisions are reached.

No Strategy in Place:

- This candy bar looks good. I feel like eating it.
- The boss is being a jerk. I feel like telling him off.
- This new stereo looks great. I feel like buying it.
- My husband isn't listening to me. I feel like yelling at him.

Strategy in Place:

- The candy bar looks good, but my strategy calls for a healthy diet. I'll grab some juice instead.
- The boss is being a jerk, but my strategy calls for working with him to enjoy my job. I'll talk to him and see if I can help him out.
- This stereo looks great, but my budget can't afford it right now. I'll have to wait a little longer to buy it.
- My husband isn't treating me right, but I want to improve our relationship. Trying to understand his mood will do a lot more than simply getting upset about it.

Reactive decisions happen constantly. Without a strategy in place, people are making daily choices that actually hurt their chances of success. Acting on your gut feeling can be the right thing to do in certain situations, but when it comes to reaching your goals, you need to have a plan. Decisions shape your life, making a constant guide essential to happiness.

Emotion-based decisions satisfy short-term desires. They gratify instantly and care nothing about the future. They ask the question, "What feels good right now?" without regard for future consequences. Strategy-based decisions ask, "What path will bring me closer to my authentic desires?" Every choice you make doesn't have to have a detailed plan. Life shouldn't be lived like an automated machine. When it comes to taking positive steps toward your desires, strategy-based thinking is crucial.

A System for Everything

There is a system for everything. From starting a business and losing weight to falling in love and enjoying happiness, there is a system to accomplish it all. Just because you can't put your finger on the exact process does not mean it doesn't exist.

A system is a specific set of steps carried out in a specific sequence to achieve a specific result. In order to get dressed, you must follow certain steps in a very particular order to achieve the desired outcome. Choosing the wrong steps (putting your shirt on backward) or the wrong order (shoes followed by socks) will not result in what you want. You must do the right things in the right order to accomplish the task.

You may find it easier to think of a computer program or operations manual as a system, but the truth is that systems surround us. It will take time, but with enough focused effort you will begin to see that every result you find in and around your life was achieved by a very specific process.

Eating dinner is a system. You have to follow a sequence of specific steps to get a desired result. First, you need to prepare dinner, which alone can include hundreds of processes. Once complete, you have to move the food to the table. Next, you have to sit down at the table. Then you pick up the food and bring it to your mouth. You chew the food and swallow it. You repeat the process until you are full or the food is gone. Everything you do can be broken down in this manner.

Not every system is a success. Putting your clothes on in the wrong order is still a process even though the desired result is not achieved. You simply achieved a different result from what you wanted. This would be an example of an unsuccessful system based on the desired result, but a system nonetheless.

What makes this perspective difficult to grasp is the fact that you can't always see what steps are taking place. If you tell someone that you love them, you can't look inside their brain to pinpoint what areas are being activated and what thoughts are being created. This doesn't mean that love isn't a system; it only means that the system is difficult to identify.

Does that stop people from trying? There are thousands of books, programs, and workshops on improving and deepening relationships with others. Even though the unique systems of love for each person may differ, there exists a more general method of receiving the affection of others. In other words, even the most complex and confusing concepts are made up of systems.

This principle gives you a new perspective on things. It creates order and confidence where confusion and fear once existed. You no longer have to look at someone and think, "How in the world does he do that?" Instead, you will say, "I know there is a system to what he does. I simply have to discover it." This is very empowering concept—there is a method to achieving every one of your desires, and when you discover and implement it, you will be successful.

To be more accurate, there are usually several methods available to you. Two unique processes can produce the same desired result. If you choose to put your shirt on before your pants while your neighbor reverses the order, both of you will be dressed for work. In a more practical sense, you can lose weight by eating different foods and following a different exercise program from someone else.

Different people require different methods. You have to find a system that works for you. I may have a hard time running in the morning, but if running at night with a friend works, that's the system to follow. Just because one specific path toward a desire doesn't work for you doesn't mean you can't find another one that better suits your style and needs.

As you think to yourself, "There is a way. I simply have to find it," you could try to discover the solution on your own, starting from scratch and learning as you go. However, it is possible to spend a lifetime seeking out the secrets and still come up empty-handed. There is another way to get what you want in half the time and with half the struggle and effort. The solution is not in reinventing the wheel, but in finding the plans to one that already exists. Modeling is the key to discovering the secrets to success.

Modeling Success

If I bake a cake using a certain number of ingredients combined in a particular sequence, you can produce the same cake by following the steps exactly. If I dial seven digits and reach my neighbor's home, you can dial the same seven numbers and get the same result. Modeling my strategy will produce for you an identical outcome. This concept is nothing new. As you recall, the idea of reproducing success was the basis for creating confidence. We are simply taking the theory and putting it to use.

Modeling allows you to bypass the guessing game of achievement. Millions of people have successfully achieved their desires and recorded every step they followed to get it done. You can benefit from the past experiences of those individuals who wanted the same things you now desire. Save yourself the time and energy of making the wrong moves. Model the strategies of success.

Each of your desires is like a combination lock. Without knowing the sequence of numbers to open it, you could spend an eternity trying to guess the right combination. What if you turned the lock over and found the numbers written on the back? Now the task is simple. Input the three numbers and the lock will open in an instant. This is the magic of modeling.

Consider one of your desires for a moment. Has a book been written on the subject? Perhaps a seminar or audio program holds the key. Chances are good that hundreds of resources have already been created to help you achieve the goal. With a quick look online, in a bookstore, or in your local library, you will find thousands of systems waiting to be modeled.

Recorded methods (books, newsletters, magazines) are only one option out of many that are available. A book is one step removed from the source, so why not go directly to the top? Speaking with others about the systems of success is the best way to learn the overall strategy as well as the intricacies that may not make it into a recorded version.

Your own past experiences are also a great resource from which to learn. If you are searching for the system to feel confident and self-assured, think back to a time when you felt this way. What were you doing? What were you thinking about? What factors increased the feelings? By examining your past, you can discover strategies that have already brought you success. You are your own best resource to getting what you want.

The purpose of revisiting this concept of confidence is simple. You will soon be creating your own strategies, and it is vital that you avoid starting from scratch when it's unnecessary. Don't waste your time! Model the successful strategies of others as well as your own to discover the system to getting what you want. You live in a world that is bursting with information, but most lack the desire to utilize its power. Don't make the same mistake. Your time should be spent enjoying life and not playing an endless guessing game of how to get what you want.

Creating a strategy will do many things, but one thing it will not do is replace authentic desire. This misconception has the potential to create feelings of frustration and disappointment. It is important to enter the process of creating a strategy with a clear understanding of what it can and cannot do.

The Vehicle, Not the Driver

A strategy is the vehicle by which you reach your goals. It is not, however, the driver. A strong desire has to underlie any successful plan. Putting together a strategy cannot make you want something. That must come from within.

From what you have learned about inauthentic goals, you can probably foresee the frustration that can result from forming a plan around something you don't really want. When a lack of internal desire is the problem, people create a strategy to cover up the fact. "All I need is a good plan," they tell themselves, "then I'll be motivated." Nothing could be further from the truth.

For too long people have preached the glory of creating a specific strategy without first giving attention to the need of authentic desire. One cannot exist successfully without the other. You cannot inject a strategy into someone who has little desire and expect positive motivation to start flowing.

It isn't hard to see why this idea has become so popular. It's a quick and easy scheme to happiness. Dissatisfied with your life? Write down a plan to make it better and you're all set. It preys on our weakness for instant gratification. Ultimately, it ends up crushing the spirit of the people who need less show and more know.

Strategy and desire are not linked because one creates the other. They are connected because strategy follows naturally once a deeply rooted desire is in place. When you have an authentic desire to achieve something, you will look to every possible tool and resource that will help you get it. Creating a strategy is one such tool, and that is why you will have a strategy in place acting as a horse to the cart of your desire.

The most useful strategy is one that is utilized by someone who has the first three pillars in place. In this case, the plan will be effective and efficient because it's serving its intended purpose and not being forced to cope with a lack of desire or belief.

Knowing the rules of the game is one thing, but discovering the methods to winning is something completely different. In the next chapter, you'll learn the six essential characteristics of a successful strategy. In a sense, you are at the make-or-break stage of success. Many people have what it takes to achieve a goal, but they lack the skills necessary to piece together a plan that actually works. By incorporating the following elements into your strategy, your desire will have what it takes to make it. Where others have failed, you will succeed.

NOTES & IDEAS

Chapter 10

The Six Elements
of a Winning Strategy

*If you have built castles in the air, your work need not be lost;
that is where they should be.
Now put the foundations under them.*

—Henry David Thoreau

A LL STRATEGIES ARE NOT EQUAL. Desire and belief are absolutely necessary to getting what you want, but you can't stop there. You have to create a workable plan that leads you, step by step, to the things you want. Forming just any plan around your desire isn't enough to guarantee success. You have to build your strategy using certain elements to give it the effectiveness and efficiency it needs to help you on your way. This is a pivotal point in the process of positive motivation, and one that deserves your attention.

The difference between a powerfully structured strategy and one that lacks the critical factors is the difference between getting what you want and coming up just short of the goal. It's not that forming a sound strategy is extremely difficult—the essentials are easy to understand and implement in any plan you create. The problem stems from a lack of education.

Most people were never taught the fundamentals of putting together a winning strategy. They know the basic idea and fill in the gaps by guessing their way from beginning to end. This haphazard method only leads to frustration and failure. To keep this from happening to you, we will examine exactly what it takes to create a plan that works for you and not against you.

We will look at six aspects of a successful strategy that should be utilized when you create your plan of action. Each element is like another brick in a wall. Every brick you add will increase its strength and stability, enabling it to withstand negative impacts and stresses as it guides you toward the things you want to achieve.

Segmented

Hundreds of miles stood between my home and our nation's capital, and I was ready to close the gap. I had always wanted to see the city, and after learning more about its history, my desire peaked. One early Tuesday morning, I loaded a few things into my car and in minutes I was on the road.

After driving the entire trip in one day, I was reminded of a very important aspect of strategy. If I had started the trip by viewing a road sign that said *Washington, DC — 850 miles*, I would have been overwhelmed. The number would seem larger than I could handle, and I would have questioned my desire to continue driving.

Instead, the distance between the beginning and the end were broken up into small pieces. I could drive 30 miles to the next town, and even 120 to reach a major city. In the end, I would drive the 850 miles, but my plan was segmented. I was able to reach the final destination in smaller, manageable steps.

Each time the miles ran down and I reached a benchmark, I felt great. It was a reminder that I was getting closer to the ultimate destination. It boosted my spirits and kept me looking forward to the next step in the process. Short-term successes paved the way to my goal.

Segmentation is a very important aspect of strategy. Each step of the way to creating positive motivation must be carefully scripted to ensure that your scales do not shift toward negative motivation. If your desire is nearing the tipping point, but is suddenly knocked off course because of an overwhelming strategy, you may never recover.

The process is useful in many ways. To begin, it provides the confidence necessary to proceed toward your desires however large they may be. While the idea of cleaning and organizing your entire home may be too much to handle, breaking the plan down into separate rooms isn't as overpowering. All along your path to success you will encounter areas that have the potential to overwhelm you. The very essence of change calls for removing yourself from what is comfortable and creating something different. To ensure you can deal with the changes that come your way, reduce a potentially massive goal into easily completed steps.

Breaking down the goal also forces you to take an in-depth look at your desire. The only way to break something down into smaller parts is to understand the subject intimately. When you gather information about your desire, you will begin to differentiate between steps that work well and steps that are less effective. In other words, you will not only learn about the desire as a whole but also which strategy is most effective.

As I mentioned before, each time I reached a new city on the way to DC, I was able to celebrate a small victory. This is another advantage to breaking down the goal. You don't have to wait until the finish line to feel that you are making progress. You can set your strategy up in a way that allows you to experience small successes on a daily basis.

Imagine having a desire that will take three years to fully materialize. It would be extremely difficult for you to stay positively motivated with only a three-year outcome on which to focus. Even the strongest of characters would begin to think, "Come on already! Give me something to feel good about!" Human beings need short-term pleasure, so why not use that fact to your advantage. Segmenting is the best of both worlds—you get the short-term payoffs and long-term rewards.

As you begin to break your desire down into manageable pieces, remember to keep the challenge involved in each step. In an earlier chapter, you were asked to discover desires that inspired you to action along with smaller goals to keep you heading in the right direction on a daily basis. The same is necessary with segmentation.

You have to create segments that are challenging and inspire you to action. If your reaction is, "So what?" after reaching each stage, you'll know that you set the bar too low. Breaking down a $5,000 savings goal into single dollars wouldn't quite inspire you. You wouldn't feel great after reaching a benchmark. You need to stretch in order to feel good about a victory.

Before we move on, I want to offer two options for segmenting your strategy. Depending on your desire, it can most likely be segmented incrementally or sequentially. These are only suggestions. The most effective way to segment is the one that works best for you and your situation.

1. Incremental Segmenting. Desires that are number-based can be segmented incrementally. The $5,000 goal from above could be broken down in $100 or $500 increments. Other incremental strategies include losing a certain number of pounds, running a certain number of miles, or cutting down a smoking habit to a certain number of cigarettes.

2. Sequential Segmenting. Desires based on unique segments can be broken down sequentially. Getting your driver's license involves several steps such as taking a driver's education course, getting your temporary license to practice with an experienced driver, and taking your driving test.

You will find that many desires incorporate both methods. Building a home would take a sequence of unique steps that could be segmented sequentially, but would also include a financial portion that could be broken down incrementally.

Creating a strategy that segments your authentic desire adds a great deal to the process of positive motivation. You will enjoy an increase in confidence, discover the most effective path to getting what you want, and experience a series of successes along the way. In short, segmentation transforms a potentially overwhelming goal into a series of easily attainable steps.

Specific

Your strategy must be specific. Specificity is among the top qualities of a plan that propels you toward your desire. You must know the exact steps involved in the process, along with the exact sequence of those steps, in order to take intelligent action toward attaining the tipping point.

Tim, and his neighbor, Curt, had been close friends for years. They worked together, played on a work softball team together, and vacationed together. One day, while talking over lunch, the two of them got the idea of installing pools into their backyards. The desire had always been there, but neither could ever afford it. After a nice-sized bonus check came in the mail, the two decided it was time to act.

A few days after the talk first came up, they met for lunch again and talked about their progress with the project. Curt wasn't exactly sure what steps to take and told Tim, "I have to talk to some people and check into some quotes. I should hear news in a few more days."

Tim, a more detailed-oriented individual, sat down the night after their first conversation and drew up a plan to install the pool. After a little research on his computer the next day, he had each step in the process laid out in front of him. Tim's plan was very specific, and pointed him in a very clear direction each day. He knew whom to call and when, what supplies were required, and a plan to ensure he had enough money to cover all of the expenses.

In short, he knew how to get it done. Anyone on the street could have figured out how to follow through with his plan, and that is why only one of the two now has a pool in the backyard. Curt's desire to have a pool was authentic, but without a specific strategy in place he didn't know what to do each day to make it happen.

When I say you have to be specific, I'm not talking about getting a few facts together. I am talking about knowing what the first, second, and sixty-fifth step in the process is. You cannot leave room for confusion. Focus on creating a strategy using Type B steps:

Type A	Type B
Call the bank next week.	Call Mr. Davis at United Bank on Friday at noon.
List a few ideas for the new novel.	Write at least five chapter topics along with three key points for each.
Contact someone about registering for adult education classes.	Call Mrs. Clancy at Brookdale Community College tomorrow at 3:15 p.m. and request an information packet, registration form, and class description list.

Aside from giving you direction, a specific strategy will increase your confidence. When you see the plan laid out in front of you in a step-by-step format, it becomes possible. You begin to think to yourself, "This is going to happen." Specificity transforms a thought into something you see and feel. It's an exciting experience each and every time you do it.

Scheduled

You can talk all you want about what you are going to do, but until you actually sit down and schedule the steps, it's just talk. Scheduling your strategy is a major step in the process of getting what you want. It is a commitment to yourself and to your desire that you mean business, and that you are willing to follow talk with action.

Scheduling your strategy transforms "someday" into "tomorrow." When you see the dates and hours written next to each segment of your goal, it will mark a turning point in your life. It is a sign that you are living up to your potential, and pushing yourself to become the person you always wished you were.

The purpose is to reach the tipping point, and thereby inspire action. This is the key component of scheduling your plan. Yes, it helps to know when things need to be started and finished, but the underlying quality of a schedule is the commitment it represents. When you know you have a deadline coming up, you will work a littler harder to make sure you meet the challenge.

You have already seen the benefits of using a schedule to keep yourself on the ball and positively motivated to take action. Term paper deadlines in college are a great example. Knowing that you must complete a project by a certain date pushes you to work harder and longer than before to make sure you finish the assignment on time.

I want you to do a little mental exercise. Ask yourself which person has a better chance of actually achieving a goal—someone who has no schedule, or someone who has included one in their strategy? Individual A will get around to it someday. Individual B will do it next Tuesday at 7:15 PM. Is there any question as to who you believe will follow through? It's painfully clear, and that's the point. I want you to realize that using these elements in your strategy are guaranteed to help, and consider them obvious aspects of any future plan you create.

There are two parts to scheduling your plan: the start and finish. Although most people focus only on setting deadlines, setting a definite time to begin each stage is critical. You will need to choose two different types of starting times. The first will be for your overall desire. You need to know when you begin the process of change. The other type of start time will be given to each segment of your goal. If you break a financial goal into four parts, you would have a time to begin the project as a whole as well as three segment start times.

When it comes to the overall desire, there is no better time to begin than right now. Of course, there are some goals that need to be put off because of certain time or financial constraints. With most desires, however, you can always do something to get started. Even the smallest step in the right direction helps.

The benchmark start times will vary depending on what comes before and after each segment. As you learn more about the subject, you will be able to gauge how long one stage should take and when the next should begin.

At the other end of the scheduling spectrum, we find the deadline. This takes away the possibility of procrastinating for weeks, months, or even years, and says, "You will do it by this time and day. Period." It's a great way to cut through the excuses and commit yourself to action.

You will need to choose a deadline for the overall goal along with benchmark deadlines for each segment within the strategy. The exact timing of these deadlines will become apparent after you get a clear and thorough understanding of the desire at hand.

When you set the schedule for your overall desire and each segment along the way, you must follow the same two rules you kept in mind when choosing your goals: keep them realistic and challenging. By shaping your schedule to take advantage of the facts of human behavior, you will be able to maintain positive motivation throughout the entire life of your strategy.

Charles Murray was always a bit on the impatient side. Whenever he wanted something, he wanted it immediately. Then one day Charles was introduced to the great game of golf, not an activity for the impatient. It was a lesson that would take several years to really sink in.

Right from the start, he set a deadline for improvement. Charles wanted to lower his score by seven shots within a single month. Without knowing it at the time, he was creating a no-win situation. A desire to improve, which was very likely with the right amount of time and practice, turned into a disappointing and frustrating failure. Charles's schedule caused the desire to self-destruct.

His score would vary from week to week, but never seven shots lower (although he did shoot seven shots higher than the goal). Each game ended with a feeling of defeat. Had Charles's schedule been stretched over several months, he would have been quite pleased with his performance. Unfortunately, the unrealistic schedule wouldn't allow for it.

You have to be careful when creating a schedule. If you set a time that is simply impossible to achieve, you will be forcing yourself to fail. Can you save $1,000? Probably. Can you do it in one day? Maybe not. The wrong schedule can transform a positive and healthy goal into a negative and self-destructive force. The solution is to create a balance. Leaning all the way to the other side will create just as many problems as an unrealistic schedule.

A schedule that offers no challenge will not inspire you to action. Imagine the timeline to achieve a six-minute mile was two years. How hard would you try? If the desire was authentic, you would still put forth effort because you truly desire the outcome, but wouldn't you push yourself harder if you knew the deadline was right around the corner? That is why a challenging schedule must be incorporated into your strategy.

Many of these aspects help to develop your confidence in your ability to achieve the goal. By failing to set a challenging timeline, you are robbing yourself of this benefit. You have to feel a sense of accomplishment and victory when you complete each segment of your plan. If the deadline to quit smoking is ten years from now, I doubt that you will give serious thought and effort to taking action today.

Remember, you can talk about your big plans to do this and that forever, but the moment you schedule it, you are making a greater commitment to success than ever before.

Measurable

Imagine bowling in the dark—no lights, no screens, nothing to let you know what happens after each turn. All you can do is take a few steps toward what you hope to be the right lane and let the ball roll. After the release, you wait a few seconds to listen for the sounds of pins falling. Was that three? Four? How are you doing so far?

This would be a slightly frustrating experience to say the least. Without knowing what pins are falling, how would you know what to do next? You would have absolutely no idea how you were doing, what you needed to change, or if you should feel good about your progress. When the lights go out in the bowling alley, so too does the positive motivation to continue trying.

Human beings need feedback. We need to know how we are doing and how to improve. It's another method to breaking up a large goal. Instead of waiting until the finish line to feel that you have accomplished something, you can enjoy those feelings all along the way.

The ability to recognize progress throughout the process plays right into human behavior. Because we thrive on short-term feedback and rewards, a strategy that can be measured for effectiveness and progress from beginning to finish will add greatly to creating and maintaining positive motivation.

It's like fuel for your car—you can't get from here to there without stopping a few times to fill up on gasoline. You need refueling to reach the destination. The small successes you'll see along the way will act as fuel to keep you going.

It is because of these advantages that you need to put together a measurable strategy. If you set it up in a way that doesn't allow you to see progress or receive feedback, you'll feel like you're bowling in the dark. Each segment of your strategy should be quantifiable in some way to allow for tracking of changes.

What does this really mean? A strategy built upon stages such as "reach financial freedom" would be hard to measure. What is financially free? What exact dollar amount is that? Without knowing how to measure "financially free," you wouldn't be able to see positive or negative feedback from your actions. You'd have to go on a hunch about whether or not your actions made you feel more or less financially free.

Instead, you could decide that financially free meant the ability to pay bills and your mortgage, and have $1,000 left over at the end of each month. After adding up each part of the puzzle, you would come to a definite amount. As you worked through the strategy, you would know exactly how far you have come and how much further you have to go.

As you piece together your success strategy, keep asking yourself, "Can I measure this? Is there a way to track my progress and get constant feedback from my actions?" This will ensure that your strategy will give you what you need: a long-term vision with short-term rewards.

Aside from giving you short-term boosts to keep going, measuring your progress is key to making positive changes to your strategy. Chances are good that you will not end up following the path you first drew up. As you begin to put your plan in action, you will undoubtedly find room for improvement. It's a learning process that involves taking two steps forward, one step back.

When the feedback starts coming in, you can use the information to help you decide whether or not a new direction should be taken. Perhaps you need to spend more time in a certain area, or eliminate a few steps of the plan. Whatever the changes turn out to be, measuring your progress will enable you to pinpoint the problem and find a solution.

Would you be happy for your friend after hearing that she now weighed 150 pounds? How about a co-worker who excitedly tells you that he can run two miles without taking a break? A neighbor whose son just got a 3.0 at school?

If you said, "I don't know," you'd be right. There is an element missing from each situation above that makes it impossible to know how much, if any, progress took place. You need to know where you're starting before you can track any progress. What if your friend from above used to weigh 145 pounds and needed to lose weight to be healthy? You wouldn't be too happy to hear that she was getting worse. What if your co-worker, before smoking, could run seven miles? That would also not be news to celebrate. Then again, if he just had surgery on his legs and was unable to walk just months ago, that would definitely be something to congratulate. A 3.0 would be great if he started with a 2.0, but not so good if it was once a 4.0.

Before you begin to put your strategy in action, you have to measure where you are at present. Progress results from knowing where you once were and how far you've come since then. If you desire to save more money, take note of how much you have right now. If you want to make more friends, count how many close connections you have in your life at the moment. The progress you make in the future will be measured from where you are now.

What do you do with the progress and feedback after setting up a strategy that is ripe for measuring? You have to have a way to take down the information and analyze it. In other words, you have to keep track of your progress.

Tracked

A measurable strategy will do you little good if you don't have a form and function for the feedback you receive. It's hard enough to remember what you ate for dinner last night, let alone remembering, organizing, and analyzing the progress of your plan.

Throughout the process, you will need to make calculations based on the data retrieved, look for trends among the results, and compare different segments and stages of the strategy. Your mind alone is not the best tool to carry out these functions.

The human brain can handle an unbelievable amount of information, but there are other methods available that make tracking your strategy a much easier process. The two methods we will focus on are the chart and checklist.

When you are dealing with an incrementally segmented strategy (number-based), the best tool to utilize is a chart. A chart offers many functions that allow you to see how you are progressing at a glance. It goes far beyond simple reflections of your progress by showing you what you are doing right and showing you where improvements can be made.

Whenever you have to keep track of some type of number, you can easily plot the points on a chart and see how you are doing and where you are heading. With today's computers, you don't have to rely solely on a paper and pencil to track your plan. The options you have with even the most basic database and spreadsheet programs give you maximum flexibility and maneuverability when working with your numbers.

Figure 12 is a simple chart tracking the progress of a savings plan. We can learn a great deal from the basic pattern of measurements in this chart alone. To begin with, the months of April and May could potentially bring the excitement of the desire to a standstill. To the uninformed, this short-term setback could be perceived as a major failure and derail the strategy for good.

When you have a chart to view not only the present, but also past statistics, you can see that April and May represent just one small dip along a heavily positive path. Utilizing a chart with your strategy shifts the focus from the inevitable small setbacks to the overall process. This is a very important aspect to tracking goals. Maintaining a strong confidence and desire during the strategy is key to seeing it through to the end.

Notice there are two bold lines included in the chart. This is a great way to designate the deadline and ultimate outcome of your strategy. In the chart above, the desired result was $1,000 and the deadline was November. This is a simple way to create a visual reminder as to what you want and when you want it.

Observe again the decline beginning in April. This represents a trend—a pattern of similar results within your measurements. Negative trends tip you off to a problem that requires your at-

FIGURE 12

tention. Perhaps your strategy needs some tweaking, or you aren't following through with your prescribed plan. Whatever the case may be, charting your progress will alert you to negative trends, giving you the opportunity to learn from your mistakes and implement improvements.

While negative trends let you know something isn't working, a positive trend does just the opposite. You need to know when you are making the right moves in order to build upon that success in the future. After a little investigating, you may discover a particular aspect of your strategy that works well and could be added to other areas of the plan. Knowing when you need to capitalize on a good thing is just as important as correcting the problems you confront.

A checklist is the tool to use when you are working with a strategy that is sequentially segmented. Whenever you have a list of unique steps or stages to accomplish, you can best track their details and completions with a simple checklist. Figure 13 was created for an individual desiring to spend more one-on-one time with each member of his family.

✔ Task	Task Strategy	Schedule
Go to a basketball game with Jeffery.	Purchase tickets online to next home game.	Friday at 12:00
Go to a movie with Jennifer.	Ask Jen which movie she'd like to see, check the times, and ask her to keep her schedule clear.	Saturday at 3:00
Take Donna to dinner and a show.	Make reservations at Donna's favorite restaurant and purchase theater tickets.	Thursday at 3:30

FIGURE 13

The first filled-in column lists each step within the strategy. The second explains exactly how the step will be accomplished. The last column schedules each step. When a task has been completed, a check can be placed in the left-hand column.

Obviously, this is only one way to format a checklist. The key is to find one that fits your needs and works best for your goals. As long as you can list your steps and track your progress, you have your bases covered.

In the end, the greatest benefit of tracking your strategy is truth. Instead of viewing a short-term setback as the end of the road, you will realize that the overall trend is positive and you can achieve the goal. It shows you that progress, however small it may be, is occurring each time you take action. Tracking takes away the unfounded negative and positive perceptions and gives you the reality of the situation, which is the greatest perspective of all.

Recorded

"What was that idea? If I could only remember what I had thought of just a minute ago." Have you ever heard someone say these words? Perhaps you've even spoken them yourself? After hearing a great idea or coming upon a new tip or technique, it's common to forget the information only moments later, making it more than necessary to record your thoughts and save them from this unfortunate fate.

Studies have shown that you will forget approximately 80% of what you learn within one to two days. Think of the amount of useful information that is lost every week, month, and year of your life. Thousands of ideas are falling to the wayside not because you don't understand them, but because you can't remember them.

Because of this inability to recall every piece of information you have learned, it is imperative that you record every element of your strategy. Each idea, question, answer, and advancement has to be written down, typed, or told to someone else. What you use to record your plan is not as important as having the information easily recalled and manipulated to serve your needs.

You may have the greatest strategy in your mind, but if you can't remember all of the steps involved, very little can be accomplished. As a human being, you have a million ideas floating around in your head at any given moment. The world we face today is in a constant state of chaotic motion. Everywhere you look, you are being pummeled with information—new and old, useful and useless. Because we can only hold so much information in our minds at any given time, some things inevitably get lost in the shuffle.

You can't afford to let your desires get lost in the shuffle. Your strategy should be at the top of your mind. Letting it fall further and further into the mix of clutter will cause a decrease in your desire and action. A "must" quickly becomes a "should," and invariably crumbles into a distant wish that will never again see the light of day.

For the sake of our discussion, let's imagine that you can recall every piece of information involving your desire. Can you quickly and easily manipulate it? How simple would it be to lay out your entire plan and make adjustments? By viewing the process as a whole, and seeing how the various stages intersect, you can easily make changes until you create the most effective strategy possible. For many, this process is one that requires outside help and shouldn't be attempted solely in your mind.

As with the previous characteristics, recording your strategy adds a tangible element to an intangible desire. Seeing your strategy written down on paper doesn't just boost your confidence, it causes it to explode. The dream you have had tucked away in your thoughts for years will finally get the chance to become something more than a wish—it will become your reality.

Get your hands on a pen and notebook, computer, or any other tool used to store and recall information, and get to work. As you begin the process of researching, learning, and taking in as much as you possibly can about your authentic desires, you will be inundated with valuable ideas and information. Ensure that they will be ready to use when needed. Record your secrets to success.

At this point, you understand what a strategy can do for your desires, and how to create one that is both effective and efficient. Now it's time to use what you have learned to create your own personal strategy for success.

NOTES & IDEAS

Chapter 11

The Triad:
Three Stories to Learn by Heart

The heights by great men reached and kept
Were not attained by sudden flight,
But they while their companions slept
Were toiling upwards in the night.
—Henry Wadsworth Longfellow

MAHATMA GANDHI AND MARTIN LUTHER KING JR. had it. So did Benjamin Franklin and Thomas Edison. The secret to success wasn't a mystery to these historic figures, nor was it a mystery to the thousands of others who have helped to shape the world in which we live.

Each of these remarkable individuals possessed something that served as a constant guide and positively motivating force throughout his entire life. It kept the drive and energy thriving, allowing him to create unbelievable change and success. The same force is available to you.

Every successful individual, from the history-makers to today's movers-and-shakers, had what is called the success triad. Everyone who has ever accomplished anything has possessed it, whether or not it was realized. You have already experienced the triad in your life, but without recognizing the force and taking complete control of its power, it has come and gone without warning.

It is possible to develop and secure your triad, giving your desires unstoppable strength; it simply takes good storytelling. As we have already seen while overcoming the rationalizations of inaction, you are already a fantastic storyteller. By focusing this ability on creating your success triad, you can put together a strategy that not only directs you, but also inspires you to action.

The success triad is the absolute understanding of what you want, why you want it, and exactly how you are going to get it. In other words, it is your strategy for achievement. You have gathered together many pieces of powerful information in the previous chapters, but up until now they have been isolated from one another. Combining and refining these resources into a single force will give you the constant source of drive and inspiration necessary to achieve your desires.

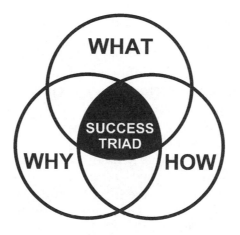

FIGURE 14

We will be revisiting your authentic desires, the pleasures and pains you associate with each, and the six elements of an effective strategy. Once your triad is in place, you will never again face the dilemma of negative motivation. Following the principles in this chapter will not only develop your desire to the tipping point, but also ensure it remains there as long as you want it to. The three stories of the triad will become the most important stories you ever tell yourself or anyone else.

What Do You Want?

You already know the basic idea of what you want, but it's time to dig beneath the surface. You have to know what you want inside and out. The prerequisite to having a specific strategy is having a specific desire. If you aren't 100% clear about what you want, you can't possibly put together a concrete plan.

Imagine receiving a call one evening while you are relaxing at home. The person on the other end explains to you that the call represents your one opportunity to share your desire and make it real; whatever you tell him will happen just as you describe. You have only five minutes to share your story and will not get a second chance to expand or alter your information.

As with most wish-granting scenarios on television and in movies, when you aren't clear about what you want, you will invariably end up getting something very different from what you had in mind. Let's say that you told the representative that you wanted world peace. Seconds later you look out your window and realize you are the only person left on the earth.

Wars, famine, and poverty are all swept away, but this isn't what you meant. "I didn't want this!" you scream, but no one is there to hear you. Perhaps you should have been a bit more specific with your wish.

What would you tell the person on the phone? Could you explain your desire in a way that leaves no room for error or assumption? Could you describe it with enough clarity and detail that any stranger off the street would know exactly what you want? Most people have a vague notion of what they would like, but that's not good enough. You have to avoid the first example below, and work toward the second.

Type 1 Desire

I'd like to find a more rewarding career.

Type 2 Desire

I will become a mechanical engineer for Menk Industries Inc., focusing on consumer goods for the household. This requires a bachelor's degree and a two-year internship.

The details could go on and on, but the point should be clear. The first desire is too weak to create action. It is a passing thought that has little to no chance of ever materializing. The second desire is ready to be executed. The goal is clear and the path is laid out before you.

The more detail you can add to what you want, the greater the chances are that you will follow through with your strategy. The picture created by type 1 desires is empty—there is no compelling future to look forward to. This leaves plenty of room for other, less important thoughts to monopolize your time.

The picture created by the second desire is completely different. You can see the logo of the company as you enter the building each morning. You can feel the atmosphere as you busily work to create a new product that will revolutionize the industry. It creates a clearly defined vision that is both exciting and achievable.

What do you see when you close your eyes and think about what you want? What excites you about the picture? What details could be added that would create even more enthusiasm and energy?

Every detail you add to your story serves as a weight added to the scales. This is yet another step toward attaining the tipping point. The fears that hold you back from acting on the things you want can be overcome, but your desires must be specific enough to make it happen.

If you have ever spoken with someone who is really enjoying life and doing what they have always wanted to do, you will find that they knew exactly what they wanted to accomplish, and had a clear vision of the future. You will never encounter an individual who has achieved consistent success through vaguely denominated desires.

What a different story you'll receive from the "wishers" of the world. Ask them about their desires and you'll get a blank stare and a lot of head scratching. The only point they are sure about is that they don't want to be where they are. After that, the conversation comes to a grinding halt. This is a fact of success: Those who succeed know exactly what they want and those who fail haven't a clue about which way to proceed.

Where do you go if you only have a foggy idea of what you think will make you happy? It's hard to make the right decisions without a crystal clear desire in place. The two hopeful career seekers from the previous example would make very different decisions based on the depth of their desires. While the first wouldn't know what to do, the second would understand which steps to take from day one.

Begin with as much detail as possible when putting together your story. As time goes on, refine and revamp your story to add to its strength and influence. You should know your story so well that you can recite it in your sleep. The next time the small talk turns to the topic of future goals, you will have a compelling story to share. Who knows, you may end up inspiring a few others to make some changes in their lives as well.

With the desire defined to the point that no one could mistake what you are after, it's time to add leverage to the equation. Knowing the "why" behind your goal is the key to ensuring that a great idea will be backed by consistent action.

Why Do You Want It?

The story of why you want it will be found in the information you gathered in Chapter Five. The pleasure of action (the good things that will result from achieving your desire) and the pain of inaction (the negative things that will result if you do not achieve your desire) will be organized and developed to complete the second stage of your success triad.

Imagine that a friend, after listening to exactly what you desire, asks, "Why in the world do you want that?" Your response will decide the future of your success. If you find yourself stumbling through a quick explanation, the desire is sunk. It will be painfully obvious that the reasons backing your desire are not strong enough nor do they hold enough meaning.

If you can't convince someone else that you truly desire the goal, you won't be able to convince yourself. The story of why you want it has to be strong enough to touch you emotionally and mentally or nothing will ever come of it. You have to believe deep down that your desire is something that will enhance your quality of life, and is well worth the time and effort it will require.

The purpose of this segment is to bring together the most compelling reasons you have backing your desire and mold them into an internal and external dialogue. People talk to themselves from the moment they wake until they go to sleep at night. The subject usually comes about by chance, not choice, and most often revolves around what isn't working. Focusing on stress, frustration, anger, worry, anxiety, and fear forces individuals to live their entire lives in a state of self-inflicted misery. It's time to change the topic of your stories.

The triad serves as an excellent replacement of this negative dialogue. Just imagine how much could be accomplished if you focused on what you wanted, why you wanted it, and how you were going to get it every single day. The results will amaze you.

Think back to the pleasure of action and the pain of inaction that you associated with your desire. You'll find on your list several reasons that are more powerful than others—these are the crux of your story. Bring together as many scale-tipping reasons as possible to build a story that makes an impact on your life.

Joseph Radcliff, a close friend and colleague, serves as a perfect example of putting together a success triad that works. Years ago, he was a heavy smoker who was never seen without a cigarette in his mouth. It got to the point where he could hardly make it up a flight of stairs without having to stop several times to catch his breath. The time came when Joe was fed up, and decided that putting an end to the habit was a must.

Joe's desire to quit smoking found strength in two compelling reasons: the pleasure of being there for his future family and the pain of not being able to run fifteen feet without gasping for air. These two factors kept him on track and enabled him to make progress each and every day until the habit was replaced with a healthy alternative.

When friends asked about his progress he would always tell them, "I have to be there for my children when I start a family. I want to be able to play with them, watch them grow, and enjoy my grandchildren. I can't do that if I have lung cancer."

Along with the reward of a happy family, Joe used the humiliating pain of not being able to run down the block as incentive.

That wasn't how he wanted to live, and he reminded himself of that fact every time the urge to smoke returned.

Joe's story brings up a great point—you will be tested. If you begin the process of change and finish it up without experiencing one setback or short-term failure, you aren't doing it right. As you go through the stages of your strategy, you will undoubtedly encounter some problems, but you don't have to let them knock you completely off course.

Situations that test your willpower can be overcome when you have compelling reasons backing your desire. By bringing together the most powerful elements of the pleasure/pain matrix to create your story of "why," you will have amazing strength on your side. You can't ignore the fact that obstacles will come your way; you must accept it, anticipate it, and make it work for you.

Your success triad is quickly coming together. You know exactly what you want and exactly why you want it, and will complete the package by discovering exactly how you are going to get it. The first two elements of the triad prepare you for action, but you have to know what to do in order for that inspiration to be of any use.

How Are You Going to Get It?

The final stage of the triad is putting together a workable plan to achieve the desired result; it is the strategy you will follow each day as a map leading to success. Your desire will only get as far as your strategy can take it. That is why an easy-to-follow, step-by-step plan that covers every angle of the desire is the best possible option.

This is where the six elements of a powerful strategy come into play. As you piece together your plan, it is important to use each of the following characteristics: segmented, specific, scheduled, measurable, tracked, and recorded. Aside from directing your focus and actions each day, an effective strategy also eliminates the chance that you will fall into the trap that has the potential to put a stop to your progress.

Whenever you reach a point in a plan where the next step isn't clear, you are opening the door to hesitation, fear, and negative motivation. The second you have to stop and ask, "What do I do next?" shifts your focus from the steps necessary to accomplish your goal to the doubts you have about your ability.

I have seen many well-intentioned individuals breeze through the first few steps of their strategy only to find themselves stuck at a point of confusion. This kills the momentum that consistent action helped create. It's like starting from the beginning all over again. The sad truth is the majority of people never start again; the single pause in their plan was enough to put an end to a worthy desire.

You can avoid this trap by creating a strategy that leaves no room for confusion or hesitation. You may be asking yourself, "What if I don't know what to do?" When you don't know how to do something, create a plan to discover the answer. It would be foolish to assume you know every stage of every desire from start to finish. There are simply too many things that will come into play as you work toward your goals.

Your list of desires should not be limited by your current span of knowledge. Letting go of ambitions that you can't accurately plan out to the smallest detail would be letting go of an extraordinary life. You can and will learn what it takes to achieve your authentic desires; you merely have to create substrategies to learn the answers to your questions. Below is a quick example of creating a doubtful plan compared to one backed by consistent action.

Strategy 1

Desire — Lose Ten Pounds

Exercise:
Run 2-3 miles at least three times a week.

Nutrition:
Unknown.

Strategy 2

Desire — Lose Ten Pounds

Exercise:
Run 2-3 miles at least three times a week.

Nutrition:
Purchase two books on the topic.
Talk with Mary about her experience with weight loss.
Visit the library to see if they have any videos on the subject.

Although both desires were identical, the two plans parted ways when it came to an unknown subject. The first individual didn't know what constituted a healthy diet and felt confused with nowhere to turn. While the second also lacked an understanding of nutrition, it wasn't left at that. Steps were put in place to discover the necessary information. Forming your strategy in this way will guarantee that your plan is in constant motion.

You don't need to know everything at this stage of the game. All too often I witness people getting excited about making a change in their life only to give up before taking the first step. "It sounds nice, but I have no idea how to do it."

Part of dreaming is striving for new experiences that are out of your current reach. If your desire is authentic, you will find a way to succeed. The answers are out there, and it is only a matter of time before you find them. The important thing is to include these answer-finding steps in your strategy.

Critical thinking is fundamental when piecing together your plan. Imagine a man seeking the answers to his weight concerns acting on the first advice he finds. What if the advice isn't really effective for his particular needs? What if the advice is harmful? Without examining all of the options and looking for the truth behind his problem, he could make it worse by not thinking critically about the situation.

This will be the case with nearly every desire you have. If you don't think critically about the information you take in, you could end up losing money, weakening your relationships with others, damaging your mental and physical health, and creating more problems than you had before. You must take an unbiased look at what's out there and choose your strategy wisely. Everyone can't be right; it's your job to tell the difference.

As you work through these processes, remember to reduce the number of roadblocks you will confront. Adding clarity and specificity is vital, but don't overwhelm yourself. People have a gift for making something they like to do sound simple and something they fear seem complex.

An individual considering an exercise program may think, "First, I have to get all my things together. After that, it's a thirty-minute drive to the gym. When I finally get there I have to find a locker that's available and change into my exercise clothes. Then, after pushing my way through the crowds, I have to find a piece of equipment that's open, which usually means a five minute wait. After the workout, it's shower time and the long drive back home." Listening to this procedure would turn off even the most committed health-conscious person.

How does someone who loves to work out describe the process? "I go to the gym after work and I'm home in no time at all." Notice the difference? You need to have a detailed strategy, but certainly not to the point of making you think twice about what you want. Write out your plan in a way that increases confidence without making you feel completely overwhelmed by the process.

The following areas will provide you with a good base from which to form your strategy. As always, do not feel limited by the categories given. If you find that a particular group doesn't fit with your desire, simply move on to the next. You may also discover other categories that better fit your needs. Each category gives you an area to think about with respect to your desire.

1. Information. What type of information would help you reach your goal? For someone desiring to quit smoking, information regarding the harmful effects of the habit would be beneficial. With your desire in mind, think of the information that you could include in your strategy that would help tip your scales and inspire action.

2. Requirements. Does your desire call for any requirements or prerequisites necessary for success? If your desire is to become an elementary school teacher, a degree in the field would be an example of a requirement. Think your way through the process and try to locate any prerequisites that you should include in your plan.

3. Skills. Does your desire call for any particular skills or abilities that need to be included in the plan? In order to become a singer, you would first need to acquire the skill. I once worked with a woman whose desire was to author a children's book. She was having a hard time choosing which avenue to pursue first, and realized that her skill of writing needed to be improved. This gave her a great place to begin planning out her strategy.

4. Resources. Are there any resources that you need to have in place in order to achieve your desire? Examples include time, money, and equipment. For instance, someone wishing to learn how to play the piano needs the money to pay for lessons, time to practice, and the piano itself.

5. People. With whom do you have to meet, communicate with, and learn from in order to achieve your goal? Most every desire you have relies in some part on another individual. Think of specific people (cousin Tom) or positions (a writing expert) with whom you should get in touch to help you achieve the desire.

6. Places. Along those same lines, can you think of any organizations that could help you? This includes for-profit companies as well as nonprofit organizations. In order to learn how to fly a plane, you would need to contact a flight school. If you desire to take night courses, you would need to get in touch with a university or community college.

Having wrapped up the categories to help you get started, it's time to revisit the topic of modeling. We can't take a complete look at forming a strategy without spending some time on this all-important aspect of guaranteeing success.

In Chapter Nine, we discussed the idea of looking to other people or organizations that have already succeeded in doing the thing you now desire. Use this information to help build your personal strategy. The answers are already out there, waiting to be revisited and repeated. Reinventing the wheel would be a waste of your time and effort. Instead, spend it enjoying the process and fruits of your success, not in blindly guessing your way to achievement.

Copying someone's strategy step for step isn't necessary. You can examine several winning strategies and choose the portions that best fit your needs. Save yourself the time of the hit-or-miss method. Confusion about where to go and what to do is unnecessary—someone has already paved the way for your success. Your job is to recognize effective models and put them to use in your own life.

In the end, your mission is to create a concrete, step-by-step strategy that leads you directly from where you are to where you want to be. Once in place, every day will bring you one step closer to getting all of the things you look forward to enjoying. It will be a work in progress, to be sure, but that is the nature of improvement. Every experience gives you an opportunity to learn something new and make your strategy that much better.

Get excited! The success triad is something that less than 5% of the people in the world utilize. If you do everything that we've talked about in this chapter, your desire will be unstoppable. Know exactly what you want, exactly why you want it, and exactly how you are going to get it, and you'll equip each of your desires with the force of a tidal wave.

You have completed the fourth pillar. Only two more stand between you and complete control of your motivated mind, but none of what you have gained matters if you fail to take the next step. You will never know what is possible until you act on your desires.

In the next three chapters, we will work to eliminate three categories of myths that often keep people from pursuing their desires. To begin, you will learn how to overcome the greatest challenge you will ever face: taking the first step.

The Motivated Mind

NOTES & IDEAS

Pillar V
Act

Chapter 12

The Essential Ingredient
of Positive Change

First say to yourself what you would be;
and then do what you have to do.
—Epictetus

UP TO THIS POINT, you have been developing the potential for change. The one thing that separates you from what you want is action. It is the link that connects you with all of the things you desire. Just as a vehicle has the potential to take you thousands of miles all over the country, it is useless if it lacks the ability to move. It's time to get moving.

Fully realizing the importance of action isn't enough. People will say, "I know I have to do something, but ..." and an endless stream of stories and rationalizations start pouring out. You may understand that taking action is the only way to create change, but you may also have several limiting beliefs and associations that are keeping you from following through.

After years of hearing the stories that hold people back from taking action, three common categories have surfaced. We will examine the first group in this chapter, with the remaining two being covered in subsequent chapters. By eliminating the beliefs you have about taking action, you can put yourself in the perfect position to succeed. Until these beliefs are recognized and overcome, you will have an extremely difficult time getting yourself to follow through with your strategy.

Each new idea you learn will help break down the barriers that hold you back from getting what you deserve. Soon, nothing will stand in your way and you will begin to act on the things that you have desired for years. Becoming action-oriented will change your life overnight. You will literally have the ability to say what you want and make it happen on your schedule. It gives you a sense of power and control over your life that very few experience. The rewards of living an action-oriented life are never-ending.

Waiting for an Eternity

Phil Parks saw the competition begin to pop up all around his business, but he figured they would never last. He took no preventative measures to improve his image or products, and chose to wait them out. In a very short time, he went from the number-one seller of sports equipment in the city to the number-four retailer.

Amanda Brown didn't know exactly what she wanted to do with her life, but there was no rush to find the answer. Years passed as she waited patiently for something to appear, but nothing ever did. After sixty-two years of waiting around for an opportunity to come to her, she realized her mistake.

Anthony Cooper had three lifelong goals: learn how to skydive, start a charity to help underprivileged children, and visit Australia. He was clear about what he wanted, but waited for the information and resources to surface. To this day, Anthony is still waiting for his dreams to come to him.

What do these three people have in common? They failed to take action and in turn missed the chance at a happier life. Waiting for better things to appear only left them waiting and wishing year after year. The cycle will never stop until you decide to stop it. Life goes on whether or not you do something about what you want.

The first belief we have to put to rest is the idea that waiting around for an opportunity to reveal itself is the surest and safest way to get what you want. If you want anything to change in your life, you must be the one to change it. Action is an absolute necessity for success.

You may know this is true logically, but you have to believe it emotionally. You can fool yourself, but reality never lies. If you don't do something about what you desire, you will never achieve it. Do yourself the greatest service and let this idea really sink in. It should be a little unsettling when the truth hits you. Instead of mumbling, "I know I have to do something to get what I want," you should firmly state, "The only way I will ever get what I want is to do something about it right now! If I fail to take action, I will never achieve my goal."

People act on their emotions even when they mentally know the opposite to be true. That is why you must feel this new belief along with thinking it. Every time I hear people say they are patiently waiting for a better opportunity to appear, I know in an instant their chances for success are minimal at best. The world would be full of successes if people began to face the fact that personal action is the only way to guarantee a positive change.

Ask yourself this question: If you change nothing about your current behavior, will you get what you want? Take the time to really think about where your life is heading and what you'll end up with if you fail to change your behavior.

Your desires will not come to you. The money, health, relationships, career, happiness, and success you are looking for will never fall into your lap. Desires are things that you must pursue. You have to overcome the two fears that hold you back (pleasure of inaction, pain of action) and do what you know you have to do.

Replace the old belief that waiting for opportunities to appear will get you want you want with the reality that you must be the one to make your desires come true. Action is a must for positive change—think it, feel it, believe it, live it.

Building Momentum

Every book in the world, from the dawn of communication up to modern times, has a single thing in common. The size and subjects may be different, but that doesn't change the fact that all books share a single characteristic: They began with a single word. Some may contain fifty words while others contain more than 150,000, but that doesn't change the fact of their common beginning.

Think of the ten most successful companies of all time. If you had the power, you could trace back the juggernauts of business to a single action. The businesses you see today, surrounded by billions of dollars, thousands of employees, and a baffling array of internal and external procedures, were set in motion because a man or woman, at some point in time, took the first step.

Every Olympian started the journey toward his ultimate dream with a single action. Every runner had to begin with a single step on the track; every diver had to begin with the first dive into the water; every cyclist, whether she can remember it or not, started with her first bike ride.

The pyramids of Egypt and the coliseum in Rome are magnificent symbols of what is possible. The thought of creating these structures from scratch is overwhelming. However, at one point in time they were only ideas. One day, long ago, both monuments that would stand the test of time began with a single stone. One action started the process that created the remarkable structures we see today.

This fact holds true for the smaller successes that aren't seen on television or read about in history books. A mother's fit body began with a single jog. A young college student's savings began with a single deposit. The relationships that a father now enjoys with his children began with the single act of listening.

The point of these examples leads us to our next self-limiting belief: Change comes through painful, massive, overwhelming steps. Anyone who believes that the pyramids or an Olympic athlete came about overnight is under an unbearable amount of fear and pressure. The myth that changing your life is too much to manage is one that creates unnecessary resistance.

It's like being given an enormous novel or textbook to read. At first it seems overwhelming, but you can only read one word at a time. Before you know it, hundreds of pages have been read and the book is finished. This is how change works. The project may seem unmanageable, but all you can do is take it one step at a time. One action leads to the next, and before you know it, amazing progress has been made. Change doesn't have to come through single, earth-shattering stages. It results from taking the right steps, day after day, in the direction of the things you desire.

Most of the things you desire are built upon several stages; rarely will you be dealing with a goal that calls for one enormous action. The problem is, most people view their desires in their entirety, focusing on the finished product instead of seeing it for what it actually is: a combination of much smaller steps.

The smallest action can be enough to get you started and keep you going until you succeed. It's like a giant boulder teetering at the peak of a mountain: A single push is all it takes to create unstoppable momentum as the rock tumbles down to the ground. Doing just one seemingly insignificant thing can create the momentum that drives you to continue taking action each day.

The model of human behavior demonstrates why a small step is enough to create massive change. People may fear taking a huge step, but if you offer a smaller action, they are more willing to carry it out. This adds weight to the positive side of the scales, and makes it possible to take progressively larger steps toward the end result.

As I was walking back to the office from lunch one day, I passed by a public swimming pool. I noticed a long line of children waiting to jump off a relatively low diving board. Next to this line was a slightly smaller one leading to a diving board that was nearly double the height of the first. Finally, there was a group of about fifteen children waiting in line for the high dive.

I noticed that the kids were following a very specific pattern. After giving the low dive a try, a certain percentage of kids would line up for the medium board. After that, several of the braver children would make their way over to the high dive. Beginning with the small step of using the low dive gave them the confidence and momentum necessary to continue through to the high dive.

Had there been a high dive only, the number of kids in line would be cut drastically. Because they wouldn't be able to test their fears and take a small step toward the ultimate desire, they would never reach the tipping point. Without having a less intimidating action to begin the process, the children would pass up the high dive.

This is how human behavior operates. Most of us are too afraid to jump in with both feet, but if given the chance to test the waters, we would eventually dive right in. Imagine that the fear of action weighs in at a six, and the initial desire to act is a three. Asking someone to take an enormous step, with the current balance, would result in inaction: The fear is too strong. However, asking for a minor step in the right direction would result in action: The resistance to a very small step isn't as great as the resistance to a large change.

This small step would increase your confidence and thereby add weight to the positive side of the scales, perhaps bringing the balance to five on the side of action (positive motivation) and six on the side of inaction (negative motivation). Taking a second small step would tip the scales even further. Eventually, a series of small steps would be enough to tip the entire balance in favor of positive motivation.

Imagine that you want to visit England. You have the time and money to make it happen, and the desire is authentic. After months of putting it off, you realize that your lack of action results from your fear of flying. If told that you had to book a trip for tomorrow, you would fail to act because the fear of flying would overpower your desire to see the country. This is where the story stops for most people, but there is another option.

You may not want to book a ticket at the moment, but how about purchasing a few books about the country and its history? This would represent a very small amount of pain (loss of money, loss of time). As you learn more about what your trip would entail, your desire to travel develops. The small steps are beginning to tip the scales.

The fear of flying is still in control, so you decide to visit an old friend who has traveled to England many times. The stories you hear and the pictures you see add more and more weight to the positive side of the scales. Your desire intensifies to the point that you are ready to make it happen. After a quick visit to some Web sites offering calming statistics about the safety of flying, you decide to get the tickets and look forward to a memorable trip.

Taking small steps enabled you to get what you wanted. Without having the option of slowly working toward the ultimate desire, you would have missed out on a remarkable experience. This is why taking small steps is sometimes the best way to begin the process of change and improvement. One action is enough to create the momentum necessary to inspire consistent action until you succeed.

Potential Power

We have one more common myth to dispel before moving on. You have probably heard the phrase "knowledge is power" many times. Although knowledge and information play an integral role in positive motivation, it does not equal power. Knowledge only represents potential power until it is backed by action.

Consider what the world would look like had the great minds of history kept their ideas to themselves. Their knowledge would certainly represent potential power, but until the ideas were shared with the rest of the world through action and achievement, they would be of little use. Only when great ideas are acted upon do we realize their true power.

"He'll never do it," my friend Chris said as he watched Carl walk down the hall. "He doesn't know what he's getting himself into."

His comments stemmed from the fact that Carl, a mutual friend, had just described his plans to join a group in New Zealand that was building a home for a family in need. "I looked into that once," continued Chris, "and I would do it, but I'm too busy right now."

Here was the all too common situation of a doer being ridiculed by a talker. I was thinking to myself, "If you know all the answers, why don't you just do it?" but instead, I held my tongue and gave Carl my best wishes. I wasn't interested in how much Chris knew because he wasn't doing anything with his supposed information. Carl may not have known every detail, but at least he was doing something about his desire.

You will never know how good your ideas are until they are

tested. You will never know how enjoyable life can be until you take your desires and run with them. Not every goal will pan out, but the ones that do will add a great deal of peace, satisfaction, and happiness to your life.

The world is built by action. One action-oriented individual is worth ten inactive geniuses. As you begin the process of achieving the things you desire most, you will experience a jolt in confidence, an empowering perspective, and a new way of life. These rewards are only possible by acting on the knowledge you have accumulated. It doesn't matter how smart you are if you don't put what you know to use.

Take Action Right Now!

Do something right now that will begin the process. It could be a phone call or an e-mail. Perhaps a trip to the bookstore or a little online investigation will get you started. Whatever it is, do something right now. It doesn't have to be massive, just a small step in the right direction.

Once you have taken the first step toward one of your desires, we will work through the second category of myths. You may have several reasons why the time isn't right to start moving, but some of those beliefs may actually be self-destructive and paralyze your ability to improve. Only when these myths are dispelled and replaced with the truth will you be free to proceed.

NOTES & IDEAS

Chapter 13

Breaking Free
from the Myths of Time

*Speech is conveniently located midway between thought
and action, where it often substitutes for both.*
—John Andrew Holmes

A GREEN LIGHT SIGNALS IT'S TIME TO GO; a red light that
it's time to stop. Reverse the order, and you'll be heading
for trouble. With most things in life, timing is critical to success.
Proposing to a complete stranger would result in failure, while
speaking those magic words to someone with whom a strong
relationship has been built would have a better chance at acceptance. The timing of your proposal is essential.

Positive motivation is no different. There is a right time to act
on your desires, and a wrong time to act. Choosing correctly
will lead you to an extraordinary life, while choosing the wrong
time to begin can spell certain disaster for your hopes of lasting
change. Knowing the difference is the key. Fortunately, your
task is simple. In the case of your dreams, there is only one right
time and one wrong time: now and later.

The minds of many are filled with reasons for putting off their
desires. Over time, these excuses have solidified into strongly
held beliefs. If you are to have any chance of success, you must

break free from myths that have the potential to cause prolonged, if not indefinite, hesitation to act.

The truth will once again shed light on the solution. You will soon realize that the false beliefs you have about the right time can safely be replaced with a proactive attitude. These myths need to be exposed for what they truly are—lies that keep you from what you deserve.

The Grand Illusion

The "perfect time" is an illusion that is holding the world hostage. At some point in your life, it is highly likely you have postponed action waiting for just the right time to come along. You'd like to focus some time and energy on your goals, but with so much on your plate already, it's just not possible. Perhaps you'll begin when:

- The kids are out of school
- The kids go back to school
- Things settle down a bit
- Things pick up a little
- The current year ends
- The new year begins

People have hundreds of time-sensitive prerequisites that must happen before they take action. And what happens when the requirements are met? Another excuse jumps in to take its place. It's a vicious cycle that ceases only when you realize that you are sentencing your desires to failure by waiting for the perfect time to appear.

The reasons backing up this truth aren't new to you. If you take a moment to reflect on your past experiences, you will come to the same conclusion. You may be searching for a time when you have nothing left to do except work toward your desires, but life doesn't work that way. You will always have something on your mind that you feel needs to be taken care of. Whether it's doing the laundry or patching together a million-dollar contract, you will always have something on your plate.

The world we face today is racing around us at a head-spinning pace. We are constantly bombarded by an endless stream of stimuli that have the potential to wreak havoc on an unsuspecting bystander. This having been said, you still have no excuse to put your desires off for a day that will never come.

Several months ago, I met with a young woman, Samantha Gibson, who wanted to go back to school to brush up on her public speaking skills. Ever since she could remember, getting up to speak in front of others was a nightmare. Sam was ready to overcome the obstacle, and was set on taking a course offered through the local community college. Her desire was authentic, but she held a belief that would stand in the way of her desires.

After she compiled the facts and put together quite an impressive strategy, it was time for action. Before the words could even leave my mouth, she had a list of reasons why she couldn't get started immediately.

"I feel great. I can't wait to get involved with the course and start to build some confidence in public speaking," she said. "And I'll get started as soon as the kids get settled in at school. This is Hailey's first year of middle school, and she'll need to readjust for the first few weeks."

As she left my office, she reassured herself that the time would soon come when she could make good on her personal commitment. I had a sinking suspicion that Sam was suffering from the "perfect time" illusion. Our conversation four weeks later confirmed my fears.

"The kids are doing really well in school, and I'm still excited about taking the course. Travis said he doesn't mind keeping a closer eye on the kids one night a week, so my schedule is pretty clear." She paused for a moment, then said, "I just have to take care of some things at work first. I've been a little overwhelmed lately and don't think I can take on anything else at the moment."

I wished her the best, and hung up the phone. There are some goals that reach this point because they are inauthentic and lack the desire necessary to create action. However, Sam actually believed that the time would come when she would have a completely free schedule. She was willing to wait it out until that time magically appeared.

Fortunately, she finally came to her senses, and decided to take action. Small steps were taken to start the process, and she eventually registered for the course. When I asked her what caused the change, she replied, "I realized how foolish I was being. I couldn't remember a day in the last twenty years when I didn't have something to do, and I knew the next twenty wouldn't be any different. If I was going to do it, I was going to do it now."

If you have a desire that you truly want to achieve, but are waiting for that elusive perfect moment to appear, stop wasting your time. You can wait for the next ten years of your life to do the things you want to do, or you can stop waiting and do something about it. It simply takes a change in perspective and mindset. By replacing a limiting word with an empowering one, you can create that mindset right now.

Small Words, Big Difference

The answer is balance. Everyone is busy, but not everyone is busy doing the same things. While some people choose to focus on the small tasks that eat away at their time, others decide to focus on the important things in life. The minor obligations still have to be taken care of, but a healthy balance makes it possible to succeed in both worlds.

Successful men and women eat, drink, shower, and shave just like everyone else. They run errands, take their children to soccer, and work forty plus hours a week. The people that have a blast living life make a conscious choice to do the things they want to do as well as take care of the daily demands on their time.

The small things will take over your life if you let them. It's possible to do the things you want to do with the time you are given. Years from now you will look back on a life that is full of completed to-do lists or a life that is full of achieved desires and fulfillment.

Twenty-four hours a day—that limit is in place for you, me, and everyone else in the world.

I have no doubt that you know at least a few people who race through their day overflowing with stress and tension. It isn't that their day is more stressful than yours—they make the choice to live their life with stress. If working mothers and fathers and CEOs of billion-dollar corporations can make the choice to live in peace and calm, so can you.

Let's bring those small words that can make a world of difference into our conversation. Time is a constant—you won't be able to find any extra hiding under some rock. If your desires are being put on hold because you are waiting to find more time, you need to rethink the situation.

Have you ever wished you could find more time? Perhaps you told your friends or family that you'll get around to your goals when you find a few more hours? Let me do you a favor—you can stop searching for lost time because you'll never "find" it.

Andy Washburn used to think he was the busiest person in the world. He was working an enormous number of hours per week, running around town taking care of errands and to-do lists, and barely had enough time to sleep. There were several goals that he wanted to spend time on, but because of his hectic schedule, Andy couldn't fit them in.

That all changed when he met David Paley—a fellow employee working the same number of hours, running the same types of errands, but also having the time to pursue the most amazing experiences. He had traveled extensively around the globe, gaining a firsthand look at the same breath-taking scenery, monuments, and culture of countries that the majority of people only read about in books. To hear him play the bass or piano, you would think he was a professional musician. David was also involved in charity work, giving his most valuable resource to others. Andy thought the list would never end.

He couldn't believe that David could fit it all in. "How do you find the time to do it all?" he asked him one day after a quick lunch spent looking at some of his pictures from Egypt.

"I don't find the time," David answered. "You can't look at it that way, or you'll never do it." He put down the picture he was holding and looked Andy straight in the eyes. "You have to make the time for the things you want to do."

What a change in perspective. Andy had been searching for lost time while David was busy using every minute of the day to do the things he desired. After taking an honest look at his situation, Andy realized that he might not have been using his most valuable resource very wisely. While David was busy helping the homeless, Andy was sitting on the couch watching television. He had to unwind after work, and couldn't be expected to use that time for extras—beliefs like that were to blame for his problems.

Realize here and now that you will not and cannot *find* more time for the things you have always wanted to do—you must *make* time. It may take a little prioritizing and rescheduling, but the rewards of reaching for your dreams are worth it. The small things will take over unless you make a conscious decision to make time for the things that matter most.

An Ageless Process

Waiting for the perfect time is only one aspect that holds people back from taking action; believing that the time to act has already passed also plays a major role in the decline of desire. The producer of a small theater company passed a story on to me that demonstrates the obstacles created by the myth of being too old.

"Oh, that would have been a nice thing to do ten years ago," Laura began, "but I'm too old for that now. The time has passed." This was Laura's reply to her friend's request that she take up acting. She had thought about getting involved in the field years ago, but never did anything about it. The "I can't find the time" myth was replaced with the false belief that "the right time had already passed." Laura was 35 years old.

"If only I had started ten years ago," Diana began, "but it wasn't meant to be. That's not something people my age do." Diana, like Laura, wanted to become an actress, but felt that she had let the opportunity pass her by. If a time machine could take her back ten years, she would explain, she would jump at the chance to act. Diana was 45 years old.

Here were two women, tens years apart in age, saying they would take action in a heartbeat if only they could go back ten years. If you feel that you are five years too late to begin now, you'll be saying the same thing five years from now.

You can't change the past. Accept the fact that you didn't act before and begin today. There are no laws to how old you have to be to chase a dream. Your decision is the only one that matters.

Edna Williams, a 77-year old woman from Connecticut, didn't let age slow her down. Upon her fifty-fourth birthday, she received her PhD, and in her late sixties became a professor. Barbara York is yet another example of what is possible if you don't allow age to limit your desires. She earned her pilot's license after she retired and flew happily for the next twelve years. If she let the "too old" myth steal her desire, she would have missed out on the thrills, joy, and satisfaction that her dream created.

From the beginning until the end, you have the right to live life as you wish. Who cares about a few naysayers who tell you to act your age? Their jealously speaks for them. In the end, it won't matter how well you fit the image that others expected of you, nor will you be remembered for following the pack. Desire is the only requirement you must fulfill. After that, the rest is up to you.

No Guarantees

What if you fail? What if the dream you have had your heart set on for years doesn't work out the way you had hoped? What if everyone laughs at and ridicules you? Questions like these form another roadblock that people face. They hesitate because of the possibility of things not working out, and pass up the opportunity to grow and succeed because of a mythical belief that a time will come when success is a guarantee.

This belief runs rampant in our world. The fear of failure is so intense that people would rather be certain of a mediocre life than risk the chance of short-term failure. This is a common theme that has been touched on time and again throughout this book: You can't get where you want to be by living solely for the acceptance of others. If that is your desire, then your path has already been chosen.

The things you desire will rarely be a sure thing. You will very likely stumble a few times as you take steps to achieve your goals, but waiting for a guarantee will leave you waiting forever.

The only guarantee I, or anyone else, can offer is the guarantee of failure if you choose to do nothing.

I'm not suggesting that you become a robot lacking feelings or emotion. It is only natural to want to succeed at what you attempt. As you already know, fear is a good thing when it is controlled and taken advantage of. Fear lets you know that something is about to happen that may be harmful and should be avoided; it is a signal that tells you to prepare.

The secret is to accept the fact that short-term failures will occur, and take steps to reduce their probability and impact. You will be amazed at the kind of life you can create when you let go of your fear of failure and proceed with confidence. It will feel as if an enormous weight has been lifted from your shoulders.

How well would a professional baseball player perform if he waited for a guaranteed hit? He would obviously never get the chance to swing because a guaranteed hit is impossible to secure. A decent baseball player fails more times than he succeeds, but that doesn't stop him from trying to hit the ball. Instead of letting the fear of failure stand in his way, he practices his swing to reduce the probability of failure occurring, while at the same time realizing that every swing can't be a homerun.

People are skilled at giving good advice, but hardly ever take it themselves. If a friend told you that she wasn't going to do anything about her goals until she could guarantee everything would work out just right, you would think she was crazy. Consider what you would tell a close friend who is living by the belief that a perfect time of guaranteed success will eventually come around—take the same advice.

Have you ever heard of Bob Hope? How about Matt Larson? My guess is that the former is very familiar and the latter is an unknown. Both men shared the same desire for a career in comedy, but only one man was able to take action every day to make it happen.

While Mr. Hope accepted the risk of short-term failure, Mr. Larson was too afraid to begin. The fear of failure forced him to remain safe and secure in his home in Atlanta, Georgia, working as a busboy for a small neighborhood diner. Did Mr. Hope fail? Of course he did, and not just a few times. But among his failures were a great many winners, which combined to bring him success, fame, and a life spent doing what he loved.

Mr. Larson will never know what he could have become because he waited his entire life for a fail-safe success. His dream, a career that would have brought him more joy and satisfaction than anything else, was never realized. It is very likely that Mr. Larson would never have reached the level of success that Bob Hope enjoyed most of his life had he acted on his dream, but that isn't the point. The process, and not the outcome, will be the thing that brings you the most excitement and fulfillment. Life is what you do between the beginning and end of your desires.

The fear of failure is natural and necessary. Everyone at some time or another has hesitated because of it. What is unnecessary is letting the fear paralyze you. Although it will be present, how you handle it is completely up to you. You'll have a much easier time inciting action if you focus on where you want to go instead of the places you wish to avoid. An absolute guarantee of constant success is a myth. Replace this belief with an acceptance of short-term failure and an excitement for long-term fulfillment.

The Option to Exit

People resist taking action toward their desires because they fear being trapped by something that doesn't actually make them happy. "What if I don't like it? What if it's not for me?" Thoughts such as these will undoubtedly shift the balance of power toward negative motivation and keep it there until these fears are put to rest.

There is a tendency to feel locked in once a plan is put into action. Because no one likes to feel trapped, most individuals would rather play it safe than risk working toward something that won't fulfill their needs. Below are a few examples demonstrating the negative impact of this fear:

> CINDY MORGAN, a retired teacher, passed up the chance to join a neighborhood association because she wasn't certain that she would fit in with the other members. She's now an outsider among a large group of happily connected friends.

ALEX MOORE never put his name in for a promotion at work because he was afraid it would turn out to be something he didn't enjoy. He was mistaken in his judgment. His friend jumped at the chance and currently has Alex's dream position.

KELLY HOGARD decided against moving to Arizona because she wasn't certain it was the right move to make. Only when the opportunity passed her by did she realize the error of her ways.

These individuals chose to miss out on potentially enjoyable experiences because they weren't dealing with "sure things." The myth that is holding them back is the belief that an opportunity will come along that is certain to create happiness. If you refuse to act on a goal until it is a guaranteed match with your needs, you'll most likely never find what you are looking for. You have to take a chance and test the desires you have discovered. You will never know for certain whether or not a goal will make you happy until you do something about it. However, taking a risk isn't the only advice to help you overcome this false belief. There is a quick and easy solution to the problem this myth creates.

You can always change your mind. It's really that simple. Whenever you fear that a particular path won't make you happy, you can always change course. You never know how a new experience is going to make you feel. It could turn out to be your passion, or it could turn out to be a dud—only time and action will tell. The option to begin with a clean slate is always there.

Children's activities are a perfect example of this principle. Many parents sign their kids up for dancing, swimming, gymnastics, soccer, piano, violin, and a host of other activities, giving them an array of potential desires to try out. Children know, at least the ones in a healthy environment, taking part in a soccer league doesn't mean they have to stick with it for the next ten years. Kids don't mind trying out many activities if they know the option to change their mind is always available.

As is usually the case, adults lose the freedom of thought and action that children possess. You don't have to pick one thing and stick with it for the rest of your life. You can pursue as many interests as you'd like, and dedicate more time and effort to the desires that bring you the most enjoyment and satisfaction.

We all live by our own guidelines whether or not we take ownership of them. Give yourself the freedom of a set of rules that allows you to change your mind and follow the path that best suits your needs. You will feel a sense of relief when you give yourself the option to alter your direction. Instead of resisting action because you fear being trapped, you will take the first step knowing it doesn't mean you will walk the same path forever. The option to change is always on the table, but you have to recognize and make use of it.

Escalating Obstacles

The last myth that we will visit in this chapter deals with the consequences of hesitation. The situations you face today will not be the situations you deal with in the future. You may postpone taking action, but the rest of the world will not. Putting off one challenge may invite many more, creating an overwhelming condition in which action is no longer an option.

The years between high school graduation and starting a family are a perfect example of the reality of hesitation. After school, the obstacles that stand in the way of a desire, let's say traveling, are minimal. As time goes on, the challenges escalate to include college and a part-time job. Several years down the road, you've got a family to take care of and a full-time career to pursue. In the end, a desire that could have been achieved is now facing enormous obstacles.

This aspect of time makes immediate action more than necessary. Do something today about the things you want before the challenges stack up against you. It might not seem like much is standing in your way at the moment, but that can quickly change. Hesitation will only serve to create more barriers to success.

Anyone who has put off balancing their checkbook has experienced this dilemma firsthand. Reconciling your account on a daily basis would make the task rather easy, but this doesn't always happen. Allowing the bills and receipts to stack up can transform a relatively simple activity into one that is impossible to tackle. The longer you wait to balance your checkbook, the more complicated and confusing the task becomes.

Balancing your checkbook is one thing, but what about a more elaborate desire? The results are just the same. I remember watching a show in which two people, a young woman and her husband, were sitting inside a small airplane on their way to an altitude of 15,000 feet. They were about to experience a tandem skydive for the first time in their lives, and the fear and tension was written on their faces. As the plane reached jumping altitude, the couple was motioned to the open door near the rear of the plane.

The woman was first to jump, and seemed to have controlled her fears rather well. She and her instructor approached the door, counted to three, and jumped. Her husband handled the situation a little differently. Instead of following her lead of instant action, he paused—and the fears began to build.

You didn't have to be a mind reader to figure out what he was thinking. "What in the world am I doing?" "What if something goes wrong?" "How can I get out of this?" Each second that ticked by as he waited ushered in a new and compelling perception of pain.

After staring at the open door for what seemed like an eternity, he decided against jumping. Hesitation welcomed in a rush of fear, and it was too much for him to overcome. His wife may have met with the same result had she paused before jumping, but she made the conscious choice to focus on the goal and follow through with the plan.

If you believe what you see today will mirror what you see tomorrow, you are only fooling yourself. Replace this myth with realty. Putting off your desires will only increase the obstacles you are up against. Consider your own goals and the escalating challenges that can result from inaction.

Practical Procrastination

While we have focused on the myths that keep people from creating the life they deserve, there is a time that actually calls for hesitation. While certain steps should be taken immediately, others need to be put off until a later date.

"I lost my entire savings in one day," explained Mr. Conner. "I didn't know what I was getting myself into." This was the beginning of a short message a colleague of mine received from a client looking to get his life back on track after a devastating investment fiasco. Mr. Conner's experience, painful as it was, serves as a prime example of what can happen when you leap before you look.

Mr. Conner took the advice of a friend and sunk his money into an extremely risky investment. He didn't think critically about the situation, and proceeded hoping things would work out to his advantage. Unfortunately, the worst possible outcome occurred and his money was lost forever.

Acting without full knowledge of the subject brought about his downfall. The situation called for prior planning and research, not impulsive action. He would have been much better off had he postponed investing and instead researched the business. A total lack of action is not the answer: The right type of action is the key.

Certain steps, in this case investing, can only be successfully completed after particular elements are in place. Seeking new employment is another great example. In order to successfully secure a new job, you must follow a specific sequence of steps to reduce the risk of prolonged unemployment.

Quitting your job and walking out of the office one day is not the way to get ahead. This action would create a world of trouble for both you and your family. Before making your move, you would be wise to research other opportunities, meet with several potential employers, discuss the move with your family, and perhaps even secure a position within another company before you take the step to actually quit your current job.

This principle, therefore, calls for intelligent action in place of impulsive behavior. Acting without full knowledge of the subject or prior to completing preliminary stages is something to avoid at all costs. This still means that something, no matter how large or small, can be done today.

Each time you confront a myth about the "right time," you have a choice to make: You can either let the false belief keep you from what you want, or recognize the truth and take action.

The former will create predictable results—more of the same. The latter will give you the chance to experience a new and exciting way of life.

The myths we have covered in this chapter are destructive elements, but they can't quite compare to a larger myth that deceives millions of people around the world. If you can overcome this limiting belief, and recognize the truth that lies at the foundation of life, you will never again worry about falling short of your potential because you will be driven to reach it every day.

NOTES & IDEAS

Chapter 14

The Most Powerful Motivator
in Your Life

The tragedy of life is not that it ends so soon,
but that we wait so long to begin it.
—W. M. Lewis

RALPH ELLIS KNEW THE SECRET. He learned it late in life, and used it to ensure his remaining years were full of nothing but joy. Ralph's secret allowed him to avoid the most dangerous myth in life—one that robs countless individuals of their hopes and dreams. The secret that set Ralph free, that brought to life the things he desired most, will do the same for you if you take it to heart.

Doing some basic arithmetic, Ralph figured that the average person has approximately 3,900 Saturdays in his or her lifetime. Being nearly 60 years old, he found that he had about 780 Saturdays left in his future. This realization gave him quite a wake-up call, but he didn't stop there.

He visited every toy store in town, and proceeded to purchase all the marbles he could get his hands on. When the trip was complete, Ralph went home with 780 marbles of all shapes and sizes. He filled a container with all 780 marbles, and taped a small piece of paper to the front that read *Saturdays*. Each week, he would remove a single marble from the jar. In effect, he could see his remaining Saturdays slowly diminish.

This made quite an impact on Ralph's life. Before he came to the realization that his days, along with everyone else's, were limited, he constantly put things off. He was much like everyone around him in that he wanted things he didn't have; he also shared their habit of hesitation. This simple exercise opened his eyes to the true nature of life, and to the limits that surround us all.

As the marble count became noticeably smaller, Ralph made sure that he savored every moment of every day. He didn't hide from the fact that his days would eventually run out—he used the fact to his advantage. He began to do the things that he used to talk about doing years before, and it dramatically enhanced the quality of his life. Ralph was a happy man.

This story was passed on to me a few years ago, and may have even crossed your path at one time or another. It deals with an extremely important principle and sets the stage for one of the most critical chapters in this book. We may vary in our personal beliefs about what happens to us after this stage of life is complete, but we can all agree that our time on earth is limited. Of course you realize this truth, but it's a matter of knowing it versus believing it. If you do nothing else but replace the myth of eternal opportunity with the truth of limits, your life will never be the same.

Throughout the rest of this chapter, we will focus on overcoming the remaining myths of action that hold you back from success. If you're looking for that last nudge in the right direction to get you moving, this is it.

You've Got One Shot

Imagine living in a world where the average lifespan is 10,000 years. Without warning, you are transported to earth and learn that the timeline shrinks to 75 years. How would you take the news? How would you behave after the initial shock has passed?

Hopefully, you would get moving! With such a short amount of time left to do the things you want to do, you would stop thinking about getting started and actually do something about it. Without the luxury of putting things off for a few thousands years, you would be driven to make the most of what time you had left.

This leads us to our first myth. People live their lives as if they have 10,000 years to do something about the things they desire. Only after watching the majority of their years pass them by do they realize their time is actually much, much shorter.

This concept is not meant to depress you. It is a fact of life that can serve you every day and give you the positive motivation that everyone is so desperately seeking. Most people would rather block this thought from their minds and live by a myth that promises forever and a day to achieve their goals. This self-destructive belief causes the postponement of real happiness and fulfillment. While the things that matter the least become the focus of daily life, the important things are put off until a later time. You won't always have a later time.

The old clichés about living each day as if it was your last hold a lot of weight. I wouldn't suggest running through the streets, looting like a madman, but I would suggest that you take the time to think about your life and its timeline. Be practical and positive about the reality of your existence.

Accept the truth. Rarely in life do you come out better for having ignored the facts. It's easy to see why people have a hard time using this principle for positive motivation. Just as people would rather eat fatty foods and ignore the fact that it is hurting them, people plan their dreams for tomorrow and ignore the fact that the day may never come.

The key isn't to live in a constant state of fear. Although life has a limit, sixty, forty, or even twenty years is a relatively long time. The point is not to feel that your time is quickly running out, but that the time to enjoy all that life has to offer will eventually expire.

Life is like stepping onto a conveyor belt that is lined with doors. Each door represents a different opportunity to experience the feelings of love, excitement, enjoyment, and fulfillment along with the many others that you are seeking. Above each door is a small sign labeling the particular desire to be found within, such as *Learn How to Speak French*, *Travel to New York City*, or *Strengthen Relationships with the Family*. The conveyor belt never ceases to move as you draw closer and closer to the exit.

How long would you wait until you began opening doors

and experiencing all of the great feelings that are easily within your reach? Would you put off feeling great for a few years? Perhaps even twenty or thirty? Of course not. You would begin opening the doors as soon as possible and continue to do so for the rest of your life.

As you can see, it's not that you lack the time to begin opening doors, it's that you shouldn't wait one second longer than is absolutely necessary to begin taking action. You can start the process today and enjoy the positive results for the rest of your life, or wait until it's too late to start opening your doors.

This life is your one shot to do it all—there are no pause or rewind buttons. There is no way to know for certain whether or not tomorrow will come. This moment, here and now, is the only certainty you have in life.

When it comes to uncertain futures, history offers the best lesson. Several years ago I had the opportunity to travel through Italy with an old friend. After backpacking through Florence, Venice, and Rome, we headed to Pompeii. It was here, in a small amphitheater located in the heart of this historic site, that I really understood the importance and power of the present.

For the most part, people haven't changed much in the past 2,000 years. The same patterns of hesitation and procrastination you find today would be found in those who came before us. It is because of this continuity in human nature that we can learn such a great deal from what has happened in the past. On a clear and sunny Saturday afternoon, a life-altering history lesson took place.

As my friend and I tired after four hours of walking, we looked for a place to rest in the shade. As we turned the corner down an old stone road, we came upon an enormous structure that seemed the perfect place to regain our energy. We walked inside the amphitheatre and found a shaded area near the upper portion of the stone seating.

I looked around to take it all in, and noticed a small window cut out of the stone directly behind us. Through the opening I could see the cause of the city's untimely end—Mt. Vesuvius. It was quite an experience. I was sitting in the same spot where a young mother or father, perhaps a shopkeeper or even a member of high society, sat watching the entertainment below when, on August 23, 79 AD, the volcano erupted and covered the entire city in a layer of lava and ash.

Although they lived thousands of years before us, the citizens of Pompeii desired the same basic things that you and I hope to gain: improved health, meaningful relationships, financial security, peace of mind, and happiness. Hundreds of people sitting in that amphitheatre filled their heads with "someday" desires, believing tomorrow to be a much better day to begin. Unfortunately, tomorrow never came.

You never know how long you have to make the most of this life. It could be fifty days or fifty years. When you go is not nearly as important as how you spend the time you have. Learn the lesson that the wishful thinkers of Pompeii have to offer; don't put off until tomorrow what you can experience and enjoy today.

You know what you want, why you want it, and how you are going to get it. The only step left is to act on what you know. Always remember, it's not the shortness of life alone that should inspire you to action, but also the amount of time you have to enjoy it. The sooner you begin putting your plans in motion, the longer you'll have to take pleasure in their results.

Windows of Opportunity

Life, as you well know, does not entail a single beginning and end; there are thousands of smaller timelines constantly in motion. The chance to reconcile the relationship with your father will not last forever, nor will the option of having a family or playing a professional sport. Your windows of opportunity will not remain open indefinitely. For many of your desires, the option to act will have a distinct beginning and end.

The previous myth dealt with the long-term while this myth focuses on the short-term opportunities you see around you. People live as if they have an eternity to act, not realizing that time will eventually expire, but they also live as if the opportunities they see today will be around tomorrow. The truth is, the current situation may allow you to act on your desires, but that isn't a long-term guarantee.

When Shea Webber was eleven years old, she had her heart set on horseback-riding lessons. Shea loved to draw horses, covered her walls with horse posters, and completely filled two bookcases with horse figurines. She was, in a word, hooked.

Finally, after years of anxiously waiting, the opportunity to follow her dream appeared. A coveted membership spot at the only horseback riding club in the area had opened. Being one of many who desired a spot, the window to take action was quickly closing. Within days the spot would be taken whether or not Shea was the new member.

She hesitated. True, she had always dreamed of this moment, but now that it was here she was afraid. "What if I mess up?" she asked her mom, worried that her lack of experience would show and be ridiculed. "Everyone will laugh at me. I'll be humiliated."

She decided to wait a few days to think about it, and finally got the courage up to follow through on her dream. Shea called the club and excitedly told them she was ready to take the open spot. Her face told the story. In a single moment, her expression changed from enthusiasm and anticipation to despair—the spot had been filled just two hours earlier.

It would be another two years until Shea got a second chance to join, and she didn't make the same mistake twice. She learned her lesson well and ever since has been proactive when it comes to the things she wants. Having experienced the loss that results from hesitation, she is no longer trapped by the myth of limitless opportunity.

This type of scenario is common. If you talk to enough people, and listen closely as they tell you stories of their past, you will invariably come across as many missed opportunities as pursued dreams. Below are just a few of the examples I have come across in the past.

Heidi Foster had her sights set on a promotion to marketing manager for nearly a year, so when the current manager suddenly retired, she knew her chance had come. Vying for the position were three other equally capable employees, each ready and willing to make the leap into management. All it took was a convincing interview with the head of the company to secure the position.

As she reached for her office phone to schedule a meeting with the president's assistant, Heidi hesitated. She had heard her share of war stories from the management staff, and wasn't sure if she was cut out for the job. She had done excellent work in the marketing department, but could she manage a staff of ten? With enough doubt running through her mind, Heidi decided to make the call after a night's rest.

Heidi snapped up in bed in a cold sweat—she realized her mistake. Had she been the only one fighting for the position, her procrastination wouldn't have been a major concern. But that wasn't the case. She was only one woman in a group of highly competitive, driven individuals. Heidi had a sinking feeling that the position was lost. Arriving to work the next day, she learned that her fears had come true.

Judy Shoemaker was browsing the Internet one day and came upon a small advertisement for a reduced airfare to Japan. She couldn't believe her eyes. Judy was taking Japanese in college, had always wanted to see the country, and could finally afford a trip that before was out of her reach. Before buying the tickets, she stopped and questioned the choice to go.

She had the time and money, but what if something went wrong? What if she couldn't make it on her own? Judy was afraid to leave her comfort zone, and left the decision to be made at a later date. Just three hours passed before the airfare deal expired along with Judy's hopes of a trip to Japan.

The chance to act on your desires will endure forever. The secret to getting what you want is taking intelligent action when opportunities present themselves. If you aren't properly prepared to make the best of the situation, prepare yourself before taking massive action. However, if you are ready to act and have the chance to do it, start right now.

Can you think of a time when something changed in your life that made achieving a goal impossible? How did it make you feel? Did you wish you could go back and do it all over again? Associate great pain with unnecessary hesitation. This will shift the balance of power toward positive motivation and inspire instant action. Think to yourself, "If I don't act now, I may never get the chance to do it again." These are the thoughts that drive positive action.

Living by the myths we have covered leads to only one place: regret. By building the pain of regret to an overwhelming level, you can ensure that you will do what it takes to avoid the experience in the future. To live without regret is to live a life of meaning and fulfillment.

Life without Regret

Near the end of his life, Ulysses S. Grant, the eighteenth President of the United States, sat on his porch with pen in hand, a notepad at his side, and a myriad of thoughts rushing through his mind. In order to support his family, Grant was writing his autobiography. He didn't have much time to finish his work; throat cancer was quickly bringing this remarkable man's life to an end.

Without the time or ability to change what he had done or what he had failed to do, Grant looked back at a life that was set in stone. He could not change the story; twisting the truth to eliminate regret was out of the question. That he was one of the most famous and beloved men in the world did not matter; he couldn't change the past. The opportunity to go back and accomplish all of the things he had always wanted to do was gone.

Ulysses S. Grant's life was not one of immeasurable regret or unhappiness; it isn't an example of what can go wrong if you're not careful. His story is an example of what will eventually come to pass in your own life. Though you may be far from it, there will come a time for reflection. You will look back on your life without the time or ability to change what has happened. When you do, you will either feel satisfied with the life you have created or regret all the things you failed to accomplish.

You may not write an autobiography like Grant did, but you will think about what has occurred over the course of your life. The major difference between your life and Grant's story is that you are still in the process of living it. You have the time and ability to change where you are heading. By using the pain of potential regret to your advantage, you can create the positive motivation necessary to choose a direction that will lead you toward a better life.

You know the reality of the situation as well as I do. As millions of people reach the point of reflection in their lives, regret is a common theme and there is nothing they can do about it. Their stories have already been written. However, you don't have to deal with the regret of lost dreams. Living a life of fulfillment is still a path for you to travel.

In order to get a sense of the pain of regret and the pleasure of fulfillment, I want to return once again to Grant's example, only this time you are going to be the one writing the autobiography. Imagine sitting in an old rocking chair on the front porch of a quiet, comfortable home. With a notepad and pen at your side, you are ready to write.

I want you to view this experience from two perspectives: regret and fulfillment. The purpose is to associate intense pain with inaction and intense pleasure with action. In doing so, these powerful links will work to develop your desires to the tipping point.

Put yourself in Grant's place. You are nearing the end of your days, and have time left only to think about the things you never did. Every desire that you promised yourself you would achieve never materialized. The career, family, body, and peace of mind you wanted so much remained something you would do "someday" for your entire life. It's too late to change it. You have to deal with the life you've created however far from your ideal picture it is.

Putting yourself in that position, how would you feel knowing you missed out on the life you always wanted to have? What would you say to yourself? What type of story would you write? Don't gloss over this point. Take a few moments to really think about how you would feel if you looked back on a life of regret. Be creative as you work to associate as much pain as possible to the prospect of missed opportunities.

Next, I want you to imagine looking back on a life in which every positive desire was fulfilled. All of the things you had your heart set on possessing, experiencing, or becoming have been achieved. More importantly, you enjoyed the process tremendously. In essence, you've lived a long and satisfying life that you wouldn't change for anything. What kind of feelings would this bring out in you? What would your story say? Again, be creative and link as much pleasure as possible to living your ideal life.

Both of these paths may come to pass depending on what you do after reading this book. The reason so many others that came before you have failed to live a life of meaning is avoidable. The cause is a miscalculated comparison of fear.

There are two basic fears that are present in this process: the fear of taking action and the fear of regret. Being the short-term creatures we are, most people associate a massive amount of pain with taking action toward their desires, and worry very little about the future regret of postponing success.

Thinking back to the definitions of motivation, remember that short-term action most often produces instant pleasure and minimal pain. Over time, however, the pleasure quickly diminishes while the pain continues to grow to an overwhelming size. This is the process of negative motivation.

Positive motivation, the long-term focus, produces a larger initial pain and a smaller amount of pleasure. Over time, the pain weakens as the pleasure grows. In the end, positive motivation gives you the most pleasure and least amount of pain.

Think about these processes in terms of a concrete example. Let's say that your desire is to ask a young woman or man out on a date. The pain of taking action is high ("What if she/he says no? What if I humiliate myself?") and the pain of putting it off is relatively low ("I'll try again later."). In the short-term, you would associate great pain with acting and a minimal amount of pain with postponing the desire.

If you follow this out long enough, the picture would begin to change. Looking back on a life of passing up the chance to find that special someone would create a greater amount of pain than was associated with taking action. In other words, you would be unhappier in the long-term. By choosing the short-term pleasure of putting it off, you would have to deal with the long-term pain that results. You may be happy in the moment because you don't have to risk rejection, but in the end you would be sad and alone, wishing you had taken the first step.

Do you have any regrets at the present moment? If so, then you know firsthand how painful it can be to pass up the chance to get what you want. It creates feelings of helplessness and hopelessness, and can take years to overcome.

One story that exemplifies the dangers of short-term thinking and long-term regret is that of Derrick Miller. He had a falling out with his father after an argument about the woman he chose as his wife; she did not practice the same religion as Derrick's family. Derrick's father did not approve of the wedding, and refused to speak with him should he continue with his plans. Harsh words were exchanged, and the scene ended with Derrick slamming the door and walking away. The ceremony took place as planned—without the presence of his father.

Several months passed without a single word spoken between them, and it was beginning to take its toll on the family. "Just call him, Derrick," his wife would plead. "You can't go on like this forever." Derrick couldn't get himself to make the call. Feeling that his father was completely out of line, he associated too much pain with being the first one to make a move. "He has to take the first step," was his constant reply.

Both Derrick and his father knew that their relationship was more important than an argument. Although his father was extremely stubborn, he understood that marriages outside of the family religion were common. He knew he was wrong, but took the same position as Derrick. "He'll apologize before I say a word," was his thought.

They wanted to reconcile their relationship, but both were too afraid to take the first step. Instead, they chose the path of least resistance and waited for the other person to make a move. In a sense, that move was made when Derrick phoned his mother about the news of their future grandchild.

Living only hours apart made a family reunion more than possible. He let his mother know that he wanted to have both she and his father at the hospital when the baby was born. The message was passed along. Unfortunately, the invitation was denied.

Because Derrick's message didn't contain an apology, his father refused to go. Unwilling to miss the chance to welcome her new grandchild into the world, his mother made the trip alone. It was a decision she would never regret, but the same couldn't be said of Derrick's father.

Years later, after reconciliation took place, the pain of missing out on the birth of his grandchild never passed. For the rest of his life, Derrick's father lived with the regret of his decision. Unable to change it, the past always provided a sharp emotional pain that was impossible to dull. The pain of regret definitely outweighed the pain of action. The lesson to be learned from this family is simple: Whatever you desire, do it today.

Michael Landon once said, "Someone should tell us, right at the start of our lives, that we are dying. Then we might live life to the limit, every minute of every day. Do it! I say. Whatever you want to do, do it now! There are only so many tomorrows."

He knew the secret, and now you know it as well. Make use of it, and refuse to let another day go by in which you fail to strive for the things you desire most in your life. You only have so much time left; you only have so many tomorrows.

You have successfully completed the fifth pillar. The myths that cause hesitation have been put to rest, and success is quickly drawing near. It's important to remember that success is built upon a series of steps, not a single act. Taking the first step is an excellent beginning, but you have to maintain the pattern to achieve your goals and ambitions. It takes consistent action over a period of time to create the kind of results that you hope to gain, making it critical that you have the tools necessary to maintain positive motivation indefinitely. The remaining chapters will show you exactly how to make this happen.

NOTES & IDEAS

Pillar VI
Maintain

Chapter 15

Five Stages to Creating
the Right Environment

*That which is not good for the bee-hive
cannot be good for the bees.*
—Marcus Aurelius

THERE ARE FIVE STOPLIGHTS between my home and my favorite restaurant, over a distance of only one mile. Most nights it seems that I would have an easier time walking than following a constant cycle of starting and stopping. Every time I find myself stuck at another red light, I am reminded of the remaining pillar of positive motivation and how important it is to your overall success.

Red lights, as safe and necessary as they are, bring a stop to progress and momentum. A great deal of energy is lost when you start and stop, start and stop. After getting everything rolling in the right direction, red lights bring you back to a standstill and force you to begin the process all over again—all momentum is lost.

Just off to the left of the stoplight-ridden road is the expressway—free and clear of obstacles. This route allows for a smooth ride at a nice cruising speed requiring only a few taps on the break or gas pedal. The expressway makes it possible to easily maintain your momentum and progress, while the city road makes for a frustrating crawl.

The same two paths are found in life. The roads littered with stoplights are packed with unhappy drivers and the expressway is sparsely populated with elated drivers cruising along toward their destination. The unfortunate thing is, the millions of people getting pumped up only to be let down are dealing with a completely unnecessary situation. The path to positive motivation is open and easily attainable for everyone to enjoy.

Have you ever started to work toward a goal with high hopes and boundless energy, ready to take on the world and finally prove to yourself and others how far you can go? Have you ever listened to a speaker or read a book that excited you to the point of taking decisive action toward the things you wanted?

Millions can claim to have experienced these things, but this isn't enough to get what you want. Taking the first step is critical, but just as important is taking the second, third, and fourth steps. This is where the majority of people drop the ball. They can get the car going, but soon find themselves slowing down to a stop before a bright red light.

The typical cycle goes something like this: You diet for a day, quit smoking for a day, exercise for a day, think nice thoughts for a day, push yourself out of your comfort zone for a day, and then the next day arrives—what a difference a day makes. After a very short amount of time, the drive and confidence to take action disappears, and you're left with unfulfilled hopes and dreams.

I don't have to convince you of this—you see it every day. People are on an endless search for quick-and-easy riches and happiness because they can't seem to find a way to stay positively motivated over time. They are sick and tired of experiencing short-term inspiration and long-term disappointment.

All of the anger and depression that is caused by diminishing positive motivation can be avoided with five simple principles. Without understanding how to maintain the positive motivation after the initial action, you will not achieve your goals or enjoy the things you desire. Nearly every single thing you want to possess, experience, or become depends on a series of actions, not a single leap.

Consider your past accomplishments. Earning a degree, starting a family, and learning how to drive are perfect examples. It didn't take a single step to achieve the goal; you had to put in time and effort over a span of several weeks, months, or years. Your current desires are no different. One shot, in most cases, won't cut it. That is why success will only come through a strategy that has elements of enduring positive motivation at its foundation.

If you have ever struggled with the frustrating ups and downs of motivation, you can, once and for all, put them to rest. To begin the process, you will learn how to manufacture a positively motivating environment. In order to stay committed to your desires over the long-term, you need to develop an internal and external setting that propels you in the right direction.

Entering Your Environment

Your environment consists of both internal aspects as well as the external world you have a hand in creating. How well you prepare your mind and body for action plays a vital role in how you feel about your desires each day. With stress and exhaustion taking control of your system, you can't possibly get inspired to work on your goals.

The space you live in and around is just as important. You don't live in a bubble, and are constantly affected by what you deal with on a daily basis. By maximizing the environmental elements that are under your control, you can not only increase your positive motivation but also remove any obstacles that have the potential to derail a worthy desire.

Before changing positions within her company, Dawn Anderson was struggling with her productivity. The drive she once experienced to excel was quickly diminishing, and she was unable to pinpoint the source of her problem. After the change, however, the reasons couldn't have been any clearer.

In the past, Dawn shared an office with a co-worker whose habits were a little different from her own. While she liked to keep the office clean and organized, he cared little for order. She could barely find her desk under all of his clutter, and when she finally settled in, finding the files and reports she needed was nearly impossible. Aside from her co-worker, the constant pressure of impending deadlines created overwhelming stress, draining her physically and emotionally every day. Without enough time to rest or even eat lunch, she was in no shape to produce positive results.

What a difference the change made. In her new position, the disorder and unrealistic deadlines were gone. Dawn was given an office of her own, working with others who closely matched her personality and ambitions. She had enough time to complete her work without stress or tension, and was able to take steps to maintain her energy throughout the day. Dawn felt like a new woman.

Without realizing her environment caused the drop in productivity, she accepted the situation and merely dealt with the problem, feeling something must have been wrong with her. Learn from this. You shouldn't have to deal with the problem. You can take control of your environment and ensure it helps you get what you want. Specifically, you will learn how to effectively manage your energy, physiology, time, space, and peer groups. If you have ever struggled with a diminishing drive to achieve your goals, now is your chance to make sure it never happens again.

Managing Your Energy

Not long ago, a young man by the name of Justin Raddant entered my office looking like he hadn't slept for a week. He seemed to be mentally and physically exhausted. After a few minutes of conversation, it was clear that his desire to become an actor was authentic. Justin also had a strong belief in his ability to succeed, and was working on a clearly defined strategy. He felt as though everything was in place, but wasn't happy with his results.

The problem Justin faced was maintaining the drive over time. He would get bursts of positive motivation and make some progress, but it wouldn't last. He realized that his on-and-off cycle of action wouldn't be enough to make it as an actor. Justin needed a constant source of positive motivation to reach the level of success he was after, but couldn't pinpoint the area that was holding him back.

After a few questions about his lifestyle, it was clear that his choices in terms of sleep, diet, and exercise were draining his energy. Every step preceding this pillar was in place and well designed, but it didn't matter if he lacked the energy to make it happen.

Justin's typical day consisted of waking up around six or seven, skipping breakfast and lunch, and eating a large dinner right before he went to sleep at four in the morning. As busy as he was, there was no time for exercise in his schedule. The truth was he didn't make the time to keep his body fit.

His desire required a great deal of enthusiasm. Justin needed to perform at his peak level to demonstrate his talent, but without the energy he needed, he was unable to carry out his plan. As Justin began making positive changes in his lifestyle, he realized a dramatic improvement in his attitude and drive.

You know how it feels to work all day without enough sleep or food—it's nearly impossible to get excited about anything. After dragging yourself around the office, the last thing you want to do when you get home is work toward a better life. However, success demands energy. Creating the life you deserve requires crisp thinking and physical vitality. The specific path to be taken is a personal decision. Being a unique individual with different needs calls for unique lifestyle choices.

The next time you are having difficulty staying motivated to succeed, I want you to consider your lifestyle choices and the impact they have on how you feel. In particular, examine your sleep, diet, and exercise patterns. There are many different areas that play a role in your energy level, but these three are a great place to begin. Most people will search endlessly for the cause of their diminishing motivation without ever considering the impact of these three aspects.

How much sleep do you get each night? If you find yourself dragging through the day, this may be an area that needs changing. Your body needs to rest in order to make repairs and regain strength for the next day. Cutting down on sleep will only cut down your productivity.

What types of food do you eat each day? How many meals and how often do you eat? Food is fuel for the body, and the better the fuel, the better the performance. Filling your body with unhealthy foods and chemicals isn't a harmless act. Using what you have learned about human behavior, it is easy to see why people choose harmful foods that give instant satisfaction instead of healthy foods whose impact is not easily seen in the short-term. Pick the fuel that is right for you, and maintain a high level of energy day in and day out.

What type of exercise do you do? I'm not just talking about a thirty-minute video or trip to the gym; I'm also talking about the general movement and activity that your body goes through on a daily basis. It's no secret that movement and exercise play a major role in your short-term and long-term health. If your daily routine lacks any movement or activity, and you don't exercise, you may be dealing with a total lack of energy and drive when it comes to achieving the things you desire. To easily overcome this problem, find a plan that works for you and stick with it.

Your body is a machine. It requires the same care and maintenance as any other high-performance instrument to run at its peak level. Failing to give your car a tune-up or refill it with fuel would result in a poorly operating vehicle. If you asked someone whether or not it was important to refuel a car, they would look at you like you were crazy. However, when it comes to refueling your body, the same people who take pains to ensure an optimized automobile are self-destructing internally.

After putting all of the pillars of your desire in place, keep track of your sleeping patterns, what you eat, and how much physical activity you get each day. Maintaining a weekly log of these areas will help you recognize and change your habits. Because most people don't really think about them, negative patterns can form without sounding an alarm. Over time, these patterns can sap your daily energy and take the excitement out of your goal.

Remember, the specific steps you should take vary from one person to the next. Do some research and discover which methods work best for you. A positively motivating environment depends on rest, fuel, and activity to ensure boundless energy and vitality.

Managing Your Movement

As you read these words, I want you to try something for me. First, let your shoulders drop and let your chest sink in. Next, let your head droop down with your eyes looking down at the page. Take slow breaths and feel your eyelids getting heavy. How does this make you feel? Are you alive and enthusiastic? Or slow moving and sluggish?

I now want you to sit erect in your chair with your chest out and shoulder back. Lift your chin up, take a deep breath, and exhale with force. Lift your eyebrows, put a grin on your face, and plant your feet firmly on the ground. Feel any different?

These factors are another element of your internal environment that, when controlled, can greatly enhance your positive motivation. The way you carry yourself has a direct connection to how you feel. Walking with an insecure posture creates feelings of insecurity, which in turn leads to insecure thoughts and actions.

However, if you carry yourself with confidence, you will feel confident. Your physical actions will communicate to your mind that you are empowered. These feelings will be accompanied by matching thoughts and behavior.

Physical action puts you in control of your feelings. A common example is smiling to feel happy. The action of smiling on the outside creates feelings of happiness on the inside. I want you to take this idea to the next level. Instead of only smiling to feel better, you can choose any emotion and create it with your posture, movement, and breathing.

If you want to feel self-assured, carry yourself in a self-assured manner. If you want to feel powerful, make explosive movements. If you want to feel excited and enthusiastic about your desire, use your physical actions to make it happen.

Although smiling to feel better can be very useful, we are concerned with the connection between your desires and movement, posture, and breathing. In particular, we will examine your current patterns followed by the most effective ways to utilize these factors. How you carry yourself with your desires in mind will play a significant role in creating the right environment for success.

To begin, think about a desire that is at the top of your list. How does your posture change? Your breathing? Are you exhibiting confident movements or are they weak and fearful? In order to benefit from the power of these aspects, it's important to recognize your current patterns in order to avoid or build on them in the future. Work your way through each of your desires, taking note of the physical responses that are linked with them.

You then need to replace limiting physical links with empowering connections. Think back to a time when you felt you were at your best—everything was going your way and you couldn't be stopped. How did you carry yourself? What movements did you make? What was your posture? What was your pattern of breathing? Get a good idea of what responses are linked with the emotions of joy and excitement. The more details you can pinpoint, the better.

Now think back to a time when you were at the other end of the spectrum—you felt miserable and defeated. How did you use your body to reflect your feelings? Where were your eyes focused? What type of movements did you make? How was your breathing affected? Just as you did before, add as much detail and distinction to these negative emotions as you can. Knowing what movements and postures to avoid is just as important as knowing which to emulate.

Your final task is to connect the positive responses with your desires while avoiding negative patterns. If, in the past, your posture reflected fear and doubt when you thought about public speaking, carry yourself in a way that communicates confidence and power. Doing this for each of your desires will help you maintain the positive motivation that you have worked so hard to create.

Maggie Bauder wanted respect. She worked at a large advertising firm, and was tired of being treated like a child by her co-workers. Her desire was authentic, but she was missing the right movements and posture to communicate both to herself and others that she deserved what she desired.

One day, while walking toward the office of a particularly abrasive supervisor, Maggie began to slip into the posture of fear. When she opened the door, her shoulders were slumped and she stared at the floor. In an instant, she communicated to her supervisor that she was insecure. Maggie's physical responses created the same effect internally, which led to passive and feeble behavior that failed to demand the respect she was looking to gain.

By recognizing her patterns and making the necessary changes, Maggie took control of her desire. She consciously chose the way in which she carried herself in the office, making sure that it communicated a sense of confidence and assertiveness. The next time she entered her supervisor's office, she looked her straight in the eye, shoulders back and head held high. It was obvious that Maggie felt confident about herself, and the message was communicated perfectly to others. The respect she had desired for so long was finally hers to enjoy.

When you manage your physical responses, you can successfully manage your motivation. Decide which emotions will help you achieve your desires, and then consciously choose your movements, posture, and breathing pattern to create those emotions. This alone will provide you with the energy and self-assurance you need to inspire action over the long-term.

Managing Your Time

There is only one resource in the world that most everyone agrees is in short supply: time. Because it is such an important asset in life, it is imperative that you make the most of your time without letting any slip through your fingers. As you become more adept at creating positive motivation and realizing the rewards it can foster, you will want as much time as possible to enjoy all the amazing things life has to offer.

Time flies, as they say, but those who succeed in life always seem to have enough of it to do the things they want to do. They seem to accomplish an unbelievable amount each day within the same twenty-four-hour period given to us all. How do they do it? The answer is control.

The next stage to creating a positively motivating environment is gaining absolute control of your time—what you do and how long you do it. Time is easily lost, and if you're not careful, you won't have enough of it to achieve your desires. The things that matter least in life have a way of taking over and eat away at your most precious resource. Following a few simple guidelines will help you break free of these negative patterns and make the most of each moment you are given.

Taking inventory is the first step to effectively managing your time. It is highly likely that a great deal of your time is monopolized by habitual routines, making it necessary to first recognize where your resources are currently flowing. Identifying these patterns will help you recover the time they have taken from you.

For at least one week, keep a log of everything you do from morning until night. No task is too small. Home-related activities include cleaning, cooking, watching television, reading, and talking with family and friends, along with your morning routine. Work-related categories include responding to e-mail, speaking with customers on the phone or in person, meeting with sales reps, or time spent in meetings. These categories are only examples; you know what works best for you.

Focus on filling your log as completely as you can. The more time you can inventory, the more opportunities you have to gain back precious minutes and hours each day. After one week of this process, you will be amazed at the results. Only when you see it written on paper does the full impact of lost time really hit you.

"I had no idea," her letter began, "that I was wasting so much time." Shari Scott was under the impression that she simply didn't have enough time in her schedule to do the things she wanted to do. She was prepared to put her desires to the side, but decided to try this method before calling it quits. After two weeks of keeping track of her time, Shari made some eye-opening discoveries and was ready to change her ways. She was finally able to make room in her life for the things that mattered most.

"I was wasting a few hours every day on petty tasks and busywork. I never realized how much time I could save if I just made the effort," she wrote. "I stopped letting my time get away from me and started to choose where I wanted to spend it. This has made all the difference." Shari went on to list a few time-wasting activities that she discovered along with the cure to her problem.

Before settling down to accomplish some actual work, she wasted nearly an hour chatting with co-workers, moving papers around on her desk, and searching for lost reports. However, Shari was most surprised by what she found at home. She watched an average of three hours of television per night. Without ever tracking and writing it down, she never paid much attention to her habits; she just did what felt good at the time and never worried about the consequences.

In total, Shari was able to take back nearly five hours of time per day—a remarkable success. She now had the time to do the things she desired most, and enough left over to really enjoy the activities. You'll never know how many hours you can steal back each day until you get out a pen and paper and keep track of your time.

You'll undoubtedly find several habitual routines that can be cut out of your schedule completely. Time-wasting activities are everywhere, and many of them can be avoided through better organization and prioritization. Sleeping an average of eight hours per night, you are left with sixteen hours of action at your disposal. Making conscious decisions about how you spend your time will make it possible to achieve a great deal of progress each and every day.

Once an inventory has been taken and you have discovered time-wasting activities that can be reduced or eliminated, you need to make a choice about what you want to do and for how long you wish to do it. Write out a daily schedule of activities, making sure to designate time for your goals. If you feel that a certain desire will require about four hours per week, schedule it. If you would rather spend one hour per night working toward the things you want, schedule it. If you would like to waste less time getting settled in at the office, schedule it. You are in control, and have the power to use your time exactly as you wish.

A lack of time is too often an excuse for the negatively motivated. Below is an example of a before-and-after schedule of an individual who was convinced he had no time to pursue his desires. After taking an honest look at his situation, he made drastic changes that gave him the time and freedom to do what he had always wanted to do.

BEFORE		AFTER	
Task	**Hrs**	**Task**	**Hrs**
Work	7	Work	7
Driving Time	2	Driving Time	2
Eat	2	Read/Eat	2
Watch TV	5	Family	3
Sleep	8	Free time	2
		Exercise	1
		Sleep	7
Total	24	Total	24

Bring order to your life. Write out a specific schedule of what you want to do and for how long you want to do it. When you find yourself veering off course, take steps to get back on track. Creating the perfect plan is a step in the right direction, but if you lack the time to implement it, what good is it? Your days are just as long as mine and everyone else's in the world—this creates equal opportunity. The difference occurs not in how many hours we are given, but in how we use them. Time is your most precious and scarce resource—treat it accordingly.

Managing Your Space

Finding everything you need when you need it—that's the purpose of managed space. Disorganization wastes time and energy, and creates stress, tension, and even illness. It's no secret that a cluttered space leads to a cluttered mind, and that is the last thing you want when working to maintain positive motivation. Everything has its place, and the best work is accomplished when you put it where it belongs.

Imagine walking into a home that is more like a war zone than a living space—piles of paper covering the kitchen and dining room tables, clothes strewn across the living room, and junk drawers emptied onto the floor. What mood would this put you in? How easily could you get your hands on the things you needed when you needed them?

Clutter and disorder are burdens to the mind, and create mental and physical stress and tension. They serve as a reminder that you still have something to take care of—that your work is never done. A disorganized space robs you of the chance to feel at peace. I'm sure you have experienced feelings of disarray in the past and realize how much of an obstacle it is to getting things accomplished.

Most people find control and comfort in an orderly space. It creates a sense of peace and a feeling that everything is settled and where it belongs. These emotions go hand in hand with a positively motivating environment. When you picture yourself working toward your desires, do you see a picture of clutter, messes, and disorganization? If not, then you can't allow it to become a part of your reality; you have to bring the picture of order and organization to life.

Time is another victim of a disordered space. When you can't find what you need, several hours a week can be wasted rummaging through the clutter. Your time is too precious to be spent rifling through piles of paper. Keep things in their place and you will have more time to do the things you would rather be doing than searching for lost information.

To effectively manage your space, begin by thinking about the places in which you spend time; your home, office, and car are obvious examples. Because each area of your life impacts the others, it is important to manage your entire space. Your office may be immaculate, but if your home is in chaos, the stress will carry over to your work.

When you have pinpointed all of the locations, it's time to get organized. This may take some time initially, but you will end up saving twice as much time in the long run. If the idea of getting organized is a little overwhelming, you can always follow the steps of a successful strategy and break the process down into smaller stages.

To get started, you will need two large bins or cardboard boxes. The first will be for the items you wish to keep, and the other is for things you will throw away. I know what you're probably thinking: "I'm not throwing away anything!" Most people have a hard time parting with possessions, but if you want to get organized, you may have to give up items that have no use or special meaning.

Beginning with the first location (home, office, etc.), choose a room and start filling up your boxes. Do your best to get as many items into your "throw away" box as possible. The less you have, the easier it is to keep your location clean. In the end, you should have a box or two full of items that you would like to keep. From here, you need to prioritize and organize.

Prioritize your items in the "keep it" box by level of usage. Using your "throw away box" and "keep it" boxes, place the items you use most often in one and the items you rarely use in the other. This will separate the things that need to be stored from the things that need to be close at hand. Be realistic. If you haven't used it for months or years, it belongs in the trash or in storage. Your goal is to minimize, not maximize.

Find storage bins or containers for the things you rarely use and put them out of sight. You can easily create a recall system by writing up a list of the stored items and in which bin or box they can be found. This will help you to get your hands on what you need even if it's stored away.

You are now free of the things you will never or rarely need, leaving you with the items you use most often. Your last task is to create a system to organize your remaining items. The key is quick retrieval. You should be able to get the things you need instantly without filing through all of your papers or drawers. Making use of alphabetically organized files and bins, for example, is a quick and easy way to store and find the things you need. After the first room is completely filtered, prioritized, and organized, repeat the cycle in the remaining rooms and locations.

It is much easier to *stay* organized than it is to continuously *get* organized. After you create the system, stick with it. The whole idea of maintaining positive motivation is to create an environment that is constantly propelling you toward the end result. Following a cycle of organized-disorganized will slow your progress. It only takes a few minutes to put things where they belong, but it can take weeks or even months to manage a space that has been left unattended.

When you receive a bill in the mail, write out your payment that same day instead of putting it off for a week. When you use something, put it back the second you are finished with it. It doesn't take earth-shattering ideas to keep your space organized. It simply takes small steps and commitment to stick with the plan.

The areas you live and work in affect you mentally as well as physically. Left on their own, there is no telling how far they will drag you down. However, when you take the time to bring order to your space, you will maintain and even increase your motivation to succeed. Take control of your space and make it work for you, not against you.

Managing Your Peer Groups

How successful do you think you would be trying to swim the length of a pool with a hundred-pound weight strapped to your ankle? How about scaling the side of a mountain chained to a boulder? Unless you have super-human strength, the weights would make it impossible to succeed.

Now imagine working toward the same goals, but instead of weights holding you back, you are given a boost to increase your speed. How fast would you cover the length of the pool being pulled by a powerful motor? How about reaching the top of the mountain in a helicopter? Under these circumstances, you would succeed in no time at all.

These two situations represent the power, both negative and positive, of peer groups. The right environment of peers can lift you up and help you reach your goals, but the wrong group can tear you down just as quickly. To round out a positively motivating environment, we will take a close look at peer groups and how the right choices can make all the difference.

People are like chameleons; they often mirror their surroundings. The need to connect and be accepted in the group is so overpowering that many will go to great lengths to share the desires, patterns, and qualities of the individuals with whom they associate at a conscious and unconscious level. They begin to talk, walk, dress, think, and act alike. Group affiliation is one of the strongest motivators of human action, and taking a quick look around will give you all the proof you need.

The influence of gangs, fashion trends, and general peer pressure among children and adults demonstrates the awesome power of the need to belong. People feel a sense of strength, importance, and safety within a group and can make extremely destructive choices to maintain or increase their position within it.

From what you have already learned, it should be easy to see that inauthentic desires and peer groups go hand in hand. Group members have such a strong wish to remain accepted that they will take on desires that are not their own. This explains why some children struggle with the choice of whether or not to smoke, drink, or cheat like the rest of their friends. Each member of a peer group may not desire the same things, but the need to belong is oftentimes stronger.

Because most people mirror their peer groups, an important decision has to be made: Do you mirror positive or negative associations? Rarely are peers consciously chosen, which has the potential to create major problems. Much of this book is about turning the autopilot off and taking control of your life. Peer groups represent an area in which people act from feeling without thinking about the consequences.

Don't get me wrong, I'm not suggesting you send out a survey to potential peers in order to find out if they are a healthy influence, but I do think it's important that you understand how much of an impact peer groups have on your future. Spending time with people who lower your standards and negatively influence your decisions can inflict just as much damage as any drug or alcohol. You have to be careful when choosing friends and groups with whom you associate because you are, in effect, choosing the person you will become.

It's a matter of expectations. Each member within a particular group is expected to follow certain standards. If you fail to keep in line with them, your membership is in jeopardy. A gang member who decides to follow his own path, a high school student who decides not to drink, and an employee who blows the whistle on corrupt business practices are taking a risk with their membership. Should they push far enough, they will no longer have the safety and comfort of the association, which, as these examples show, isn't always a bad thing.

Six years ago, a close friend of mine, Andrew, paid me a visit while on leave from the military. It had been a while since we last saw each other, and I couldn't believe what I saw standing in the doorway. I barely recognized him. Andrew was twenty pounds lighter and in the best shape of his life. He had a certain energy about him, and had to keep pushing his glasses up his nose because his face was too skinny to keep them in place. Andrew was a new man.

Fast forward six years and you'd find a slightly different picture. Since completing his military duty, Andrew has gained back the lost weight plus another fifteen pounds, and his glasses fit just fine. His new figure doesn't resemble his past image in the least. Again, he is a new man.

What happened? What could have caused such a dramatic change in behavior? Expectations. While in the military, he was expected to live up to a certain standard. His group was one of strength, discipline, character, and commitment. Andrew followed the group and satisfied the standards placed upon him. When the expectations were removed, he found new ones and worked to satisfy them just as well as he had the military's.

Up to this point, we have looked at extreme situations and obviously negative peer groups. My hope is that you never have to deal with gangs or corrupt businesses. What you will deal with, however, is spending time with a group of friends or co-workers on a consistent basis. It is in these situations that your life is altered. Choose the right group or organization to associate with and your life will be lifted up to a new level of success; choose the wrong one and you may end up further from the things you desire than you are today.

If your desires do not match those of the group, and you act on them, you will create fear among the other members. Your friends don't want to lose you, and see any difference in desire as a potential separation. A group, by definition, shares common characteristics and if you begin to want different things than the group, it may mean you are getting ready to leave them behind.

Without meaning to sabotage your progress, this fear can be exhibited in thoughts like, "Why in the world would you want that?" or, "That's a dumb idea. You'll just make a fool of yourself." They don't intentionally keep you from what you want; they are just afraid of losing a member of the group.

Intentional or not, this won't create a positively motivating environment. Constantly being reminded how crazy or foolish your desires are will only increase the fear and doubt you may already be fighting. What you need are standards and expectations that drive you to be your best. Positive peer associations will help you become the person you want to be. The need to belong is natural and cannot be denied, but when it comes to which groups you wish to emulate, the choice is yours.

There are other people who desire the same things you want for your life. Aspiring speakers have speaking associations, inquisitive students have universities and colleges, and loving mothers and fathers have friends and family members wishing them the best. The type of people who are seeking success can become positive peers if you take the steps to find them. Communicate with people, join clubs and organizations, get involved with your interests, and become an integral part of groups that inspire you to reach your potential.

Your friends are good people and want you to be happy. They react the same way anyone else would when confronted with the prospect of losing a close connection. You can remain connected to the people who don't share your vision. You simply have to let them know that having different desires doesn't mean you are going to leave them behind; it only means that your goals, and not the friendship or connection, are changing.

Be sure to have the same conversation with yourself. Maintaining friendships with those who have lower expectations is fine as long as you stay committed to what you want. Your desire has to be strong enough to withstand a little poke here and there. If you don't think you can continue toward the things you want with negative peers, you may have to rethink your situation. As always, this is a decision that only you can make.

Positive peer groups raise your expectations and inspire you to be your best. Negative peer groups lower your expectations and keep you from reaching your potential. These are the facts. Whatever you decide to do, find positive peer groups. These associations will help you time and again as you work to achieve a better life.

With your energy peaking, your movements communicating confidence, your time and space prioritized and organized, and your peer groups inspiring you to reach new heights, you will enjoy the endless advantages of a positively motivating environment. After all of the time and effort you put into your success triad, you can rest assured that your environment will propel you forward to the life you have imagined.

Following these principles alone would be enough to change the picture of success forever, but there are still many tools for you to discover. Another key aspect of maintaining the drive to succeed is the power of focus. Taking control of your thoughts will equip you with the ability to turn your brain into a twenty-four-hour-a-day machine, providing a constant stream of new and exciting ideas to help you create the changes you desire.

NOTES & IDEAS

Chapter 16

Creating Success from the Inside Out

All that a man achieves and all that he fails to achieve
is the direct result of his own thoughts.
—James Allen

WHAT DO YOU THINK ABOUT EVERY DAY? It's a simple question, but don't let that fool you. The thoughts that constantly run through your mind will eventually become your reality. Much attention is given to the foods we put in our bodies, the furniture we put in our homes, and the best fuel to put in our automobiles, but seldom is any attention given to the thoughts we put in our minds.

For many, the idea of thoughts affecting their life doesn't even occur to them; they just think about whatever jumps into their head. After years of witnessing the extraordinary impact focus has on success and failure, I have learned that what we put in our minds deserves more attention than anything else. You will soon experience the same realization.

Uncontrolled thoughts can tear at your positive motivation every minute of the day. They can transform a small fear into an overwhelming terror and a low level of doubt into a total lack of confidence. You cannot succeed with a negative or uncontrolled focus.

Controlling your focus gives you an unending source of positive motivation. It not only boosts your confidence, but also allows you to see opportunities and solutions everywhere you look. A positive or controlled focus removes obstacles and puts success easily within your reach. If you want to create a better life, you have to learn how to harness the power of focus.

The Shaping of Reality

How carefully would you regulate your focus if every thought that popped into your mind appeared before you? Worrying about people laughing at you would instantly cause others to point and laugh hysterically. Fearing that you'll lose a sale instantly turns away your prospective customer. Whatever thought comes into your mind is instantly created. How careful would you be?

My guess is that you would be extremely careful when it came to your thoughts. You would ensure that only positive and empowering things crossed your mind, and would take great pains to focus on the things you want to achieve and not on the things you wish to avoid. Feeling the instant impact of your focus, you would treat your daily thoughts with the respect and importance they deserve.

This is exactly how your thoughts and focus work. Although it's extended over time, the things you focus on each day eventually become your reality. The reason most people do not recognize the importance of focus is the delay in results. If you can't see an instant effect, most people pay no attention. Just because you can't see the impact of your thoughts the moment they enter your mind doesn't mean they won't come to pass in time.

Your focus consists of things you see, say, and hear in your mind, as well as things you see and hear around you (these external factors cause you to think internally). When any reference is made to controlling your focus, I am referring to the things you visualize, the things you say to yourself, the things you hear in your mind, and the objects you see and hear in your external environment. Each of these factors is under your control, giving you many options when it comes to utilizing your focus.

To break it down one step more, focus is made up of two main categories: general and specific. Your general focus deals with the things you think about throughout your day. It includes what you focus on when you get up, eat breakfast, head off to work, and drive back home. Your general focus is what you think about when you are not attached to a specific activity.

Your specific focus is what you think about when confronting a particular situation. For instance, the thoughts that run through your mind when you are about to propose, shoot a free-throw, or give a presentation on your latest marketing data are specific to the situation.

Both types are critical to the success of your desires. Bringing one under control while allowing the other to run rampant won't solve your problems. With that in mind, let's take a closer look at the inner workings of thought and discover exactly what you need to do to take control of your general and specific focus.

Specific Focus: Equal Input, Equal Output

This factor consists of two distinct processes: the fear focus and the success focus. The first describes what most people have and need to avoid; it is thinking only of the irrational fears that cause hesitation and failure. The latter is what you should be shooting for; it is thinking about what needs to be done in order to achieve the desired outcome.

A fear focus will bring to life the things you wish to avoid. If you find yourself running through an internal dialogue of worry and doubt when you think about your goals, you will head in that direction; you will do the very thing you fear because that is where you are focusing all of your attention, energy, and action. This is exactly what the majority of people do when it comes to improvement. Instead of getting excited and thinking about the best strategy to implement, they make themselves sick with worry about what might go wrong.

Just before giving a speech to a large group of potential clients, William Rogers began running through every fear he associated with the action. He began thinking to himself, "What if I forget what I want to say? What if it doesn't go over well? What if I fail?" Fortunately, he had a good understanding of this topic, and after snapping out of the fear focus he asked the only logical question of the night: "Why on earth am I focusing on everything that I don't want?" The change in focus led to an excellent presentation.

It's really odd behavior when you think about it. He wanted to give a good talk and help his listeners benefit from the information he was about to share. Instead of preparing himself to give the best possible speech, he filled his head with everything that he didn't want to happen. In effect, he told his brain he wanted to succeed and proceeded to fill it with every imaginable fear he could create. These two elements don't work well together. The goal is to align a positive desire with a positive focus. If you say you want one thing but think about another, you will find that your internal focus overpowers your spoken desire.

A success focus will bring to life the things you desire. When you have succeeded in the past your mind was focused on what you wanted and what you needed to do in order to make it happen. You thought about the best way to implement your plan along with the rewards of achievement. This is how the power of specific focus should be utilized—decide what you want and then focus intensely on getting it.

The reason you get what you focus on is simple. You can't type a bunch of gibberish and expect to print out a masterpiece. In other words, you can't think negative and get positive.

Your brain operates just like every other machine; it works with what you give it. It doesn't matter how good your actual chances are for success if the only information you input is fear and doubt.

A computer can only process and create with the information it receives. You can't install a word-processing program and expect it to do the work of a database—it simply isn't possible. The computer doesn't have the power to say, "Hold on a minute. Don't you need a database for this project? Let's install a different program." It simply sits in its place and does what it is told.

Your brain operates in much the same way. There are no barriers to negative information or a self-limiting focus. Your brain cannot say, "Stop! Inputting this garbage will only create trouble." It works with the information you give it and nothing else. What's more, it can't always tell the difference between fact and fiction.

An intensely imagined experience is treated as reality in your mind. Visualizing yourself succeeding with great detail and clarity will make your brain think it has happened. This will create the confidence and certainty that actual success develops. Picturing a failure has the same effect. If you see yourself failing, and focus intently on the pain it causes, your mind will treat it as reality. This develops the feelings and actions of a failure before it has even occurred, and places an enormous amount of weight and importance on the power of focus.

This power is nothing new to your life. Whether you realize it or not, you have already dealt with the process many times. I can remember a very specific event in my childhood that demonstrated the principles of focus firsthand. It was my first year in little league, and I couldn't wait to get out there and play. The first game arrived and everything seemed to be running along smoothly in the top of the first inning. And then it was my turn to bat.

As I pulled my foot into the batter's box, a cold chill ran down my spine. My heart started to race as the fear focus took hold. I was terrified. My every thought centered around being hit by a pitch. My internal dialogue included thoughts like, "What if I get hit in the head?" After visualizing vivid images of being toted away in an ambulance, I had convinced myself that I would fail to hit the ball, but the ball would not fail to hit me.

I looked up to meet the pitcher's eyes and thought, "Why does he look so angry?" As I lifted the bat off my shoulder, I repeatedly told myself, "I can't do it. I can't do it. I can't do it." The pitcher started his windup, launched the ball toward the plate, and fearing I would be hit in the head, I ducked. That was the last thing I remember.

After coming to on the ground next to the catcher, I was informed that my ducking maneuver placed my head directly over the plate and in line with the ball. If I had kept my head where it was, I would have been fine. I was afraid of being hit and did everything I could to bring my fears to life.

Most batters have some amount of fear when they step up to the plate, but they don't focus on it. Instead, they focus on the right technique, their coach's words of wisdom, and the feeling of hitting the ball out of the park. Successful batters focus on the things that will help them hit the ball. Failures focus on the fear of striking out, or in my case, being knocked out by a pitch.

I knew how to hit the ball, and after refocusing my thoughts in the upcoming games, I actually did. But everything you know how to do can be blocked by a fear focus. If you invest the time and effort in learning how to succeed, you owe it to yourself to use that knowledge when the time comes to act. It would be a terrible waste to have all of your knowledge and experience blocked out while every doubt and worry is welcome to walk right in.

What possible chance of success does an individual whose thoughts reflect the following ideas have?

I can't do it.	I've never done it.
It's impossible.	I am a failure.
Everyone will laugh at me.	What will they think when I fail?
Why am I doing this?	This is a dumb idea.
I shouldn't get my hopes up.	I give up.

It's easy to see that anyone whose mind is filled with thoughts like these will fail each and every time. How can anyone succeed when they have already convinced themselves of failure? They can't, and if you allow your mind to be overrun with negatives, neither will you. It's simply impossible to get what you want when your thoughts are focused solely on the things you fear. You must take control of your thoughts if you want to succeed. But we're not ready for that stage of the game just yet. Along with understanding how your specific focus operates, you need to fully comprehend the general focus and how it can help you get what you want.

General Focus: A Radar for Success

Have you ever experienced the phenomenon of thinking about something and then seeing it all around you? Perhaps you were looking to purchase a new home and soon overheard people talking about new homes, noticed advertisements in the newspaper and television about them, and saw a constant stream of houses for sale everywhere you drove. It seemed like the entire world was crazy about new homes the instant you became interested in purchasing one.

Your experience was not uncommon. This happens to every-one, and the cause is your reticular activating system. In short, this system acts as a filter of information. Every minute of every day you are inundated by thousands of messages of sight, sound, touch, taste, and smell. Because your brain can't possibly take in each piece of information, it filters out the aspects that you have deemed unimportant to your success and safety.

As you take in new information, the system makes you con-scious of the most urgent messages and sends the rest to your subconscious mind. The best example of this process is one that you have probably experienced many times. You're talking with a friend in a packed room, and can barely hear a word she is say-ing above all of the noise. All of a sudden, from the other side of the room, you hear someone say your name. Until that mo-ment, you couldn't make out what people directly around you were saying, but when your name was spoken, you recognized it instantly.

At this very moment, your mind is filtering through incom-ing information looking for messages that you deem important. Imagine the messages that get through to an individual who is completely focused on fear. The brain will begin to pick up infor-mation in the environment that substantiates the fear, causing it to increase in size and strength.

Two people walking down the same street will pick up totally different aspects of the environment because their general focuses differ. If one side of the street was filled with failing businesses, and the other with thriving companies, a businessman with out of control thinking would realize what terrible shape the economy was in while the man with a controlled general focus would be inspired by the health of the business world. You will find what-ever you focus on.

Below are two examples of general focuses. One is controlled, while the other is left to random thoughts. With both types, however, the desire is the same: to find a new career.

Out of Control Thinking	Controlled General Focus
It's hot out today.	What do I want to do with my life?
I hate it when people cut me off.	I like math, to draw, and to create.
I would really like a nice cold soda.	What careers incorporate the things I enjoy?
I can't wait to get home.	I should ask John about his new job.
I hate traffic jams.	I've got it! Engineering has it all.
That guy should get a haircut.	I'll look into it tonight.

At the end of the day, the pattern on the left will get you nowhere, but the controlled general focus gives you something with which to work. By thinking about what you want, you can create plans, recognize opportunities, and get excited about making changes in your life.

This puts an amazing power in your hands. By consciously choosing your focus and communicating to your brain that a particular desire is important, you can turn your mind into a radar for success. With your desire as a top priority, you will begin to notice everything in your environment that may help you achieve your goal. Your brain will be aware of useful information that before was hidden in your subconscious.

The thoughts in your mind are under your control. You don't have to feel depressed and dwell on past failures or future fears. You can pick and choose what you want to place in your mind, and use it to help you bridge the gap between where you are and where you want to be. Now that you know what you are dealing with, it's time to discover exactly how to benefit from a controlled specific and general focus.

A Conscious Choice

It all begins with a decision. You have to make a conscious choice to think about the things you want. This may be a new habit for you, and one that can take a little while to really set in.

No one wakes up in the morning and says, "I am going to think about this," and then goes on to think about their chosen focus, but that is exactly what I am asking you to do. You will have to force yourself to think about your goals until it becomes an ingrained habit.

You're fighting an uphill battle. Ever since you were born, you probably haven't made a choice about what to think—it just happened. A span of ten, twenty, or even fifty years of random thinking has passed, creating an embedded behavior. However, you can replace the routine of haphazard thinking with conscious choice.

How do you control your specific focus? By making the decision to focus on what you need to do in order to succeed and blocking out the irrational fears that hinder your progress. Whenever you confront a situation that has the potential to cause fear, force yourself to focus on doing the right things, at the right time.

It's a matter of taking a fear and focusing on its remedy. If you fear rejection as you make your way to an audition, focus on how you can make your performance strong enough to be accepted. If you fear humiliation after forgetting the words to an important speech, focus on proper speaking and preparation techniques to ensure success. If you've done your homework, you'll know how to succeed. When the time comes, your job is to remember what you have learned and put it to use.

This brings up an important point about fear. Fear is a good thing—it serves as a warning to potential harm. Without fear, you wouldn't be able to succeed. You need to know when and where preparation is needed. When I talk about blocking out the fear of action, I am talking about irrational fear. In other words, choosing your focus is not the absence of fear, but rather controlling it. By focusing on the solutions to your problems, you will be able to handle fear in a constructive way.

How do you control your general focus? By making a choice to think about what you want every single day. You have to visualize the things you desire, talk to yourself about achieving them, and create an environment full of positive triggers. Instead of thinking about whatever happens to fall into your mind, you have to regulate your each and every thought.

Begin each day with a conscious decision to think about your goals. Your time in the shower, getting ready for work, the drive to the office, and lunch are perfect opportunities to develop and direct your motivation. This process will also help you recognize solutions to problems that have been holding you back. When you begin to consciously choose your general focus, you will be amazed at how quickly your situation improves. The amount of progress that occurs each day within a mind that is focused on success is astounding.

Just as you may have experienced the phenomenon from the opening of this section (wanting a new home), the moment you tell your mind that your desires are significant you will begin to notice helpful resources all around you. Imagine how many new ideas, answers, and opportunities will cross your mind when you focus on the things you want twenty-four hours a day. The number is easily in the thousands. You will find it impossible to fail when you have a constant flow of positively motivating messages entering your mind.

When you catch yourself thinking negative thoughts during the day (general focus) or focusing on the things you fear when confronted with a particular situation (specific focus), stop yourself immediately. Make the decision to change your pattern of thinking and refocus on what you want to accomplish.

Focus on what you want and you'll get it. Replace random thinking with intention by making a conscious choice to allow positive and empowering thoughts into your mind while blocking those that cause fear, hesitation, and failure. With your general and specific focus in control, the life you desire will begin to appear before you. Always remember the undeniable truth Henry Ford shared with the world: "Whether you think you can or think you can't, you're right."

This chapter has dealt with a constant. In some form or fashion, you are always thinking, but there is another technique that comes in bursts of inspiration whenever the need arises. Focus is like a constantly flowing stream while the other is like an explosive fire hose that can be turned on and off at will. The process is called linking, and it will soon become one of your most effective motivational tools.

NOTES & IDEAS

Chapter 17

Linking: Inspiring Action in an Instant

Your imagination is your preview of life's coming attractions.
—Albert Einstein

IF YOU CAN PINPOINT the common characteristic among movies, mountain climbers, books and bicycles, you will have discovered a motivational tool that can get you to take action within seconds. It may seem a little far-fetched, but it's true. Recognizing the similarity among these elements will make it possible for you to overcome the fears that have been holding you back in an instant. It will become one of your most valuable motivation techniques.

Let me give you a hint—think link. Each of these things uses the power of links to accomplish their objectives, and you can do the same. A movie creates a link between emotion and pictures, a mountain climber relies on links to keep him safely connected to his ropes, a book creates a link between emotion and words, and a bicycle uses a chain of links to propel you forward. In each case, a link is at the center of success. Without it, they would all fail to do what they were meant to do.

A movie that fails to connect with its viewers will usually find the majority of them walking right out of the theater. A mountain climber relying on a set of broken links and frayed ropes will find it difficult, if not impossible, to safely scale the mountain. A book that doesn't connect with its reader will be put aside, never to be read again. A bike with a broken chain would be as useful as a car without an engine. When the links are working, however, the power and influence they have is remarkable.

Just as a movie can move you to tears or screams with pictures and sounds, you will be able to move yourself to action with the power of linking. Thousands of individuals have reaped the rewards of linking for many years, and have personally experienced how quickly and effectively it inspires action. It's time to share the secrets and rewards of this motivational tool, and give you the ability to transform a mental desire into a physical reality.

Linking 101

Watching the Olympics always leaves me in awe of the athletes who dedicate themselves to their sport and strive for perfection 365 days a year. I am amazed at their ability to stay committed to a single desire for such a long span of time. How do they do it? What is their secret?

Their answer is in your hands. These individuals and others like them are able to control their motivated mind and implement each pillar with excellence, but they are particularly gifted in the final stages of the process. After researching and speaking with successful people from all walks of life, I soon discovered that the majority of them share a talent for linking.

Whether it was a teacher, athlete, business owner, or full-time mother, each one used the technique to maintain an amazing amount of drive and energy over a span of weeks, months, and years. You can enjoy the same results; you're already halfway there. You know what you want and why you want it; the only thing missing is the link.

After discovering and clearly defining your goals in previous chapters, you ran them through the pleasure/pain matrix. This gave you a long list of compelling reasons to act on your desires, but having a written list of reasons isn't always enough. While some can read a sentence and get inspired to act, others need a stronger message. This is where linking comes into play.

In essence, linking is the process of associating tangible and intangible elements in your environment with your desire. In doing so, your positive motivators (pleasure of action, pain of inaction) are instantly recalled and you are inspired to act. It brings all of the power, passion, and joy of future achievement to the present. When your link is put to use, you immediately focus on all of the reasons for wanting to achieve your goal and are driven to implement your strategy.

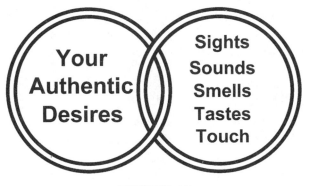

FIGURE 15

Before we get into the heart of the matter, let's take a look at some examples to get a better understanding of linking and how it can help you get what you want.

Anti-smoking commercials are a prime example of motivational linking. The purpose is to get you to quit, or never begin, smoking. Writing these words on the screen wouldn't have the impact required to connect with the viewer. Instead, linking is used to motivate people to action (to quit smoking or turn down any requests to start). Knowing that continued life and happiness are among your most deeply rooted desires, the commercial links these needs to the pictures and sounds you see and hear, reminding you of your desire for a long and healthy life.

Images, phrases, facts, and figures are also used to associate great sadness and pain with smoking to create a powerful and emotional link. Testimonials from widows and widowers, orphaned children, and grief-stricken parents create feelings of loss and despair. The purpose is to link cigarettes with long-term pain and motivate you to say "No" or give up the habit.

Telephone commercials are another great example of motivational linking. Instead of focusing on pain, they mix it up with the positive and negative aspects of calling your loved ones (pleasure if you do, pain if you don't). By showing scenes (visual links) of families reuniting, couples in love connecting over long distances, and young children laughing with their grandparents (auditory link), their hope is that an association begins to set in between using their phone service and good feelings. But it doesn't end there.

Flashing their logo on the screen along with the pleasant scenes creates another link; in this case, it's a visual one. The goal is to create a strong connection between their logo and pleasure. When you see their logo, you are reminded of how great it feels to call your mom, and you pick up the phone and use their service.

This is the purpose of all advertising, and some companies are better than others. The ones that create strong emotional links with their consumers will always win in the end. I'm sure you have associated certain feelings, both good and bad, with many well-known companies, even if you aren't aware that it is happening. The world is swimming in motivational linking. You can find it in television, radio, magazines, newspapers, the Internet, songs, paintings, photographs, people, and places, to name a few. Anytime one person wants to get another person to carry out a particular action, motivational linking is used at the conscious or unconscious level. The exciting aspect is that it's just as effective when you wish to influence your own behavior.

Consider someone who wants to lose weight. This individual could read his list of positive motivators for inspiration, but for many people, this wouldn't be enough to motivate action. On the other hand, he could tape up a picture of the body he wishes to achieve. In an instant, all of the reasons he has for getting in shape are brought to life in a single image. The desire is a fit body and the link is the picture. It's fast, effective, and keeps him going day after day.

By linking your desire with elements such as images, sounds, and physical objects, you can retrieve all of the compelling reasons to act in an instant. Merely closing your eyes and visualizing the achievement of your goals can be enough to get you off the couch, out the door, and working toward a better life. It happens so quickly that you will no longer struggle with the grip of negative motivation.

Linking bridges the gap between where you are and where you wish to be. It is because of this gap that so many people fail to create the life they deserve. If it's not instant and easy, very few wish to pursue it. The secret is to associate great pleasure with taking action, and inspire yourself to do whatever it takes to get what you want. Below are several examples of how linking has been used to do exactly that.

Desire	Link
Write a book	A finished book on a shelf
Learn how to fly a plane	Repeating, "Now or never!"
Travel to Europe	Visualizing being in Europe
Reunite with mother	A family picture
Learn how to play piano	Listening to Beethoven
Overcome shyness	Visualizing being alone

In each case above, the link recalled all of the pleasures of action and pains of inaction that the desire would fulfill, and in doing so, tipped the scales toward positive motivation. Just looking at, hearing, picturing, or saying each of the above would remind you of the reasons you desired the goal in the first place. It would bring the work you completed with the pleasure/pain matrix to the surface in seconds.

Looking over the list of links, you will notice it includes tangible objects (book, picture), self-talk ("Now or never!"), visualizations (Europe, loneliness), and sounds (Beethoven). These elements fit into one of two categories: internal or external linking. Utilizing both types will give you an unlimited number of linking options.

Internal Linking

Barry Fischer was the youngest of nine brothers and sisters. His parents were hard-working individuals who relied on nothing but their own perseverance to provide for their children, but with a family that size it wasn't always easy to make ends meet. College, at least for the first eight children, was out of the question.

Barry was a unique child. Being the youngest in the family, he learned early on that being self-sufficient was the surest way to get what he wanted. Nearing the end of his junior year in high school, Barry informed his mother in no uncertain terms that he was going to college. She had been waiting to hear those words her entire life. She always wanted one of her children to get a college degree, and until Barry made his decision to go, no one in the family even considered it an option.

With tears in her eyes, she hugged him and said, "I am so proud of you. I know you can do it."

Barry's choice of colleges required not only a large financial aid package, but also several prestigious academic scholarships. It would take an unbelievable amount of willpower, dedication, and persistence to secure the scholarships and fulfill the demands set before him.

There were times when his commitment was put to the test. He was surrounded by people who didn't think he could do it. Friends, family, and even his own high school teachers warned him that he was setting himself up for a major letdown, but all the naysayers in the world couldn't stop Barry and his desire. After a year and a half of hard work, sacrifice, and overwhelming odds, Barry was admitted to Stanford University—he achieved his dream.

When asked what kept him going day after day, Barry had one answer: his mother. "Whenever I felt like giving up, like the odds were against me, I remembered what my mother said to me years before. That was all it took to get me back on track."

Barry found the drive and inspiration to achieve his goal in a link. Recalling his mother's words of encouragement provided the inspiration he needed. The desire was to achieve a college degree and the link that inspired action was the voice of his mother. Today, Barry runs a non-profit organization whose goal is to help disadvantaged children succeed in the future. His work is helping make the world a better and brighter place, and it all started with the power of a link.

Barry used an internal sound for his link, but internal linking also includes sights. A portion of your links may include just one type, but the majority will incorporate both. We'll now take a closer look at each, and put the power of the internal link in your hands.

Sights. The first category consists of the visual images you picture in your mind. The various forms of visualization are an effective way to quickly recall your positive motivators (pleasure of action, pain of inaction) and drive you to action. There are countless characteristics that you can incorporate into your internal sights including size, color, sharpness, intensity, etc. Aside from these traits are two larger distinctions that we will examine below—still images and scenes of movement.

What images can you link to your desire? What picture can capture the feelings of elation that will result from finally achieving success? What visual link can effectively remind you of the reasons you are working toward your goals in the first place? Think of as many different pictures as possible; you can always edit them down at a later time.

Remember that you are a creature of emotion. Your images must pack a punch in order for them to be of any use to you. You could picture yourself giving a handful of money to a charity to motivate the act of donating, or you could see yourself surrounded by thousands of grateful children and their families enjoying a better life because of your help. While the first may not diminish your positive motivation, the second will definitely enhance it.

Effective examples that I have encountered in the past include an aspiring college professor picturing his own classroom full of students, an adventure seeker visualizing the next mountain she was to climb, and a high school student seeing the silver convertible he wished to purchase.

If you have trouble finding the link that works for you, keep your eyes open for examples that could possibly fit with your situation. Everyone visualizes in some way. The people close to you may have just the link you are seeking. It's an evolving process, and you may discover more powerful images over time.

The important thing isn't to wait for the perfect picture—it's to get started now.

Each one of your desires can have a unique link (or set of links), or share one with another goal. It doesn't matter exactly how you set up your system as long as it works for you. If one image is enough to motivate action toward all of your desires, more power to you. The key is to find what fits best with your particular needs.

Moving on from still images, think about what scenes you can link to your desire. What mini-movies can you play in your mind that will motivate you to act? Just as still images need to connect with you emotionally, the scenes you play in your mind require detail to create an effective link.

A past client found that linking a scene of winning the local golf championship helped motivate him to practice every day. Another visualized herself walking through the front door of a new home to motivate the action of saving money for a down payment. The possibilities of internally linking scenes to your desires are endless. If it inspires you to follow through with the things you want, use it.

Once your link is in place, and it successfully recalls the rewards of action, it's yours to use whenever the need arises. Sitting on the couch, but know you should be doing some research on your dream job? Close your eyes, picture your link, and action ensues. This will only happen, however, if it is strong enough to change your state of mind. If not, try adding more life to the picture or scene, or consider using another in its place. When you find the winning link(s), you'll have the solution to every moment of negative motivation you encounter.

Sounds. The second group of internal links consists of sounds. This includes self-talk/internal dialogue (the sound of your own internal voice) and the recollected sounds of other people or things (Barry's mother, a favorite song, the sound of a car crashing). Together, these internal sounds are extremely effective at transforming a situation of negative motivation into one of positive action and progress.

Your internal dialogue is a common theme in positive motivation, and for good reason—it is the longest conversation you will ever have in your life. With such a personal and influential communication, you have ample opportunity to create amazing changes in a relatively short period of time. Unregulated, self-talk can be your own worst enemy, but when brought under your control and used as a link to the things you desire, it can be your new best friend.

Take some time to think about a word or phrase that could be linked to your desire. In some cases, simply internally repeating your objective is enough to inspire action. A man wishing to learn how to fly a helicopter could successfully motivate himself to follow his dream by repeating the phrase, "Learn to fly," over and over in his mind. If this failed to do the trick, he could add a little more depth to it by saying, "Fly over San Francisco at night with my wife." This new twist may add the needed punch to put his strategy in motion.

Another common example is a link that children use to endure the remaining weeks of school. "Twenty more days," they will repeat to themselves, maintaining the motivation to stick with their homework and continue studying for their exams. Would a short phrase counting down the days to completion work for your desire?

Follow the same process of brainstorming and editing as you did with image linking. Ask around, pay attention to what others say, and exhaust as many options as possible. The right word or phrase spoken internally can serve as the last nudge necessary to get the boulder of action rolling down the mountain.

The second type consists of the sounds that you recall from sources other than yourself. The voice of Barry's mother was an example of this type of link. Think about what possible sounds could be matched with each of the desires you have. Would another person's voice work well? A song? The sound of people cheering your victory? Any sound that comes from someone or something else can be used as an internal link.

I know of a little boy who is extremely motivated to brush his teeth because of the horrible cries he overheard while at the dentist's office. Every morning and night he is in the bathroom doing his best to keep his teeth shiny and clean, and far away from the pain of having his teeth drilled. What pleasurable or painful sounds can you take advantage of?

When you have discovered a link that proves successful, give it more leverage by adjusting volume, tone, pitch, and speed. A whisper telling you to get moving is not as effective as a booming voice that demands action immediately. Be creative with your linking. There are very few rules to this game, and winning has never been easier.

In the end, the best link is one that incorporates both sights and sounds. Just as the addition of sound into silent films revolutionized the industry and the impact a film had on its audience, you can revolutionize your life with a link that combines the power of pictures with the influence of sound.

External Linking

There is no better way to introduce the subject of external linking than with the story of Dr. Paulson. As an emergency room doctor, he has seen his share of tragedy and the deepest of sadness. Many times in his recent past he became overwhelmed with the position and felt like giving up. With fear and doubt in his heart, Dr. Paulson was unsure if he was the right man to hold the lives of others in his hands.

In the midst of Dr. Paulson's struggle, a young boy was carted into the emergency room after a violent car crash left him unconscious. Hours passed by as Dr. Paulson and the nurses worked to save the child's life. When they did all that was possible to rescue him, Dr. Paulson collapsed on the closest chair, exhausted and full of emotion. As far as he was concerned, that was his last operation.

Several days later, after the boy had regained consciousness and was able to walk without assistance, he approached Dr. Paulson with a gift. He dropped an old penny into the doctor's hands, and gave him a hug. In his ear he whispered, "Thank you for saving my life." He then walked away with the largest grin you've ever seen and returned to his room.

The penny turned out to be the young boy's good luck charm—an item he had kept close for the past five years. It was his way of giving thanks to the man who gave him back his life, and performed the greatest of all human deeds. Dr. Paulson was moved by the boy's gift, and decided then and there that he would continue doing all he could to save the lives of others.

Every overwhelming moment that Dr. Paulson experiences is now put to rest with a simple glance at his lucky penny. In an instant, he is reminded of the unparalleled rewards of being a doctor, and finds his energy renewed and spirit lifted every time he sees the gift he was given.

The small external link that was passed on to Dr. Paulson was much more than a lucky penny. It was hope, meaning, and inspiration. These gifts can be yours when you unlock the power of external linking. The motivation to continue seeking the fulfillment of your dream can be maintained over a lifetime when the rewards are linked to an object in your environment.

Sights. The method of linking externally with sights is much like that of internal linking. The only difference is where the viewing of the pictures or scenes takes place. When it comes to external linking, everything you see with your eyes is included. Again, the two areas of sights are static images and scenes of movement. We'll begin our talk with still images.

You can never run out of visual external links. Every single person, place, or thing you see around you can serve as a powerful link to inspire action; it all depends on your particular desires. Some may be obvious, such as pinning up a picture of a rival football team in a college locker room, while others will require a little more time and thought. Either way, you can always find a link that works for each of your desires.

Can you link a person to your desire? Perhaps a role model or an admired friend or family member? People serve as excellent linking resources, and carry with them the advantage of all five senses rolled into one. You could find a picture of your chosen person and pin it up in your home or office, carry it with you in your purse or wallet, or even keep it in your car.

Many thriving organizations use the face of their founder as an external link to inspire success. The first thing employees see as they walk through the doors of WN, Inc. is a framed portrait of Mr. Nicholson, the company's founder and visionary. As a man of integrity and impeccable character, just the sight of his picture is enough to put people in a positively motivated state of mind before their workday begins.

Can you link a place to your desire? Places, like people, bring much more than a single sense into the equation. They offer magnificent sights, soothing sounds, and refreshing scents that have the ability to change the way people feel and act. What places can you use to recall the rewards that achieving your desire will create?

Several revolutionary America history writers visit Philadelphia for the inspiration and positive motivation necessary to create literary masterpieces. Viewing firsthand the liberty bell, Independence Hall, and the same cobblestone walkways that men like Benjamin Franklin, Samuel Adams, and John Hancock walked along sends shivers up their spines. For them, Philadelphia represents one of the strongest links available.

What objects can you link to your desire? Remember the penny given to Dr. Paulson. This item helped remind the doctor why he chose his profession in the first place, and reminds of the gifts he is given and shares with others on a daily basis. When you think of your desires, what items jump out as possible links?

If you'll recall my experience in Pompeii, I picked up a rock from the amphitheater floor before leaving the site. This small object is a reminder that tomorrow is never promised. If the things in my life are to be achieved, they must be acted upon now, in the present. Merely looking at this rock on my mantel immediately communicates this sense of urgency.

Written phrases can also be effective links. If you have come across a moving passage in one of your favorite books, writing it down and posting it around your home or office can recreate the positive feelings whenever you need a boost. Jotting down a few choice words on a slip of paper works just as well. Place the reminder where you'll see it often and you'll have no trouble staying dedicated to the goal.

Have you ever left a movie theater feeling pumped up and ready to take on the world? If so, then you already know the power of viewing life in motion. Viewing a film that moves you is an excellent way to use a visual link to inspire action. Movies are only one option among many that are right outside your front door.

Many artists, authors, and musicians are inspired by observing normal people living normal lives. You don't have to pay money or watch a screen to experience life in action. You can sit on your porch, go to the park, or take a walk around your neighborhood. Another option, although it does include paying and sitting, is attending a live seminar. This can cover all of your linking bases and provide not only positive motivation but also useful information.

When you give it a few minutes of thought, you will begin to recognize hundreds of possible sights to use as links. Anything you see around you is fair game. Brainstorm, ask around, and experiment with different ideas. When you find a link that works for you, keep it close and out in the open so it can do what it does best: motivate you to action.

Sounds. We now move to linking with sound, which includes the things you say to yourself out loud as well as any sounds you hear from other sources. If listening to a song has ever brought you back to a moment in your past, including the thoughts and feelings you had at the time, you already know how effective this type of linking can be.

As we have discussed with internal dialogue, your own voice is a very powerful linking tool. The only difference here is the impact you can have on your emotions. While thinking a phrase in your head can be effective, screaming it can double the result. It is easy to input passion and power into your voice when you speak out loud. This provides your internal language with muscle.

What words or phrases can you link to your desire? Simply repeating the steps that make up your goal, or the end result itself, can sometimes be enough to get you going. You can also use a few words to sum up the essence of what you are working for and why you are working for it. Reading through your pleasures of action or pains of inaction will give you a great place to start.

Be sure to inject passion into your words; speaking softly won't quite seal the deal. You have to say it like you mean it, without doubt or fear in your voice. Speak your external links with clarity and confidence, convincing yourself and anyone within ear shot that it is only a matter of time before you succeed.

Dr. Martin Luther King Jr.'s speech from the steps of the Lincoln Memorial will forever be remembered as one of the most moving and influential uses of the human voice. With words alone, he held thousands of people in awe, hanging on his every word. It was not the use of movement or pictures (aside from the man himself) that captivated the crowd—it was the passion of his message. Closing your eyes, having only his voice to carry the words, would create the same feelings that stirred the masses that day.

His message touched a place in people that few could reach. His words served as a link to the reasons why the movement for equality began in the first place. The speech reminded people of what they were fighting for, and why the struggle, patience, and perseverance were all necessary. You can catalog Dr. Martin Luther King Jr.'s speech as the perfect example of external linking. Hearing the speech today has the same affect on people that it did more than forty years ago.

Listening to the words of others is only the tip of the iceberg when it comes to using outside sounds (as opposed to your own voice) as links. Anything that you hear can be used to tie together what you must do today in order to get what you want tomorrow. Do any sounds stand out as obvious links for your desires?

Do you find that certain songs, speeches, soothing sounds of nature, or combusting sounds of industry connect with you and your goals? Perhaps you can link a painful sound to a habit you'd like to replace or avoid. An old friend of mine, upon hearing the hacking cough of a smoker, always found renewed commitment to his promise of remaining smoke-free.

I once saw an interview with a prominent baseball player who shared his secret of maintaining the desire to practice all day, every day, year after year. "All it takes is hearing the crack of a bat hitting a ball out of the park. Just the thought of it makes me want to get out there and play," he said with an unsettled tone hinting at his desire to finish the talk and continue playing. "I can't explain it. There's just something about that sound."

When you find the answer, don't waste it. If you find that a certain song motivates you to act, get a recording and keep it close by. If it's the sound of classical music that maintains your dedication to learning how to play an instrument, go to the store and purchase a few classical tapes or CDs. When you know what it takes to succeed, do what you can to keep those items easily accessible.

Smell, Taste, Touch. Not as common as sights or sounds, you can link externally using your senses of smell, taste, and touch. I know of one man who used to rub dollar bills between his fingers as motivation to invest 10% of his income into a retirement plan. The feeling of the money against his skin brought to life all of the rewards of retiring financially sound. I also heard about a teenage girl who purchased a spray to keep cars smelling brand new. This served as motivation to stick with her part-time job and continue to build her savings until she could afford her dream automobile.

Like I said, you probably won't use these links that often, but if it works, it works. You never know what link will be the one to set off a burst of motivated action toward your goal. It could be something you smell, taste, touch, see, or hear. The more links you have, the better your chances are of maintaining the motivation to achieve your desire.

There will be moments, as you know all too well, when you don't feel like doing the things you know you should be doing. You know you should exercise, but you're just not in the mood. You know you should put that cigarette down, but it's just one more. You know you should make some progress on your strategy, but tonight just isn't the right time. Enough thoughts like these and your desires are as good as gone.

Linking keeps you going. It brings the energy and enthusiasm you feel for your desires to the front of your mind, reigniting your passion to succeed. After a short time practicing the technique, you will literally be able to snap out of a negatively motivated state in seconds. You will have the ability to take your desire in mind, utilize your link, and be driven to take action in an instant. The power of linking is an amazingly quick and easy way to drive your desires to the tipping point.

Linking, along with the other tools to maintain positive motivation, will help inspire you to consistent action, but there is one thing they cannot do: guarantee a 100% success rate. Due to the nature and course of life, you will meet with setbacks at some point—it is inevitable. The key to success is not doing everything right, but maintaining the flexibility to overcome and learn from the setbacks you encounter. This is an asset you cannot be without if you are to create the changes you desire.

NOTES & IDEAS

Chapter 18

Taking Advantage of Your Greatest Obstacle

We shall draw from the heart of suffering itself the means of inspiration and survival.
—Sir Winston Churchill

A BEND-BUT-DON'T-BREAK DEFENSE has always been a mainstay of the most successful athletic teams. Although progress may at times be slowed or lost, the majority of steps are in the right direction. By accepting the up and down nature of the game, preparing for their opponents, and developing a game plan that incorporates past lessons to avoid future losses, the momentum necessary to win is maintained. The relationship between your desires and the motivation to achieve them is no different.

Life is a game. Winning the game demands the same bend-but-don't-break mentality while working your way through the strategies you have created to achieve your goals. In the end, if you are to create the kind of life you desire, you must effectively deal with the losses that are certain to occur. In particular, the ability to use negative change and short-term failure to your advantage will ensure that the positive motivation you have developed remains intact.

Change can be seen as both a good and bad thing. A positive shift would be working your way from rags to riches. This type would create an improved situation in your life. A negative change would be unexpectedly losing your job. In this case, the new situation would create pain. Throughout the remainder of this chapter, the word "change" will be used to define an unexpected and unfortunate shift in plans that leads to obstacles within your strategy.

The winning defense that bends to allow for short-term losses, but refuses to completely break, relies heavily on one characteristic: flexibility. If you are a flexible person, and can deal with minor setbacks, you will have an easy time maintaining a constant drive to act. When an obstacle arises, you will find a way to overcome it and carry on. If your strategy is built upon a weak foundation that will crumble with the smallest of glitches, your chances of success are virtually nonexistent.

The Facts of Life

Things will not always work according to plan. These are the facts of life, plain and simple. This isn't meant to bring you down, it is meant to set you up with a strong foundation. Ignoring gravity, no matter how much you want to believe it doesn't exist, isn't going to keep a dropped glass from breaking. Gravity pays no attention to what we believe. It exists whether or not you understand or accept it. Ignoring the potential for setback is just as dangerous as ignoring the laws of physics.

To succeed, you have to deal with the facts that you are given. There are many people who are playing with the wrong rules, and are suffering because of it. To ensure this doesn't happen to you and your desires, we'll begin by laying out the rules by which the game of life can be won. The inevitability of change and short-term failure are two rules that cannot be ignored. Recognizing and accepting these laws will equip your strategy with the staying power necessary for success.

You can control most things in your life, but you can't control everything; some things are simply out of your hands. You have little say over what the other six billion people on earth do every day. This leads to a great deal of uncertainty in your life that is impossible to see coming.

Change is a constant. From the economy to the policies at

your daughter's high school, what you see today rarely reflects the reality of tomorrow. With everything around you shifting on a daily basis, what are the chances that your life will never encounter an unexpected change? What are the chances that the circumstances on which you rely for the success of your strategy will forever remain in place? I can almost guarantee that certain shifts will take place in your life that affect how you go about achieving your desires.

Rebecca Dorn's goal was to become a mentor. She had always had a soft spot in her heart when it came to children, and after researching a local organization whose mission was to improve the lives of those in need, she was ready to get involved. Rebecca called the group and set up a time to meet with the head counselor about possible volunteer positions. With her meeting only a week away, she couldn't wait to get started.

The meeting, however, never took place. Three days after scheduling her interview, Rebecca received a call from the organization. Due to a lack of funds, the program could no longer remain open. Her hopes of joining the mission and giving her time to young children were dashed.

This presented quite a change in plans for Rebecca. Upon hearing the news, she couldn't believe her luck. "Just when I thought I was doing something good," she complained to her husband, "everything goes wrong."

Rebecca put the desire aside, believing that getting her hopes up a second time would only lead to more frustration and disappointment. Achieving her goal was still a possibility—there were many other groups and organizations with the same mission and volunteer positions—but Rebecca gave up on the entire idea because one avenue didn't work out exactly as planned. She could have made a difference in the lives of hundreds of children, but her lack of flexibility put the desire to rest.

Rebecca didn't control the future of the youth organization. She wasn't at fault for its closing, and could do little to reverse the situation. At times, this is the nature of change. It happens without your consent, and pays little attention to your complaints and wishes that things would be different.

Changes will occur in and around your life that call for an

adjustment in your strategy. Even the most thoroughly planned strategies encounter unforeseen circumstances. It doesn't matter who you are or what you want; shifts will occur that you cannot control.

Ilka Chase once said: "The only people who never fail are those who never try." She couldn't have been more correct in her assessment of the facts of life. Failing is an essential part of any success. Anyone who has accomplished anything most likely stumbled a few times along the way. Failing, like the changes that are guaranteed to occur, is a rule of the game that you must abide by in order to get what you want in the end.

Why do Ilka Chase's words hold such undeniable truth? Because people don't know everything. It is impossible to know with absolute certainty how to do every step in every strategy for every desire you will ever have. Everyone, from the most gifted talents to the average Joe down the block, fails in the short-term when they try to accomplish a goal.

The experience of a baby learning to walk is a perfect example of how success is achieved. Every parent expects his child to fail as she develops the skill to walk. Not only that, but everyone around the baby expects the same thing. It isn't an issue of concern because everyone knows that taking a few steps and falling is the only way a baby will develop the skill.

Think about how many babies would be walking if perfection was expected upon the first attempt. Instead of an encouraging group of family and friends, you would find a disappointed crowd wondering why in the world a baby can't walk the first time she tries. It's crazy to think that a baby will never fall while learning how to walk, and it's just as crazy to think that you will do everything right while achieving your goals.

The answer isn't to tell you that you will never fail. I'm telling you that you have to fail to get what you want. It's not just a feeling or slight possibility—it will happen. Understanding that failing is all part of the process will enable you to overcome any setback, and move on with your plan.

A portion of your desires probably includes new experiences or skills. You can't expect to know how to do everything right when you have just begun the process of learning. That's like someone stepping up to bat for the first time expecting every swing to result in a homerun—it's doubtful.

We would be swimming in Olympic athletes and Pulitzer Prize-winning authors if success was a smooth and easy road. The fact that more people are looking for happiness than experiencing it is proof that obstacles line the path to achievement. This isn't negative news—it's merely a caution that a few easily handled bumps may find their way into your plan.

You aren't a machine that can be programmed to do something in just the right way and repeat the process without the slightest adjustment indefinitely. You will make mistakes just like everyone else. You and I are not perfect, and will sometimes go left when we should have gone right, sometimes fall down when we should have worked our way up. You know just as well as I do that this is true, but like most good advice, it's much easier to give than take.

Thinking back to past successes will give you a handful of situations that were full of short-term failures but resulted in ultimate success. Chances are good that you received a high school diploma. Were you expected to answer every question on every test in every grade correct before you were allowed to graduate? No. The school staff understood that expecting perfection from each student was absurd. Take this lesson to heart.

Imagine a friend comes to you and says, "I want to learn how to build homes, but only if I do it perfectly, right from the start." How would you respond? My guess is you would explain how learning new things takes time, and that mistakes are bound to happen in any goal. Think about the advice you would give to a friend about the inevitability and acceptance of setbacks, then follow your own wisdom.

The first stage, realizing that change and failure in the short-term are inevitable, is complete. The next stage is learning how to use that fact to your advantage. You don't have to agree that perfection is unrealistic and leave it at that. You can use the rules of the game to strengthen your strategy, develop your desire, and drive you toward a better life.

The Art of Flexibility

Using a simple four-step process, you can overcome the fear of negative change and failure and use the setbacks to your advantage. As you will soon see, falling down can sometimes create more positive motivation than staying on your feet. Mastering the skills of expectance, preparation, acceptance, and utilization will provide your strategy with the flexibility it needs to endure.

Expect. The first step toward gaining a flexible mindset is expectance. Knowing that setbacks must happen from time to time, your strategy needs to make room for them. Obvious difficulties will arise if you enter into the deal expecting perfection when reality demands occasional changes and small failures. You must bend to match reality because it will not move for you.

Two problems are eliminated when you expect setbacks. The first is the debilitating fear that you might fail. We hear about this all the time. People are so afraid to fail that they would rather give up their dreams and settle for a mediocre life. They end up seeking safety in their daily routine of wanting, wishing, and waiting. In time, usually when too little is left to reverse the damage, regret replaces desire as they realize playing it safe only solidified their unfulfilled and unhappy existence.

"But what if I make mistakes?" was the question Duncan McGregor asked me as we worked through his plan to get his GED.

"If?" I replied. "Duncan, short-term failures aren't a possibility, they're a certainty." In order for him to succeed in the long-term, he needed to expect mistakes in the short-term.

You have to make a choice—do you want to avoid setbacks at all costs, or do you want to live a better life? Deciding to improve requires an expectance of setbacks. You no longer have to worry that things may not go according to plan because they won't. Take comfort in the fact that we all have to deal with unforeseen changes and short-term failures; it's a reality that all successful people must expect.

If action is eventually taken, the second problem appears. Expecting perfection, most people give up at the first sign of trouble. I can't tell you how many times I've heard people tell me, "Well, I tried it once, but it didn't work out." Once?! You would have to be all-knowing to get everything you wanted on the first try. Just as you put the fear of failure behind you, the belief that a single setback spells the end of your plan can be forgotten.

Expecting setbacks ensures that minor mistakes won't catch you off guard and devastate your hopes for success. When circumstances change without notice, or a wrong move is made along the way, you'll be ready to make the best of things and try a second time.

Fear is rooted in uncertainty. Scary movies instill fear in people because they aren't sure what to expect. Is someone hiding under the bed? Who made that noise? They would lose their impact if you knew that someone was, in fact, under the bed. When you expect the problem, like expecting someone to be hiding in your room, the fear is diminished. But this is only the beginning of the process. After expecting the short-term setbacks to occur, your next task is to prepare.

Prepare. What could potentially go wrong with your strategy to achieve your desire? What changes could take place that would cause you to have to change your plans? What areas are likely to involve short-term failures? These questions lead to the element of preparation.

When a student is called to the office after starting a fight, he expects the worst. The next step after expecting to get into trouble is preparation. He thinks about what he is going to say to get himself out of trouble, or what he can say to reduce the severity of his punishment. These two measures—reducing the risk and reducing the impact—are the same areas you will need to focus on in order to best prepare yourself for the road ahead.

What steps can you take today to reduce the risk of setbacks occurring in the future? An aspiring writer can research the publishing industry or create contacts with people in the field to reduce the risk of his manuscript being rejected. A salesman or woman can enroll in a course or study the strategies of successful sales organizations to reduce the risk of poor performance. What can you do to improve your chances of success in potentially difficult areas within your strategy?

Instead of worrying about your plan not working, focus on what you can do to ensure it succeeds. Replace, "What if this doesn't work?" with, "How can I make this work?" It goes back to the principles of focus. If you think about what you don't want, you'll end up getting it. The key is to think about steps you can take to make sure the things you fear never happen in the first place. However, if they do, you need to move on to the second facet of preparation.

What steps can you take to reduce the impact of negative changes or short-term failures? In other words, when something bad happens, what can you do to minimize the damage? It's insurance for your desires. When you get in a car accident, your insurance company will help decrease the amount of money you need to pay. It doesn't give you anything until a problem occurs, but when something does go wrong, they are there to minimize the negative impact. What can you do to insure yourself against the negative impacts of likely setbacks?

After taking steps to reduce the risk of trouble and its impact on your life, the next stage is acceptance. When things change or you make a wrong turn, you have to accept it and move on. Doing so will bring you one step closer to a mindset and strategy based on flexibility.

Accept. Denial, in all its shapes and sizes, is never a good thing. You can only ignore the facts for so long before the truth comes crashing down on you. The faster you are to accept what has happened in your life, the faster you can get back to enjoying it. Your time is too precious to waste on wishing something didn't happen. Setbacks will take place; when they do, accept it and move on.

Not long ago, a group of friends and I were working late on a new idea we were piecing together. We finally wrapped up our work around midnight, and together made our way out to the parking lot. We knew something wasn't right the moment the door closed behind us and we looked at the row of cars parked only ten feet from the building. One of the car's interior lights was on, and the door was slightly ajar. "I know I didn't leave that door open," my friend said, looking understandably worried.

He hadn't left the door open—he left it unlocked. Nothing was damaged, but the contents left in the glove compartment were gone. For reasons they will never understand, John and Derek (the two who had driven to the office in that car) left their wallets inside the glove box. Thinking the meeting would be over quickly, they both reasoned that it would be easier to leave their things in the car. "After all," John explained, "we're right in front of the building."

What happened next reinforced a valuable lesson about accepting setbacks. Realizing their things had been taken, John and Derek immediately took action. One sat in the front seat of his car staring at the floor while the other went back into my office. "How could I have left the door open?" John asked himself, sitting there in disgust. "What was I thinking?"

I followed Derek into the office to see how he was doing. He was sitting at a small desk making a phone call, looking as calm as he had hours before. "Just making some phone calls to cancel credit cards," he said. "Hope you don't mind my using the phone."

While Derek was taking care of safeguarding his money and information (credit cards, bank cards, social security card, etc.), John was still in the car blaming himself for his mistake. "I can't believe I did this," he repeated over and over.

It happened. Like it or not, the door was left unlocked and someone had stolen their things. All of John's guilt and disbelief couldn't turn back time and change the reality of the situation. Both men had experienced the same setback, but only one accepted the situation for what it was. As the evening came to a close, Derek felt settled and John felt terrible. John hadn't contacted anyone, even though he had several credit and bank cards. My only hope was that someone wasn't already using the contents of his wallet for a personal shopping spree.

When something doesn't go your way, accept it. Your only other option is to wish it didn't happen, and that only makes matters worse. After you have accepted the facts of the situation, it's time to benefit from the experience.

Benefit. Imagine sitting in front of a beautiful grand piano. You are instructed to play Middle C, but have no idea where it is. With eighty-eight options, you take a wild guess and hit a key. After the note fades, you are told it was incorrect. You have one of two choices: You can randomly strike another key, or you can benefit from your failure.

Let's say that you immediately hit another key. Looking almost identical, you may end up hitting the same key twice without even knowing it. This means that you could fail more than eighty-eight times. This is the typical response of failure. An incorrect move is made, and without learning from the experience, another incorrect move quickly follows. This cycle continues until the entire strategy is abandoned.

Keeping the final principle of flexibility in mind would create a very different outcome. After striking an incorrect key, you learn from your mistake. Placing a small piece of tape on the key reminds you to avoid it on your next try. Using this method, you can only fail eighty-seven times, but you are assured success. You know the right key is there, and learning from each of your failures guarantees that the correct note will eventually be played.

Failing in the short-term is a gift. You cannot learn without failing, and without learning you cannot succeed. It's not always easy to pinpoint the cause of success. It could be that you said the right things, made the right moves, or were in the right place at the right time. Without knowing the reasons why it is impossible to repeatedly succeed, you are left to guess at what works and hope you are making the right decisions.

When you do something wrong, on the other hand, the reasons are more easily discovered. After touching a scalding pot, you immediately learn never to repeat the action. Discovering every way not to do something leaves you with the answer you are seeking. Every time you fail, you are given another piece of valuable information that brings you one step closer to getting what you want.

There is no better example of benefiting from setbacks than a complaining customer. Any company that loathes a complaint needs a lesson in running a successful business. The benefit of a satisfied customer can't compare to that of an unhappy patron. Ten thousand happy customers can come and go without saying a word, and you are left to guess at the reasons for their pleasant shopping experience. Why were they satisfied? What did we do right? How can we build upon their pleasant experience to ensure future customers are just as pleased? A satisfied customer, entering and exiting your store without a word, leaves you guessing for answers.

However, a complaining customer tells you exactly what you can do to improve service. Guessing is unnecessary because you are told firsthand what you are doing wrong. With every wrong move, you are given the opportunity to make a right one. A complaining customer is literally handing you more money and growth on a silver platter. A satisfied customer offers nothing to build upon whereas a complaint gives you the secret to improvement.

It is because of this principle that successful people fail more than they succeed, and they do it with a smile. Now that you know failing is the best way to improve and get what you want, you will join the group of short-term failures who eventually became amazing successes. Every success, from the business moguls to the parents of happy and healthy children, has repeatedly met with failure. It was their steps backward that allowed them to progress so far forward.

Who is in a better position? A salesman failing once and giving up or a salesman failing one hundred times? It should be obvious that failing one hundred times gives you one hundred opportunities for improvement. In the end, the salesman who fails but refuses to give in will always be more successful.

Setbacks have a great deal to teach you, but only if you learn from your mistakes. You have to take steps to discover what you did incorrectly and how you can avoid the error the next time you take action. One hundred failed sales calls are of no use to a salesman who doesn't take the time to learn why his product or service is declined. Only when you learn the cause of failure is a setback an opportunity.

We now come to what I believe to be the most useful by-product of a setback: pain. Experiencing the pain of failure or unexpected change gives you the leverage you need to tip your scales toward positive action. The pain that results from things not working out right can drive you to ensure that you succeed your next time around.

"I was so embarrassed," she said. "I will never put myself in that positive again—ever." These were the words that Cynthia used to describe her first competitive diving event. She was positively motivated, but not to the point that she knew was necessary to excel at her sport. It wasn't until the first meet that she found the pain to push herself further than ever before.

Every time Cynthia felt like giving up, she remembered the pain of doing so poorly at her first competition. Immediately, she was back to taking positive action and training to become her best. The pain of failure served her well. It tipped her scales and inspired her to never give up.

As you can see, setbacks are not something to fear. Rather, they are something to take advantage of. Benefiting from unexpected change and short-term failure gives you the opportunity to achieve your desires in less time and with fewer struggles. There is a final benefit that obstacles present, a benefit that makes feeling great about yourself and your life possible. Without it, you would never know the joys and thrills of success.

The Challenge

If you could have everything you desired in the blink of any eye, without the least amount of effort or sacrifice, would you want it? You might, at first. The promise of unearned rewards sounds good on the surface, but you wind up losing so much more than you gain in the end. If you're still not convinced, a closer look at the subject may help change your mind.

Do you value the ability to move your arm up and down? Do you give thanks each day and truly appreciate how easily you can move your arm in all directions? My guess would be that you do not really think about it, and many people with whom I've spoken have confirmed that assumption. It's easy to move your arm, always has been and always will be. Because it comes so easily and without much attention, it is not valued as heavily as, say, the ability to hit a golf ball three hundred yards.

What a difference you would find with a man or woman who had just regained movement in his or her limbs after years of enormous struggle and pain. Every inch of movement would serve as a reminder of the adversity and great odds that had been overcome. You would find a man or woman who felt great about him or herself and never took the simple things in life for granted.

Compare the feelings between a gold medal winner at the Olympics and someone who received the same medal in the mail, a raffle winner. No effort or sacrifice, no obstacles overcome or rivals defeated, just luck of the draw. There really is no way to compare the two.

One of the major reasons gold medal winners are so overwhelmed with emotion on the podium is the hard work and sacrifice that made it all possible. After pushing themselves beyond the limit every day, their persistence finally paid off. The recipient of the mail-order medal would certainly be grateful, but the Olympic medal would hold no real meaning for them. It would look nice on their mantel, but it wouldn't make them feel good and give them the fulfillment everyone is so desperately seeking.

You may have personally experienced this last example. When I was about twelve years old, I had my heart set on buying a new bike. Two of my friends had just received new bikes as birthday gifts, but seeing that my birthday was nearly nine months away, I had to find another way to get it. After pleading my case for an early birthday present, I was told it had to be earned.

Throughout my childhood, I was given everything from food and shelter to toys and clothes. I appreciated what I was given, but they didn't create feelings of pride or satisfaction. This wasn't the case with my new bike. After saving the money I had made from odds jobs around the house and mowing lawns in the neighborhood, I bought the bike with my own money. To this day, I can still remember how proud I was of that bike. Through my own hard work and dedication, I was able to get what I wanted, and I was ecstatic. I felt great about what I had done and looked forward to the next opportunity to face any challenge that might come my way.

These short examples all lead to the same conclusion: Esteem and pride for yourself can only be experienced when you do things that challenge you, things that require effort and sacrifice. Overcoming obstacles proves that you are able to confront incredibly difficult odds and win the fight. It creates feelings of worth, confidence, and respect for yourself. Rewards that come unchallenged are stripped of these feelings. Instead, they make you question whether or not you deserve them in the first place.

Think back to a time when you felt good about yourself. Were you given something or did you have to work for it? Degrees, relationships, and careers don't magically appear when you snap your fingers. These things present real challenges that need to be overcome. Positive feelings about who you are and what you have accomplished arise when you are tested physically, mentally, and emotionally, and emerge as the winner.

Unexpected changes and short-term failures present you with a challenge. Accepting and meeting these challenges gives you satisfaction and pride. Without the presence of setbacks in your life, you would be robbed of the chance to feel the excitement of victory. Never be afraid to fail or encounter change, and never let the occurrence of them stop you short of success. Expect, prepare, accept, and benefit from the truly remarkable gift known as the setback.

One final principle stands between you and complete control of your motivated mind. A constant flow of positive motivation requires another constant: information. Following a pattern of continuous improvement will give you the edge you need to create the life you have always imagined.

NOTES & IDEAS

Chapter 19

The Driving Force
Behind Lifelong Achievement

*The man who graduates today and stops learning tomorrow
is uneducated the day after.*

—Newton D. Baker

IF YOU'RE NOT GROWING, you're dying. If you cease to learn and improve, you don't stay in the same place; you sink. There are only two choices at hand, and you have to decide whether you wish to sink or swim among your desires. It's the natural course of things, and taking the road to growth brings us to our final installment of maintaining your positive motivation.

Success demands growth and improvement. A never-ending cycle of discovering, experiencing, and understanding more about your desires and your life is absolutely necessary to getting what you want. You can't stop watering a plant if you want it to grow, just as you can't stop providing your desires with the fuel they require if you want them to develop. What you know at this moment may not be enough to get it done; you need a constant flow of new information.

Perhaps you already take steps to learn and experience new things in life. If so, keep it up and put more energy in that direction. However, more people than not have been force-fed facts for so long that they have put an unnecessary and uninformed stop to education. You have probably experienced the difference between having to do something and wanting to do it for yourself. Learning is one such area that adds to life when chosen, but frustrates it when a chore. It's no longer a chore.

Every person worth admiring follows a philosophy of constant growth. It's time that you stop admiring from a distance and instead join the ranks of success. It's absolutely essential to understand and experience more today than you did the day before if you are to rise above the wishers of the world and live the life you have imagined. And believe me, once you start the process of constant curiosity and growth, you'll never want to stop.

Something New Every Day

Information is fuel for desire. Every single ounce of new information you absorb enhances your ability to inspire action. Large or small, any progress in your understanding brings you one step closer to realizing your goals and dreams. That is why a habit of constant learning and growth is so vital to the ultimate achievement of what you want.

The reality we face today is built upon a majority of people for whom education ends the day after graduation; for the remainder of life a steady decline in understanding, curiosity, and satisfaction occurs. The people who enjoy life most live by a philosophy of learning for a lifetime. There is never a point at which you should say, "I know enough."

Constantly learning electrifies your life. Without change and improvement, we begin to lose our purpose. We were meant to grow and prosper from day one until the last moment. It is through an unstoppable curiosity that the life you dream about will materialize. There is no question about it: If you want success, fulfillment, and a life of meaning and gratitude, you must never put a stop to the learning process.

There are many avenues you can follow to fulfill this need. Some follow a general principle of increasing their knowledge of the entire world around them, taking in new information from every possible area. Others look for a more focused improvement, learning as much and as often about their particular dreams and goals as time allows. A third group uses a combination of both, increasing their understanding about life and the world in general while at the same time focusing on the improvement of their specific desires. Each type of growth adds to the quality of life as well as to the speed of success. Your particular style will vary according to your own needs, but make no mistake about it: You must follow one of them to fully realize what your life can become.

Any resource that provides information is a possible means to growth and improvement. The obvious forms include books and classes, but these only scratch the surface of learning. Merely talking with a few strangers while you are waiting in line at the post office can enhance your understanding of your desires and life in general. Watching a few kids playing games next door can offer valuable lessons if you are willing to look for them. You are surrounded by opportunities to improve. It is more difficult to block information out than it is to let it flow into your head.

You have already started the process. Reading this book and digesting the principles within it has added to your knowledge base and enhanced your understanding about your life and the things you desire most. In effect, your job is not to begin the process of constant growth, but to continue it for the rest of your life. Read, speak, and most importantly, listen to those around you who have something to share.

Never stop learning. Never stop growing as an individual, a friend, a co-worker, and a member of your family. Life wasn't meant to be ignored. Don't race through it blindfolded and ignorant. Open your eyes to the possibilities around you, and soak up the experience of living within the facts of history, the joy of the present, and the excitement of the future.

The greater enjoyment of life is reason enough to be curious and inquisitive, but the rewards don't stop there. There are countless benefits to following a philosophy of constant improvement, but three in particular stand out with regard to our focus of positive motivation. We will end our time together by taking a closer look at each of these three powerful advantages.

Building Momentum

For the millions of people who can't seem to get themselves to take action, their desires are like a long stretch of delicately placed dominoes—a single push in the right direction is all it takes to start an unrelenting flow of movement. You never know how close your scales are to the tipping point, and every new gem of useful information (pleasure of action, pain of inaction) could be the one to start the chain reaction.

Alyssa King was dealing with a nearly tipped desire, and one early Saturday afternoon she received the small nudge her dominos needed to tumble toward success. Like most people, she knew she needed to exercise, but did a lot more thinking about it than anything else. Alyssa would repeatedly tear herself down for her inability to do what she knew she had to do to remain healthy. She was at the point of giving up and accepting her so-called laziness.

Then something happened. It was at a gas station just down the road from where she lived that she read the words that shifted the balance of power. Standing in a long line of impatient customers, Alyssa glanced down at the newspaper rack and noticed a headline about reducing the risks of disease through exercise. It was nothing new—everyone knows exercise is beneficial—but it was a certain figure the paper used to demonstrate the point, a graph to represent the jump in illness that results from a lack of exercise.

Alyssa was a little shocked—she didn't know that exercise made *that* much of an impact. She bought the newspaper, cut out the article, and has been exercising ever since. It was that last bit of information that made all the difference. As time passed, the more she learned about the benefits of exercise, the easier it was to inspire consistent action. The same can happen to you if you never stop educating yourself about the things you want.

If you have a negative habit that you'd like to replace, never stop learning about the pain and suffering the behavior creates. If you'd like to do something that is good for you, never stop learning about the rewards of success. It always comes back to the scales. The moment you add enough weight to the side of positive action to outweigh the obstacles, you'll do what it takes to achieve your goals.

You can think of the process of constant learning like reading a good book. Each page pulls you deeper and deeper into the story, making it hard to put down. Your interest and desire grows with each new word, and before you know it, the story is successfully completed. When you are on the lookout for new information about your desires, you will be pulled deeper and deeper into the story of your dream, finding it hard to turn away from taking action. In what seems like no time at all, your dream is successfully completed.

You are at the beginning of your story. It's now time to begin turning pages, and learning as much as possible, as often as possible, about the rewards of success and the penalties of ultimate failure. All around you are books with your desires printed on the cover. Whether or not you pursue their story is up to you. Your desires can be left to gather dust on the shelf, or followed with passion to success.

Intelligent Action

If my desire is to make more friends, pinching every new person I meet isn't going to get the job done. I have the desire, but my strategy isn't right. With a strong enough desire, I would eventually find a method that works, which leads us to the second benefit of constant growth and improvement. The strategies you have in place, or are currently piecing together to achieve your goals, need to be accurate and up to date. Only through constant education can you ensure that you are working from a plan that gets the job done effectively and efficiently.

All strategies are not equal. Two people with the same desire will most likely use completely different methods, with one probably outperforming the other. Having a plan doesn't necessarily mean your plan will work well, let alone at all. It could do just the opposite. Many people desiring to lose weight and make more money have learned this lesson firsthand. Instead of finding the answers to their problems, they were sold a get-happy-quick scheme that offered a strategy that not only didn't work, but made matters worse. Having a plan in place isn't good enough; it has to work, and work well.

The first strategy you put together may not actually create the results you are seeking. This isn't a criticism in the least—I have created many strategies that didn't work, but I kept learning until I got it right. Every idea out there can't be right, and it's your job to make your way through the garbage to discover the gold.

Constant improvement guarantees that you will find a strategy that works. If you are always on the lookout for new information about your desires, you will undoubtedly begin to learn how to put together an effective plan. It goes back to our talk on critical thinking. Believing the first thing you hear can lead to a lot of damage down the road. You have to view both sides of the story before you can zero in on what actually gets the job done.

Kirk Branson wanted to become a successful salesman. He had just started working for a life insurance company when a veteran saleswoman took him under her wing. The veteran was rude, abrasive, intimidating, and pushed her products onto unsuspecting customers. Without knowing any other strategies, Kirk listened patiently to the tactics she used, believing her way was the right way.

For the first few months, he had a difficult time selling policies, and began to feel bad about the way he was treating potential clients. Kirk started to question whether or not the "veteran" actually knew what she was doing. Checking with a few others in the company, he soon realized she was, in fact, one of the least successful salespeople in the firm.

Her intimidation techniques turned customers off, and those who did purchase policies never referred friends or family to the company. Kirk had made a mistake in choosing an ineffective strategy. After reeducating himself about the industry and respectable salesmanship, he was able to turn things around and gain the success he was after from the start.

This type of thing happens all the time. Unsuspecting individuals, quick to listen and learn, pick up the wrong strategies and never think twice about the information they hear. Don't be a skeptic about everyone and everything; just take steps to ensure you are working with accurate information to form your plan.

Constantly improving your understanding of your desires will lead you to a strategy that works, but it doesn't end there. This will also guarantee that you are using the latest methods and techniques available. With the rapid pace of advancement in the world, today's ideas will be tomorrow's history. As we speak, people are discovering how to do things in less time, with less effort, and for much less money. Following the principle of a never-ending education will keep you aware of these developments.

Tangents to Happiness

People are forever searching for happiness. Knowing where to find it, which door to open and which to pass by, is not always an easy decision to make. However, the decision becomes far less complicated with constant learning and growth. This is the third and final benefit of a curiosity that refuses to quit.

As you learn more about the things you want, you will invariably come upon information that sparks your interest in other areas. Intent to learn more about painting could lead to a career as a fashion designer. A desire to rekindle a relationship could unlock a passion for marriage counseling. Educating yourself about one thing can open the door to many more.

The process mirrors the structure of a large tree. Your initial desire is the trunk. As you learn more about that specific area, you may stumble upon a new area of interest that was never before considered. As you follow that branch, you may again recognize a new subject. A single desire can spawn a hundred more. The only way to take advantage of this aspect of success is through constant growth.

Having worked with many individuals who have found their purpose in life, I am convinced that discovering your true calling doesn't always begin with the initial desire. Often it is a tangent to what had first been pursued, a tangent that led to true happiness.

For Ashley Jenson, it started out as a desire to be a preschool teacher. In an amazing string of events, a position as a teacher led to an eventual leadership position at the school. It didn't take long for that role to ignite a passion to help children in need.

Ashley was happy as a teacher, and the feelings grew when she took the lead. Each successive step on her path brought more intense feelings of fulfillment and meaning. Her final stage, a pediatric nurse, sealed the deal. Ashley has found her purpose in life, and the level of happiness she now enjoys cannot compare to anything she has ever experienced before. The curiosity of a hopeful preschool teacher led to the reality of fulfillment.

You can find your purpose in life, not because you were born to fit one mold, but because of the vast possibilities and opportunities today's world presents. There is literally something for everyone. Every new piece of information you discover will bring you one step closer to finding that calling. Every door opened is one less barrier standing between you and a life of meaning. No one can say with certainty when it will happen to you, but I can tell you without hesitation that you will never find your purpose in life if you sit and wait for it to come to you. Life rewards action, and action is what it takes to attain your desires.

Living is about growing, and to grow you must learn. Following the philosophy of constant improvement will inspire action, improve strategy, and help you discover what you were meant to do with your life. More importantly, it will allow you to drink fully from the cup of life. You cannot stand still. Refusing to move ahead, you will soon find yourself far behind. You have only one choice to make, and a simple one at that: grow or decline. While one is guaranteed to create pain and misery, there is no telling how far the other will take you.

You have successfully completed the final pillar of *The Motivated Mind*. The ability to maintain the force you have created is within your hands. No longer will you experience the roller coaster of success. Instead, the unstoppable drive of positive motivation will forever take you toward the life you have always wanted to live.

NOTES & IDEAS

Afterword

Wheresoever you go, go with all your heart.
—Confucius

WE ALL DREAM. We all want to change and improve, to become the person we know we are capable of becoming, but dreaming is the easy part. What separates the dream from reality is action. Only those who act on their desires fully recognize and seize the infinite number of opportunities and possibilities that life has to offer. Fortunately for you, inspiring action is no longer a mystery.

With an understanding of motivation and your behavior, a desire to change and an unshakable belief in your ability to make it happen, a plan of action and action toward that plan, and an effort to maintain the drive toward success, there is nothing you can't achieve. More importantly, taking complete control of your life will provide you with the meaning and fulfillment everyone hopes to experience.

What happens next is up to you. The path is painfully clear if you do nothing, but there is no telling how extraordinary your life will become if you choose to take control of the motivated mind within you. Using the tools in this book and the desire in your heart, you have what it takes to create the life of which you have always dreamed.

I thank you again for allowing me to share these ideas with you. They have enriched my life more than words can ever express, and I have no doubt they will soon do the same for you.

While our time together has come to an end, your time is just beginning. As you set in motion a life by your design, I wish you the best of success and the greatest of happiness now and forever in the future.